RELEVANT FINANCIAL STATEMENTS

This is a volume in the Arno Press collection

THE DEVELOPMENT OF CONTEMPORARY ACCOUNTING THOUGHT

See last pages of this volume for a complete list of titles.

RELEVANT FINANCIAL STATEMENTS

Joshua Ronen and George H. Sorter

With An Introduction

ARNO PRESS
A New York Times Company
New York • 1978

Publisher's Note: This book has been reproduced from the best available copies.

Editorial Supervision: LUCILLE MAIORCA

Reprint Edition 1978 by Arno Press Inc.

THE DEVELOPMENT OF CONTEMPORARY ACCOUNTING THOUGHT
ISBN for complete set: 0-405-10891-5
See last pages of this volume for titles.

Manufactured in the United States of America

Library of Congress Cataloging in Publication Data

Ronen, Joshua.
Relevant financial statements.

(The Development of contemporary accounting thought)
Includes bibliographical references.
1. Financial statements. I. Sorter, George H., joint author. II. Title. III. Series.
HF5681.B2R63 657'.3 77-87318
ISBN 0-405-10930-X

ACKNOWLEDGMENTS

All selections from *Objectives of Financial Statements, Vol. 2, Selected Papers,* copyright © 1974 by the American Institute of Certified Public Accountants, Inc., were reprinted by permission of the American Institute of Certified Public Accountants.

"An 'Events' Approach to Basic Accounting Theory" by George H. Sorter was reprinted by permission of the American Accounting Association.

"Relevant Accounting" was reprinted by permission of *The Journal of Business of the University of Chicago.*

RELEVANT FINANCIAL STATEMENTS

Joshua Ronen and George H. Sorter

Introduction

The authors have long been concerned and involved in attempting to define what relevant financial statements should consist of and how such information is to be provided within a specific framework of objectives. Financial statements have long been provided, of course; however, the rationale and use underlying such statements and their usage have largely remained undefined and unexplored. Much has been written about specific items in financial statements; there has been much advocacy of specific quantifications and procedures, but rarely within the context of an integrated framework suggesting why such rules or procedures should be preferred.

In this volume we compile several previously-published works of the authors, individually or collectively, that bear on the subject. In addition, we have included several new papers which augment, elaborate on and refine the central theme. We view the central theme of relevant financial statement information as one that addresses the question of what set of information, what levels of aggregation and what modes of presentations can best facilitate the accomplishment of the pre-defined objectives of accounting. This theme is dealt with the full realization that accounting information is only one among numerous alternative sources of data that are utilized by market agents. We believe that accounting information is an important input into the decisions of market transactors, but in no way a sole input. Because accounting information is used in conjunction with other information, joint effects are produced. The overall objective of accounting we believe, should be the promotion of efficient resource allocation in the economy in a way that is consistent with individuals using accounting information so as to maximize their own wealth. Furthermore, we subscribe to the specific objectives derived from this overall objective as articulated by the accounting objectives study group. In particular, we believe that the objective of accounting is to provide information that helps predict cash flows and the uncertainty associated with such flows. We believe that this primary objective is consistent with the promotion of resource allocative efficiency in the economy as a whole. The works contained in this volume call for a greater level of disaggregation than presently employed in existing financial statements or suggested by existing accounting theory.

Accordingly, we start this volume with two papers concerning the purpose and need for objectives. The first is a general discussion of why objectives are needed for accounting; the second deals more specifically and in a more detailed fashion with the need for specifying accounting objectives within an efficient market. In the note, following these papers, we comment on the apparent irreconcilability between the specification of normative accounting objectives and the problem of social choice subject to the implications of the well-known Arrow impossibility theorem. Having, to our satisfaction, established the need for accounting objectives, the question arises as to how these objectives should be identified. The last paper in this section explores whether a normative approach or a descriptive approach is more appropriate for this purpose. Not surprisingly, while we conclude that both the normative and descriptive models should be considered, we believe that at this stage, a normative approach deserves priority.

The second section of the book explores what these objectives should be. The section starts out with an early article advocating a disaggregated approach to accounting information. The next article develops a framework for determining the type of disaggregated information that is likely to satisfy the objectives. This is followed by an article that discusses why it is important to separate the concept of accounting and economic income and the following article suggests the disaggregation of information to be reported in the balance sheet and income statement and suggests that they need not articulate in a simple manner. The section concludes with a paper suggesting what the objectives of financial statements should be.

From the general frameworks developed in the previous section as to what disaggregated information would in general be useful, we turn in the next section toward statements that accomplish these purposes. The first paper "Relevant Accounting" provides an elaborate system to provide disaggregated and comprehensive information that is consistent with the framework and the objectives developed earlier. The statements included in this paper provide disaggregated information concerning not only past transactions, but expectations of future events as well. Economic income and accounting income are distinguished, as well as disaggregations that enable assessment of the changing risk posture of the firm. Moreover, the disaggregation into past transactions and future expectations provides means for the validation of expectations and assessing their reliability. One of the central features of this paper is the communication of forecasts in the form of discounted cash flows. The concept of discounted cash flows is discussed more elaborately in the next paper and a case study is then provided to demonstrate the feasibility of implementing this approach. Both these papers refer back to the concepts developed in "Relevant Accounting". The next two papers call for even further disaggregations than envisioned in the "Relevant Accounting" paper but that are consistent with the theme of that paper. These two papers deal with providing information alternatives to the currently popular replacement cost system. The alternative information is thought to be a) more appropriate in terms of accomplishing the objectives identified earlier and b) less costly to implement. Finally, in the conclusion, we suggest an update to the ideas suggested in "Relevant Accounting."

CONTENTS

I THE NEED FOR AND THE PURPOSE OF ACCOUNTING OBJECTIVES

Sorter, George H., in collaboration with Martin S. Gans, Paul Rosenfield, R. M. Shannon and Robert G. Streit
PURPOSE AND NEED FOR OBJECTIVES (Reprinted from *Objectives of Financial Statements, Vol. 2, Selected Papers*) New York, 1974

Ronen, Joshua
THE NEED FOR ACCOUNTING OBJECTIVES IN AN EFFICIENT MARKET (Reprinted from *Objectives of Financial Statements, Vol. 2, Selected Papers*) New York, 1974

Ronen, Joshua and George H. Sorter
A NOTE ON ACCOUNTING ALTERNATIVES AND SOCIAL CHOICE

Ronen, Joshua and George H. Sorter
THE DESCRIPTIVE AND THE NORMATIVE (Reprinted from *Objectives of Financial Statements, Vol. 2, Selected Papers*) New York, 1974

II DEVELOPMENT OF A GENERAL FRAMEWORK

Sorter, George H.
AN "EVENTS" APPROACH TO BASIC ACCOUNTING THEORY (Reprinted from *The Accounting Review*, Vol. XLIV, No. I) Menasha, Wis., January, 1969

Ronen, Joshua
A USER ORIENTED DEVELOPMENT OF ACCOUNTING INFORMATION REQUIREMENTS (Reprinted from *Objectives of Financial Statements, Vol. 2, Selected Papers*) New York, 1974

Sorter, George H.
ACCOUNTING INCOME AND ECONOMIC INCOME (Reprinted from *Objectives of Financial Statements, Vol. 2, Selected Papers*) New York, 1974

Sorter, George H.
THE PARTITIONING DILEMMA (Reprinted from *Objectives of Financial Statements, Vol. 2, Selected Papers*) New York, 1974

Sorter, George H., in collaboration with Martin S. Gans, Paul Rosenfield, R. M. Shannon and Robert G. Streit
ECONOMIC DECISION-MAKING AND THE ROLE OF ACCOUNTING INFORMATION (Reprinted from *Objectives of Financial Statements, Vol. 2, Selected Papers*) New York, 1974

III DEVELOPMENT OF A SPECIFIC FRAMEWORK

Ronen, Joshua and George H. Sorter
RELEVANT ACCOUNTING (Reprinted from *The Journal of Business of the University of Chicago,* Vol. 45, No. 2) Chicago, April, 1972

Ronen, Joshua
DISCOUNTED CASH FLOW ACCOUNTING (Reprinted from *Objectives of Financial Statements, Vol. 2, Selected Papers*) New York, 1974

Ronen, Joshua
A TEST OF THE FEASIBILITY OF PREPARING DISCOUNTED CASH FLOW ACCOUNTING STATEMENTS (Reprinted from *Objectives of Financial Statements, Vol. 2, Selected Papers*) New York, 1974

Ronen, J[oshua] and G[eorge] H. Sorter
PROVIDING RELEVANT FINANCIAL STATEMENT INFORMATION IN A PERIOD OF CHANGING PRICES (A Paper Written for the Committee for Economic Development)

Ronen, J[oshua] and G[eorge] H. Sorter
REFLECTING THE IMPACT OF PRICE CHANGES AND INFLATION IN FINANCIAL STATEMENTS: AN APPLICATION (A Paper Written for the Committee for Economic Development)

IV CONCLUSION

THE NEED FOR AND THE PURPOSE OF ACCOUNTING OBJECTIVES

PURPOSE AND NEED FOR OBJECTIVES

George H. Sorter
in collaboration with Martin S. Gans, Paul Rosenfield,
R. M. Shannon and Robert G. Streit

Purpose and Need for Objectives

George H. Sorter, Research Director, *in collaboration with*
Martin S. Gans, Paul Rosenfield, R. M. Shannon and Robert G. Streit

The Need for Objectives of Financial Statements

The definite need for explicitly stated objectives of financial statements has been inferred again by the appointment of the Study Group on the Objectives of Financial Statements by the American Institute of Certified Public Accountants. By implication, the following question deserves summary analysis: Why should objectives of accounting and accounting's basic output, financial statements, be rigorously defined and explicitly communicated in the absence of similar statements of objectives by many other areas of trade and professional endeavor? Consider, for example, the cobbler whose services are limited exclusively to the repair of shoes. It is generally agreed that there exists a one-to-one relationship between the cobbler and *each* individual customer in relation to services rendered, i.e., no third parties are involved. The objective of the cobbler is thus a *private* one of satisfying a specific customer who directly requests, and pays for, the shoe repair services.

The relationship described above, which can easily be extended to professions such as law or medicine, can be compared and contrasted with the rendering of services by the certified public accountant. Accounting services are commissioned by specific customers or clients. However, there is more involved in this particular relationship. Financial statements of publicly held corporations are produced by client companies but are not intended to primarily benefit these companies or its management. The primary purpose of financial statements is to serve the needs of various third parties. These third parties, such as existing or potential stockholders, creditors, suppliers, or employees, have diverse needs and do not directly employ the preparers or attestors of financial statements. In most instances these third parties also cannot directly nor effectively communicate their needs, desires, or requests to preparers or attestors of financial statements.

Financial statements are responsive, and accountants are responsible, to third parties who rely on information contained in financial statements. To satisfactorily discharge this responsibility and to establish the responsiveness of financial statements to users' needs, it is necessary that there be an explicit statement of objectives of the accounting profession, a statement that is not necessary for other trades or professions in which responsibility does not extend beyond the individual direct customer or client level.

It is most important for objectives of financial statements to be stated explicitly to provide for effective evaluation and evolution of financial accounting standards, and to respond to the challenges posed by public criticism of the financial accounting process. Stated objectives should set forth the function of financial statements and provide an overall framework for determining financial accounting principles or standards. The objectives should also facilitate the determination of implementation techniques and formats.

Objectives and Financial Accounting Standards

Financial accounting principles or standards indicate

> . . . which economic resources and obligations should be recorded as assets and liabilities by financial accounting, which changes in assets and liabilities should be recorded, when these changes should be recorded, how the assets and liabilities and changes in them should be measured, what information should be disclosed and how it should be disclosed, and which financial statements should be prepared.[1]

They are guides to be followed in the preparation of financial statements.

Objectives of financial statements, on the other hand, are the functions that financial statements are designed to serve, the policies to which financial statements should conform, and the qualities financial statements should have to serve their functions and conform to established policies.

Financial accounting standards, which represent specific choices for preparation of financial statements, should be selected to promote the objectives of financial statements. "Financial accounting and reporting . . . must rest on . . . standards designed to achieve what are perceived to be the desired objectives of financial accounting and reporting."[2] Agreeing on the objectives and stating them explicitly is indispensable to that process. Ideally, the objectives should be identified, and then methods of implementing the objectives should be selected as financial accounting standards.

Stating objectives facilitates the following activities:

1. Evaluation of present financial accounting standards.
2. Adoption of proposed financial accounting standards.
3. Evolution of financial accounting standards to respond to changes in objectives or in implementation technology.

---

[1] APB Statement No. 4, *Basic Concepts and Accounting Principles Underlying Financial Statements of Business Enterprises* (New York: American Institute of Certified Public Accountants, 1970), Paragraph 137.

[2] Study on Establishment of Accounting Principles, *Establishing Financial Accounting Standards* (New York: American Institute of Certified Public Accountants, 1972), p. 19.

Evaluating Present Financial Accounting Standards

Present financial accounting standards can be effectively evaluated only if the objectives which they are supposed to fulfill have been specified first. Without stated objectives, present financial accounting standards can only be evaluated against inconclusive criteria, such as the number of enterprises that follow the standards or whether the standards conform to traditional ideas. It is, however, impossible to determine whether a given standard is accomplishing the intended goal if that goal is not known or stated. "Articulation of social goals is important for ascertaining whether they are being reached and even for reaching them. It is improbable, to say the least, that any goals can be reached by chance."[3]

If a financial accounting standard were adopted, for example, which specified a single method of depreciation as the only acceptable method, conformity of accounting practice to that standard could be determined. Whether the method was accomplishing the implicit objective which led to the adoption of the standard, however, could not be determined in the absence of an explicitly stated objective. Furthermore, whether practices such as changing estimates of depreciable lives have subverted the implied objective from which the standard was developed also could not be determined. Whether or not practices subverted the intended objective could only be determined if the objective has been previously specified.

Adoption of Proposed Financial Accounting Standards

Specifying objectives is necessary to reach agreement on sound changes in financial accounting standards or the adoption of new accounting standards. How can an analysis of proposed changes in standards proceed in a logical or rational manner unless the objectives to be served by these standards are explicitly stated and agreed to? If objectives are not explicitly stated, it is difficult to establish whether disagreement results because of differences in implied objectives of financial statements or because of differing conclusions concerning the efficacy of the proposed standards in achieving agreed-to objectives. The explicit statement of objectives allows for a more structured investigation of proposed standards and should facilitate resolution of conflicting positions. Disagreement may remain but would be confined to questions such as those concerning the efficiency of proposed standards in achieving objectives or the resolution of conflicts between objectives.

Responding to Changes in User Needs or Technology

Financial accounting standards at any time may be the best available means to achieve the objectives of financial statements, given existing needs and the implementation technology available. Both needs and technology may later change however. Stating the objectives of financial statements

---

[3] Nestor E. Terleckyj, "Measuring Progress Towards Social Goals: Some Possibilities at National and Local Levels," *Management Science*, August 1970, p. B-765.

and the available implementation technology permits systematic re-examination of financial accounting standards in the light of changed circumstances. In the absence of stated objectives and without consideration of changes in implementation technology, financial accounting standards may become dogma, appearing as ends in themselves rather than as the pragmatic means aimed at accomplishing objectives. Enveloped in tradition, the original justification for the standard is forgotten and the standard becomes impervious to change.

Conservatism is an example of a financial accounting standard that originally might have been a sound response to proper objectives. Since the objectives that the standard of conservatism was intended to accomplish were never made explicit, however, conservatism has achieved the status of an end and, as such, defies and hinders re-examination and revision. The following speculative analysis may be plausible: If the primary audience for financial statements originally were credit grantors, then conservatism may have evolved in response to an objective to provide useful information to credit grantors. Credit grantors must make decisions as to whether to grant loans. In making a loan, the credit grantor receives the benefit of interest payments but risks the principal of the loan. Since principal is almost always larger than interest, the lender has more to lose by making a bad loan (in which he loses the principal) than by not making a good loan (in which he foregoes the interest he could have earned). He therefore needs information that will minimize his chances of making a bad loan, even at the cost of not making loans that could and should have been made. Conservative accounting information may have resulted because of creditors' preference for information that would minimize the probability of making a "bad" loan.

Since the audience for financial statements has shifted to a large degree from creditors to investors, the standard of conservatism may no longer be responsive to users' needs. Investors have as much to lose by not making a good investment as from making a bad investment. In fact, they have more to lose from not making a good investment since market appreciation is unbounded, whereas market loss is limited to the price paid for the security.

It was never stated that conservatism was a standard intended to be responsive to creditor needs or any other objective. Instead we inherited a dogma, and no vehicle for modifying this standard is available to respond to a changed audience of users. Conservatism may, of course, have evolved in response to different influences. In any event, since the objectives originally to be served by the standard of conservatism were not identified or are now lost, no methods are available to determine if the objectives originally justifying the standard are viable or obsolete.

Another example may clarify this point. One of the most vexing problems confronting the accounting profession in the past decade has been the problem of leases or, more generally, of executory contracts essentially unperformed by both parties. Since the early twentieth century, accountants have accepted with little questioning the dogma that executory contracts essentially unperformed by both sides shall not be recorded. They have not seriously questioned why this practice was adopted or what ends it was meant to serve. It is entirely possible that when this practice was adopted in the early twentieth century it represented a proper response to a valid objective: Information should only be reported in financial statements if the benefit of that information exceeds the cost of reporting it.

In the early twentieth century most executory contracts were of short duration and essentially recurring. A typical example might be a one-year lease. Obviously any payments demanded by the lease contract were recorded as they occurred. Similarly, the utilization of lease facilities and the incurrence of any liability as a result were also recorded. Thus the question concerning leases at that point of time was not whether they should be recorded by the accounting process but rather how often. Payments under the lease were recorded, and utilization of lease facilities was recorded. The questions of whether the signing of the lease or the entering into the agreement should also be recorded became appropriate matters for consideration. Since under the conditions stated all three of these events were likely to happen within one year, the legitimate question could be raised whether the costs of recording the lease agreement as well as the payment and utilization of lease facilities were justified by the informational benefits of reporting such agreements. Very likely, a proper response would have been that there was little informational benefit to be gained by reporting the signing of the lease under such circumstances. However, no reasoning leading to the adoption of the standard was given and it was never specified what objective was meant to be served by the practice of not recording executory contracts essentially unperformed. Thus, as the nature of executory contracts changed from essentially short-term recurring contracts to long-term leases or long-term employment contracts, it was impossible to determine whether such changed circumstances should result in changed practices. Obviously, if the objective that led to the adoption of the rule that executory contracts essentially unperformed shall not be recorded was related to informational benefits and costs, then that relationship is drastically altered when the contract is a fifty-year lease rather than a one-year recurring agreement.

Response to Challenges and Criticism

Stating objectives of financial statements is necessary not only to evaluate and change financial accounting standards but also to preserve those standards that facilitate the achievement of proper objectives. Without stating objectives explicitly, proper standards cannot be effectively defended against challenges. Stating objectives of financial statements would strengthen the accounting profession's position for establishing financial accounting standards in the private sector. Demonstrating that the objectives of financial statements legitimately differ from objectives of fiscal or tax policy would provide a sound rationale for financial accounting standards that differ to some extent from rules of tax accounting, for example. Demonstrating that financial accounting standards represent appropriate and feasible implementation of stated and desirable objectives of financial statements would reduce opportunities for political interference in financial statement construction.

Court decisions have recently held that conformity with generally accepted accounting principles or standards is not necessarily a valid defense to a challenge against financial statements. The courts themselves have implicitly established objectives of financial statements and have determined whether given financial statements under challenge adequately meet the objectives. If the accounting profession agreed to and stated the objectives of financial statements and demonstrated that financial accounting standards serve those objectives, it could more easily justify the position that conformity with financial accounting standards should be the criterion to judge financial statements. In other words, the profession can then legitimately argue that principles and standards are generally accepted because they are proper and right rather than that they are right and proper because they are generally accepted.

The public has criticized the accounting profession for not being a positive force in the public sector. Stating objectives of financial statements clearly and establishing financial accounting standards that are responsive to objectives seem the best way to meet that criticism. The accounting profession could then be identified and evaluated in terms of the appropriateness of visible goals and its effectiveness in achieving these.

THE NEED FOR ACCOUNTING OBJECTIVES IN AN EFFICIENT MARKET

Joshua Ronen

The Need for Accounting Objectives In an Efficient Market

Joshua Ronen

In light of the American Institute of Certified Public Accountants' recent appointment of the Accounting Objectives Study Group to formulate the objectives of financial statements, some questions were raised regarding the propriety of regulating accounting information through specifying the objectives of financial statements. Arguments were put forth stating that, in view of the generally demonstrated efficiency of the marketplace, Adam Smith's invisible hand will cause the appropriate kind and quantity of accounting information to be communicated; and that therefore the regulation of accounting information by a group of interested preparers and users will be wasteful. The purpose of this paper is to examine whether—in view of the theory of, and the empirical findings related to, efficient markets—there is a justification for the specification of accounting objectives.

The first part of this paper discusses the implications of the efficient market hypothesis and its related research with respect to the choice of a "best" accounting system. The second part is addressed to the question of whether there exist market incentives for firms to produce an optimal amount of accounting information which would eliminate the need for regulation. The issue is examined first by assuming that no disclosure laws exist, and then the existing disclosure laws are explicitly taken into consideration.

The Implications of Efficient Market Research On the Choice Among Accounting Alternatives

Recent research effort in accounting[1] centers on the implications of the efficient market hypothesis and the empirical capital market research for

[1] Ray Ball and Philip Brown, "An Empirical Evaluation of Accounting Income Numbers," *Journal of Accounting Research* (Autumn 1968), pp. 159-178. W. Beaver, P. Kettler, and M. Scholes, "The Association Between Accounting Information and Market Valuation of Securities," *Accounting Review* (October 1970), pp. 654-682. William H. Beaver, "The Behavior of Security Prices and Its Implications for Accounting Research (Methods)," Supplement to the *Accounting Review* (1972), pp. 407-437. R. E. Dukes, "Market Evaluation of Alternative Accounting Information Systems" (Unpublished dissertation, Stanford University). Nicholas J. Gonedes, "Efficient Capital Markets and External Accounting," *Accounting Review* (January 1972), pp. 11-21. L. L. Lookabill, "A Study of the Relationship Between Accounting Information and Market Valuation of Securities" (Unpublished dissertation, Stanford University).

choosing among accounting alternatives. For example, it is stated that "observations of the market reactions of recipients of accounting outputs should govern evaluations of the actual informational content of accounting numbers produced via a given set of procedures and the informational content of accounting numbers[2] produced via an alternative set of accounting procedures." The underlying contention is that in the context of competitive and efficient markets, transactors in the aggregate will not react to accounting information[3] unless the accounting numbers have informational content.[4]

Not much harm is caused by the assertion that when accounting numbers are used (as manifested in movement of stock prices), they have informational content. This is descriptive of a definition of what constitutes informational content and of actual phenomena, i.e., movement of stock prices. When it is asserted, however, that market reactions should govern the evaluation of accounting alternatives, the underlying implication is that when accounting numbers are used (i.e., the market reacts to them) they are also useful in the sense of satisfying the objectives of accounting. The problem with this approach is that it uses a definition and the manifested results of a descriptive process to make a normative judgment (that market reactions should govern the evaluation of accounting alternatives).

The assertion that market reactions should govern the evaluation of accounting alternatives is primarily justified by acknowledging that—assuming that individuals are rational and that markets are efficient (as defined and shown in the efficient market literature)—one cannot expect the market to react unless accounting information is useful. However, the kind of usefulness that should be inferred from (a) the proposition that individuals are rational and from (b) the findings that markets adjust efficiently and unbiasedly to information, may not necessarily be the kind of usefulness that we might care to require from accounting information.

Evaluation of Usefulness In Light of Accounting Objectives

Certainly, the kind of usefulness that is desired can be derived only from the objectives of accounting. For example, if among the criteria or objectives

---

[2] Gonedes, "Efficient Capital Markets and External Accounting," p. 12.

[3] Reaction to accounting information is generally measured via movements in the stock price through which the aggregate behavior of market transactors is manifested.

[4] Informational content of accounting output is usually implicitly defined as those attributes of the accounting output that trigger market reaction. For example, Ball & Brown argue, "If, as the evidence indicates, security prices do in fact adjust rapidly to new information as it becomes available, the changes in security prices will reflect the flow of information to the market. An observed revision of stock prices associated with the release of the income report would thus provide evidence that the information reflected in income numbers is useful." (Ball and Brown, "An Empirical Evaluation of Accounting Income Numbers," pp. 160-161.)

of accounting there is listed the efficiency in resource allocation and perhaps some criteria relative to the distribution of wealth,[5] it may be discovered that the kind of usefulness inferred from market reactions does not necessarily satisfy these two objectives. In other words, the kind of market equilibrium consistent with presently available accounting information and the degree of efficiency of the market's reaction to this kind of information may not necessarily be the desired equilibrium. (Note that equilibrium is a descriptive phenomenon and not in itself an indication that some normative criterion has been satisfied.) Thus, the manifestations of a present equilibrium which may be undesirable cannot be used as a normative criterion for choosing the accounting alternative which best satisfies an objective. The satisfaction of the specified objective may well require a different kind of market equilibrium which—if extant—would produce entirely different manifestations.

To put things somewhat differently, imagine that there are two market equilibrium systems, *A* and *B*, and two distinct systems of accounting procedures resulting in sets of accounting signals *X* and *Y*, respectively. Then assume that *X* and *Y* are evaluated on the basis of the market's reactions. Suppose it turns out that under system *A* the market reacts to *X* but not to *Y* (thus indicating that *X*, and not *Y*, has informational content) while under system *B*, the market reacts to *Y* but not to *X* (thus implying that *Y*, and not *X*, has informational content). Which is the better accounting system? Clearly, in this situation the market reaction is not a sufficient criterion. There is still open the question of which equilibrium system, *A* or *B*, better serves the objectives. This illustration could also be applied over time rather than across market systems. Presumably, a different market equilibrium system existed 100 years ago and the accounting system undoubtedly was somewhat different from today's practice. How can the two systems be evaluated if the market reacted to both systems? How can a descriptive phenomenon be used to make normative judgments?[6]

Exploration of the descriptive phenomenon is valuable in understanding the market mechanism and in generating hypotheses about the nature of decision-making in the marketplace. The descriptive phenomenon is also useful in testing the implications of hypotheses about how decisions are made in the marketplace. However, it cannot be the sole test of which

[5] While the means of achieving allocation of resources in the economy are subject to debate, probably none would question the desirability of efficient resource allocation as a goal. As to equity criteria relative to the distribution of wealth, they are clearly implicit as objectives. For example, Rules 10b-5, 10b-6 and Section 16 of the Securities Exchange Act of 1934 and the Court rulings in the Texas Gulf case relate to insider trading and the disclosure of information.

[6] Indeed it may be argued that technological changes modify the nature of the equilibrium over time. The proposition of an accounting alternative whose test of usefulness is not derived from extant equilibrium can be viewed as a technological change in itself.

accounting alternative better satisfies our goals and should therefore be preferred. The appropriate test should depend, among other things, on pre-specified accounting objectives.[7]

The Argument That Accounting Operates In a Competitive Context

The contention that accounting alternatives should be evaluated on the basis of market reactions is partially defended on the grounds that the accounting process provides information only in a competitive context and that there are alternative sources of information that investors could use.[8] The contention that accounting operates in a competitive context is based on (a) the assumption that accounting numbers include information that reflects economy-wide events and industry-wide events that can also be obtained from other indicators such as industrial production reports and national income reports, and (b) the evidence of the existence of anticipatory price movements that precede the announcement of accounting numbers.[9] Thus, it is argued that if there were no other sources competing with accounting information, one would expect to observe rapid price movements when accounting data are disseminated. As a result, it is postulated that ". . . market transactors in the aggregate do not blindly accept and use accounting numbers only" and therefore "the market's reaction to accounting numbers (e.g., the anticipatory reactions noted above) provides reliable indication of accounting numbers' informational content."[10]

There are several problems with these contentions. Alternative sources of information with respect to economy- and industry-wide events that affect the value of the firm may well exist, but the likelihood of alternative sources of information about the existence of a firm's specific events is minimal. It is indeed possible that the latter does exist since such events usually constitute transactions involving other entities which, potentially, could provide the information. However, the cost of reconstructing the firm's specific events from numerous and possibly scattered sources is probably prohibitive. As a result, such a reconstruction of events may not be undertaken by investors since

---

[7] A framework for the formulation of accounting objectives is discussed by the author in "A User Oriented Development of Accounting Information Requirements," pp. 80-103, this volume.

[8] See, e.g., Gonedes, "Efficient Capital Markets and External Accounting," p. 14: "In particular it appears that the accounting process—qua supplier of information—does not possess strict monopoly power over the supply of information pertinent to the evaluation of a firm. Instead, it appears that the accounting process—qua supplier of information—functions within a competitive context."

[9] For example, Ball and Brown, "An Empirical Evaluation of Accounting Income Numbers."

[10] Gonedes, "Efficient Capital Markets and External Accounting," p. 16.

the cost may exceed the perceived benefits.[11] Thus, if some firm-specific information is not provided by the firm, even if it is available in the market it may not be used. This fact is consistent with an efficient market in which transaction costs are assumed to exist.

Moreover, a market equilibrium in which transactors do not seek information because of the high cost of search, even when they know that it exists, is consistent with the evidence collected about efficient markets. And when accounting information is provided about firms' specific events for which alternative sources of information are too costly to seek out, transactors are justified in relying on the accounting information.

Thus, if it is found that transactors accept and use accounting numbers (this phenomenon has occasionally been referred to as functional fixation,[12] although the term has never been rigorously defined), this does not necessarily imply that they do so blindly. Use of the accounting numbers by transactors may be explained by one or both of the following propositions:

1. In equilibrium, investors rely on accounting information whenever the cost of seeking alternative sources about the same events exceeds the benefits of searching. This is likely to be the case in particular with respect to firms' specific events.[13] Thus investors' reliance on accounting information does not imply that they do so blindly, but rather that they make rational decisions about when to stop seeking information.

2. The accounting system is a vehicle for management to communicate its expectations about the firm's cash flows, and it is likely that investors view accounting information as a surrogate for management expectations which they utilize since there are no alternative sources.

A social organization that requires firms to report probably results from an implicit decision based on information economics. Delegation of the information provision function to the firm makes sense if the firm can produce the information at a lower cost than outsiders. This is consistent with the evidence that accounting information is anticipated through price move-

---

[11] This is consistent with the phenomenon, for example, that in some developing countries the state enforces the disclosure of minimal accounting information (apparently because individuals find it too costly to produce the information themselves). Turkey is a case in point. See Var Turgut, "The Turkish Uniform Accounting Plan," (Unpublished manuscript, University of Kansas).

[12] Yuji Ijiri, Robert K. Jaedicke, and Kenneth E. Knight, "The Effects of Accounting Alternatives on Management Decisions," *Research in Accounting Measurement,* edited by Robert K. Jaedicke, Yuji Ijiri, and Oswald Nielson (Evanston, Ill.: American Accounting Association, 1966).

[13] The cost to the firm of processing information about its specific events and transactions is probably lower because of scale economies. While no evidence exists on this hypothesis, it is clearly empirically testable. It is also consistent with the observation that the SEC and other governmental agencies increasingly require more accounting information to be disseminated. To provide evidence against this hypothesis, it must be shown, for example, that anticipatory market reaction is caused solely through sources other than the firm and that the anticipatory reaction explains all reaction to accounting information (which has yet to be shown).

ments prior to the announcement date. There probably exist cheaper outside sources for information about economy-wide and industry-wide information that are tapped in advance of the announcement of accounting information. Some firm-specific events could also be anticipated as a result of announcements by the firms' managements through releases issued by market newsletter services and through reports by the firm to the SEC, etc. These "leakages," however, all come from the firm itself and could well be viewed as part of its information or accounting system. In fact, it might be advisable to incorporate such announcements formally into the accounting system, since they would then be subject to audit and verification.

In sum, the existing evidence on efficient markets may well be viewed as being consistent with the following statement: Market transactors, in the aggregate, accept and use accounting numbers as well as any additional information that they can obtain at reasonable search costs. Had accounting numbers not been provided, market reactions might have been different since the information contained in accounting numbers might then have been too costly to obtain elsewhere. Thus, market reactions alone do not provide a criterion for evaluating information alternatives.

In particular, individuals' reliance on accounting numbers does not indicate irrationality or psychological conditioning. Rather, it may reflect rationality within the context of a competitive market in which information is costly and in which expectations about the value of different data are heterogeneous. Individual rationality is thus consistent both with the reliance on accounting data (without testing their informational content through seeking other sources), and with a competitive equilibrium that assumes costly information and heterogeneous expectations. And while the evidence from the efficient market research (both the weak and the semi-strong form) is consistent with that efficient market hypothesis which assumes costless information and homogeneous expectations, it is also consistent with an efficient market hypothesis that assumes costly information and heterogeneous expectations.[14]

The Argument That Stock Prices Eventually Reflect "Inside Information"

Finally, the argument is usually made that market reaction is a reliable indicator since it impounds any existing information, even that not made publicly available. It is contended that since there must be at least one person possessing the information who recognizes the inefficiencies that result from its nonpublic availability, he would—being rational—exploit this opportunity either by transacting directly in the market or by selling the information. Thus, the knowledgeable person (possessing the information)

[14] Stigler, for example, argues: "There is no imperfection in a market possessing incomplete knowledge if it would not be remunerative to acquire (produce) complete knowledge. Information costs are the costs of transportation from ignorance to omniscience, and seldom can a trader afford to take the entire trip." (George J. Stigler, "Imperfections in the Capital Markets," *Journal of Political Economy* (June 1963), p. 291, as quoted in Gonedes, "Efficient Capital Markets and External Accounting," p. 20).

will, through his own action, help to eliminate inefficiency in the market.

However, while it is true that any new existing information is apt to be impounded eventually through an arbitrage mechanism, this mechanism may not be the most desirable process through which information should get impounded in market prices. This is particularly true from the standpoint of social optimum (considering both allocative and distributive criteria). The undesirability can result for several reasons:

1. Assuming that inside information exists,[15] there is uncertainty about the length of time needed for the arbitrage process to rectify the allocative inefficiency (resulting from nonpublic availability of the information). Since the time lapse is likely to be greater than it would be if such information were required to be immediately available to the public, the allocative inefficiency is apt to continue for a longer time period than if such a requirement were made.

2. Insiders possessing information not available to the public or superior forecasting ability are likely to cause the information to be impounded in market prices with less efficiency than if they were to make the information immediately available to the public. This is likely to be the case for at least two reasons. First, they may not have the sufficient capital immediately available to carry out the volume of trading necessary to rectify the inefficiency. Second, they are not likely to have a comparative advantage in selling information or in offering portfolio management services. In comparison, if such information were required to be made immediately available through the accounting system, the process is likely to be more efficient, since there is a greater likelihood that individuals with sufficient capital and those who possess comparative advantage in selling information would be included among the recipients of the information.

3. The likelihood of a single individual or a small knowledgeable group being able to interpret inside information properly is less than the likelihood of the same information being ably interpreted if it were available to many persons and many groups, i.e., if it were publicly available. In other words, the greater the number of participating rivals in the marketplace, the more efficient is the process of competitive equilibrium.

4. Finally, the prospect of insiders becoming wealthier may not be palatable to those for whom criteria for desirable distribution of wealth are considered to be important.

Existing Incentives to Communicate Desirable Information

It is assumed in the efficient market literature,[16] that the existence of super-analysts will eventually insure that actual market prices are, on the

[15] Some evidence on the existence of inside information is provided by Myron Scholes in "A Test of the Competitive Market Hypothesis: The Market for New Issues and Secondary Offerings" (Unpublished Ph.D. thesis, University of Chicago, 1969).

[16] See, for example, Eugene F. Fama, "The Behavior of Stock Market Prices," *Journal of Business* (January 1965), pp. 34-105.

basis of all available information, best estimates of intrinsic values. But notice that the identity, on the average, between security prices and the intrinsic value ultimately depends on the ability to consistently predict the appearance of new information and the subsequent prediction of its impact on intrinsic values. Suppose there is new information which is neither made available to sophisticated traders nor predictable on the basis of presently known information (possibly because it does not fit into the familiar pattern of information dependencies learned by the analyst). It is conceivable that, had this information been made available, the stock price would have been changed as a result of impounding the content of the new information. It could be argued that, since equilibrium is reached in the absence of this information and the relative wealth of the investors is preserved, it is not crucial that the new information be reflected in actual prices. However, in that event, resource allocation is sub-optimal. Thus, from the standpoint of stating accounting objectives, the relevant questions are:

1. What are the likely sources that possess new information which may not be made immediately available publicly?
2. Does the existing market system provide incentives for those sources to make the information available?

A likely source of new information is the firm itself. The new information consists of prospective cash flows that result from the decisions and plans being made continuously within the firm.[17] These plans and decisions are first known to the management; they are the endogenous factors—peculiar to the firm—responsible for the firm's unique rate of return. Because management is the first to know its plans, it is also the first to make a prediction of the cash flows that result from these decisions. Thus, by systematically and periodically communicating expectations of cash flows, management can provide valuable information that is not, at the present time, made available systematically.

The second question can best be examined by considering the system of incentives offered by the market that may induce the provision of such information with and without disclosure laws.

Incentives for Producing and Communicating Information in the Absence of Disclosure Laws

This question was investigated directly by Fama and Laffer[18] and indirectly by Hirshleifer.[19] In spite of the different approaches, the two discussions reach many of the same conclusions. Since Fama and Laffer's

---

[17] While management's expectations of these flows may be communicated publicly, they are not part of the systematic and periodic accounting reports and they are generally communicated in an ad hoc and sporadic fashion at the present time.

[18] Eugene F. Fama and Arthur B. Laffer, "Information and Capital Markets," *Journal of Business* (July 1971), pp. 289-298.

[19] Jack Hirshleifer, "The Private and Social Value of Information and the Inventive Activity," *American Economic Review* (September 1971), pp. 561-574.

discussion is, however, more germane to the role of information produced by the firm vis-à-vis other sources, it is used as a basis for discussion. Their main conclusions are briefly stated, and their underlying assumptions are examined.

The Fama and Laffer Conclusions And Assumptions

Fama and Laffer conclude that the production of information for trading purposes only[20] is not consistent with Pareto optimality. The production and communication of this information is costly since it uses resources merely to redistribute wealth and not to generate it. Thus "investors as a whole would be better off (and the producer would be no worse off) if they could simply pay the monopolist in order to induce him not to produce information. . . ."[21]

Since high transaction costs are associated with such side payments, the authors predict that, in general, there will be some socially sub-optimal information output. Other conclusions of interest are as follows:

1. In equilibrium there will be a single producer of a certain type of information about a firm, and when this producer is an independent outsider (vis-à-vis the firm) his profits will always be greater if he sells the information rather than use it for his own trading.
2. Under competitive conditions of producing information, a producer can cover his costs only by selling to investors.
3. As a rule, under monopolistic conditions information will be sold.
4. When a firm produces information about itself, it produces less than an independent outsider, since the firm considers the effects of its information production on the firm's shareholders.
5. In the interests of its shareholders, the firm has strong incentives to have all the information produced at its discretion.

---

[20] That is, information that neither reduces risk, thus reducing the supply of a non-desirable commodity, nor improves operating decisions of the firm—thus bringing about savings in resources through their improved allocation. The authors concentrate on "information, as yet unavailable to the market, about decisions already made" ("Information and Capital Markets," p. 291) that affects investor trading profits as a result of private access to new information. This type of information parallels what Hirshleifer ("Private and Social Value of Information and the Inventive Activity," pp. 563-564) describes as prior information about the true states of the world in a simplified world of pure exchange, in which all productive transformations among entities and commodities are ruled out and in which the endowments of individuals can be modified only by trading. This is the type of information that can affect only the wealth distribution and not the resource allocation.

[21] Fama and Laffer, "Information and Capital Markets," p. 294. While Fama and Laffer discuss the incentives to produce information under both monopolistic, competitive and partially competitive environments, the thrust of the conclusion is not significantly affected by the economic environment assumed. In all environments, it is concluded that socially sub-optimal information will tend to be produced, and only the extent of sub-optimality and the identity of the producer may be affected.

In summary, Fama and Laffer conclude that, except in the case of monopoly or partial monopoly, and when the monopolistic producer is an independent outsider rather than the firm itself,[22] the firm will tend to produce information about itself and prevent others from doing so.

The Fama and Laffer assumptions of primary concern to our discussion are as follows:

1. Firms are perfectly competitive in their product markets, and the capital market is perfect in the sense of zero transaction costs (costless access to publicly available information) and the existence of perfect substitutes for the firm's securities.
2. Investors can trade in the market without identifying themselves as possessing new information.
3. Investors have "homogeneous expectations" in that they agree on the implications of any given information set for the equilibrium prices of securities.
4. A seller of new information insists that the purchaser guarantee against resale of the information.

Moreover, it is assumed that any potential producer of information about a firm knows the probability distribution of market value changes associated with different levels of information expenditures, and that—should these distributions have a zero mean—this fact is costless information. As a result, market prices impound it, and the consequence of going from zero to some positive level of expenditure is a probability distribution of market value that has a zero mean.

Implications for Accounting

To examine the implications of the conclusions for the need to specify accounting alternatives, assume first that the firm is the sole producer of information. If the firm is a monopolistic producer, it will benefit its shareholders by enabling them to sell their stock in the case of negative foreknowledge information. Positive information would eventually come to light anyway and will not affect the expected gain to the firm's shareholders. But in the case of discovery information[23] the firm will release positive information and either suppress negative information or give shareholders the oppor-

[22] Which is an unlikely situation when the type of information produced is one that relates to a firm's specific events (see discussion below). Moreover, Fama and Laffer state that "the firm is not limited to direct competition with independent producers for sales to outsiders, since the cost to an outsider of producing information about a firm is likely to be somewhat in the firm's control." ("Information and Capital Markets," p. 298.)

[23] The dichotomy between foreknowledge and discovery information was first made by Hirshleifer ("Private and Social Value of Information and the Inventive Activity"). Foreknowledge consists of events that will become known whether or not information about them is generated. Discovery involves things that would not become known without information production.

tunity to sell before the information reaches the market.[24]

When information generation is competitive, the firm will prevent entry by independent producers, give its information output to its shareholders, and recover its costs entirely from sales to outsiders. In this case, since the information will be available both to the firm's shareholders and to outsiders, no investors will have expected trading gains. In the case of partial monopoly, the firm will act like a monopoly with respect to incremental information that the firm produces for which the marginal cost is below that of the next cheapest producer.

Thus, except for the case of competitive generation of information[25] there are likely to be trading gains or losses, i.e., redistribution of wealth. In the absence of a requirement with respect to immediate dissemination of information generated or known to the firm, and given all the Fama and Laffer assumptions,[26] there are incentives that induce firms and outsiders either to sell information or to trade on its basis—thus causing redistribution of wealth. This shift of wealth may violate social distributive criteria of welfare aside from waste of resources. Thus, a requirement that information known to the firm must be disseminated can help in preventing shifts of wealth that could be socially undesirable even when the information produced is assumed to have no allocative effects.

It is apparent from the foregoing that production of information which has allocative effects[27] may be consistent with Pareto optimality in the sense that the benefits resulting from production decisions based on the information generated may well exceed the costs of producing the information. Indeed, given the Fama and Laffer assumptions, both the firm and outside independent producers would have the incentive to generate the information and either act upon it or sell it.[28]

It now becomes important to carefully examine the Fama and Laffer assumptions to determine whether, indeed, there is enough incentive to generate socially beneficial information that has allocative effects. Indeed, it seems unlikely that any information would have only a distributive effect and would not improve production decisions or the consumption-investment opportunities of individuals. For example, positive information (whether

[24] Fama and Laffer, "Information and Capital Markets," p. 294. Notice that in the case of discovery information, negative information may be suppressed. In a case where discovery information has allocative effects (in that it leads to improved operating decisions), on the other hand, it probably would not be disseminated, thus causing sub-optimality even under the strict assumptions made by Fama and Laffer.

[25] As indicated, this is unlikely with respect to the firm-specific information since the firm has first access to the transactions giving rise to such information.

[26] "Information and Capital Markets."

[27] Notice that Fama and Laffer postulated that discovery information may well be of the type that can improve production, i.e., have allocative effects.

[28] Except in the case of negative discovery information which, once generated, may be suppressed by the firm.

foreknowledge or discovery) released by the firm will bring about a positive revision in the prices of securities which in turn would reduce the cost of capital-raising. This, in itself, is bound to have an effect on resource allocation decisions within the firm.

The assumption that the capital market is perfect and that producing firms are perfectly competitive in their product markets is needed so that information about a specific firm will not affect the consumption-investment opportunities of individuals except through its effects on their wealth. This is analogous to Hirshleifer's assumption of pure exchange[29] in which only the endowment vector of individuals, rather than production, is affected by the information generated. But information about a product or an industry is likely to affect consumption-investment opportunities through its implications for changes in relative prices. Thus, in the case of nonperfectly competitive product markets or a nonperfect capital market or in the case where information is generated about an industry rather than about a single firm, the information generation will probably affect consumption-investment opportunities of investors, and thus affect the reallocation of resources and not merely the distribution of wealth.[30]

Another set of assumptions that is not likely to hold is (a) that investors can trade without indicating that they possess new information and (b) that the seller of new information insists that the purchaser guarantee against resale of the information. The first assumption (nonidentifiability of a possessor of new information) insures that returns from exclusive access to information can be maximized. Through the second assumption other potential purchasers can be guaranteed exclusive access to the information sold. To the extent that either of these assumptions does not hold, which is the likely case, the incentive to generate and to communicate new information is significantly lessened. It is usually difficult to observe the selling of information about a firm, especially accounting information. Accounting information is provided at zero price. This is probably so because the transaction costs of guaranteeing exclusive access to the information and of maintaining the unidentifiability of the possessor of new information are very high.[31]

Even if information were sold at a positive price, the ability of the resulting price to provide an appropriate signal and incentive for the genera-

---

[29] "Private and Social Value of Information and the Inventive Activity."

[30] These are probably the situations that Hirshleifer considers as "the more realistic regime in which production and exchange both take place." (Hirshleifer, "Private and Social Value of Information and the Inventive Activity," p. 566.)

[31] While information in the nature of "consulting advice" is sold by consulting and management-services firms, the costs of policing the right and the exclusive access of the purchaser to the information are much smaller than those associated with guaranteeing access to information in the nature of "facts" about a firm. This is particularly true if we allow for heterogeneous expectations governing at the market place so that there is disagreement about the implications of facts. The interpretive processing by "advisors" can be viewed like any other commodity that commands a non-zero price in the market.

tion of information would be very limited. This is so because the ability to enforce the right to exclusive access to the information purchased determines, to a significant extent, the value of that information and its price. The ability of such enforcement is likely to be very limited in the case of information about a firm (including accounting information), and thus the private benefit for the seller is apt to be significantly below the social benefit.[32]

The observance of zero prices for information about a firm (primarily accounting information) and the regulation of the amount and nature of information to be included in reports issued by the firm about itself are consistent with the assumption that the costs of policing information are excessively high. In other words, the reason that accounting information is presently regulated is probably because the property policing costs are too high to allow the market to generate accurate information on the social benefits of accounting information. In this situation, the SEC's, or preferably the profession's, determination of the objectives and nature of desirable accounting information may be the most practical way of coping with the nonfeasibility of guaranteeing exclusive access to information about the firm, just as government non-price rationing may be the most practical way of coping with high exchange costs. It should be noted, however, that the SEC's or the profession's rationing of information about the firm is costly and only second best to a market in which exchange and enforcement costs were low. Regulation, essentially a political process, would result in less efficiency than reliance on a market with low transaction costs. But, in the absence of the latter, regulation may be the only efficient way of ascertaining the social value of information about a firm unless the cost of regulation per se exceeds the benefits from rationing, in which case regulation should be eliminated.[33]

Finally, the assumption of homogeneous expectations makes possible the proposition that there can be general agreement on the probability distributions of market value changes associated with different information expenditures and, if these have non-zero means, market prices will adjust unbiasedly. Once we allow for heterogeneous expectations, this will not hold and the likelihood that incentives for generating information would exist will not be assessable.

If the above assumptions do not hold there may not be incentives in the market for generating information nor for overproducing information. In this case, and when the information has allocative effects (i.e., when information affects resource allocation for productive purposes), the systems of incentives presently provided in the market may not induce the generation and communication of socially desirable information.

---

[32] For a lucid discussion of issues related to the impact of enforceability of rights to property on prices, see Harold Demsetz, "The Exchange and Enforcement of Property Rights," *Journal of Law and Economics*, VII (October 1964), pp. 11-26.

[33] This "truistic" statement merely indicates the desirability of an extensive cost/benefit study of accounting information regulation. Such a study itself is not costless.

Effects of Disclosure Rules

We now examine the possible effects of disclosure laws and regulation of information on the incentive for producing information about firms. If information that could potentially be produced by a firm has only distributive effects (e.g., for trading purposes), the present disclosure laws may lead to a social optimum.[34] If the firm is a monopolistic producer of information it will generally lose its incentive to produce the information, since under the disclosure regulations it is prohibited from discriminating in favor of its shareholders or from selling the information. This is also the case when the firm is able to produce the same information that an outside producer can generate at a lower cost. But as Fama and Laffer comment,[35] there may be situations in which the disclosure laws can lead to inefficiencies in the sense that an outsider produces information that the firm could produce more cheaply were it not for the disclosure law that destroys the firm's incentive to produce. A more detailed analysis of the effect of the particular disclosure law in existence may help to clarify these points. For this purpose it will be assumed that the information discussed has potential allocative effects.

Under the Securities Exchange Act of 1934, profits made within six months by a firm's officers through trading in the firm's stock inures to the firm [Section 78p(b) of the 15th U.S. Code]. Moreover, Rule 10b-5 (of Title 240 of the Code of Federal Regulations) prohibits the use of manipulative and deceptive devices, which are broadly construed to include making "any untrue statement of a material fact or to omit to state a material fact necessary in order to make the statements made, in the light of the circumstances under which they were made, not misleading . . . in connection with the purchase or sale of any security." Rule 10b-6 of the same regulation prohibits trading in securities by parties interested in their distribution.

Under these rules a firm's officer, who is either in the possession of information or of the means to produce information which is either not likely to be revealed by an alternative source outside the firm within a period of six months[36] or whose effect on price is expected to persist beyond six months, would have an economic incentive to maximize his gains from the information by either trading in the stock himself or by selling the information to potential traders. (Notice that the law does not affect profits made through trading within a period that exceeds six months.) This does not mean that such an attempt to capitalize on information is costless. The attempt may be

---

[34] See Fama and Laffer, "Information and Capital Markets," p. 298.

[35] Ibid.

[36] The information could not likely be revealed by an outside source either if the insider has monopolistic access to it (as a result of his position or decision-making function within the firm) or because the insider can produce the information more cheaply, thus enabling him to deter the production by outsiders. Notice that much of the relevant information possessed by firm insiders is an already manufactured by-product of decision-making within the firm (e.g., cash flow forecasts necessary to make investment or divestment decisions), and the marginal costs of producing this information for the firm insider (or decision-maker) is zero.

strictly illegal under Rules 10b-5 and 10b-6, and the expected consequences of illegal action must be perceived as part of the cost of trading or of otherwise selling the information by the insider. In addition to this cost, there is the risk of the insider being held liable for misleading the firm's stockholders, thus jeopardizing his position in the firm.

At any rate, the incentive for acting on inside information that is likely to be profitable within a period exceeding six months is greater than the incentive to act upon the information whose usefulness is limited to a period of six months, since in the latter case the profits—by law—would inure to the firm. To the extent that the insider acts upon it, the information will eventually be impounded in market prices[37] thus securing allocative efficiency. Such trading, however, would violate the distributive goals implied in the Securities Exchange Act.

When the profits from using information are expected to be made if trading is completed within a period of six months, firm insiders would have no economic incentive to trade in the firm's stock, since the profit from trading will inure to the firm. An insider can, of course, sell the information to outsiders (not including the firm's shareholders since a major shareholder of the firm is also considered as an insider by the law), although the transaction costs of selling such information to outsiders are apt to be high both economically and legally (due to Rules 10b-5 and 10b-6). To the extent that insiders would sell such information in spite of the economic and legal costs, the information will be impounded in prices, although in the process some resources will be wasted through higher costs (as well as through increased risk to the sellers). To the extent that insiders would be deterred from selling information in this case, there may still be an incentive to generate the information (if it is not already known) and to make it available. In the absence of a direct economic incentive for the insider either to trade or sell the information, it would be to his benefit to make it available to the firm's shareholders so as to enable them to maximize their wealth and thus indirectly reinforce the insider.

But a distinction must be made between positive information (i.e., information which if known will push stock prices up) and negative information (information which if known will bring prices down). If the information is positive, it benefits the shareholders if the information is made publicly available immediately since the market value of their holdings[38] will be increased. In fact, firms' officers do seem to make positive information available immediately through press releases, analysts' conferences, and speeches. Such

[37] Subject to the inefficiencies that may result from communicating the information through insiders' actions for profit maximizing purposes versus immediately making the information available publicly, as discussed earlier.

[38] In the case of foreknowledge, the only benefits of immediately making available positive information from the point of view of shareholders is temporal, i.e., the price increase occurs immediately rather than later in time. In the case of discovery information, however, the benefits consist of the total increase in wealth as a result of prices going up, since if information is not generated and communicated, it will not be known.

releases tend to be timed shortly before new issues or secondary issues of securities are offered even though this practice is illegal. This is understandable since the impact on prices of new information tends to reduce the firm's cost of raising capital. From the point of view of social optimal allocation, the public may be able to make more informed allocation decisions if specific information about a firm is periodically and systematically released so that it can be compared with information about other firms released at about the same time. The social benefit of such presentation which enables this comparison across firms may well exceed the private benefits perceived to inure to the firm as a result of such periodic reports. Thus, the firm may not have an incentive to communicate its information in such a manner, although such periodic and systematic communication—in addition to facilitating the comparison across firms—could enable potential investors to monitor and audit the information and thus assess its reliability.

In the case of negative information, the firm will have no economic incentive to make the information public.[39] It is again useful to make the distinction, however, between foreknowledge and discovery information. In the case of foreknowledge, since the information will become known later to the public, the firm will have an incentive to generate the information and make it known to its shareholders so that they can avoid capital losses by selling their stock. Because of the existence of the disclosure law, however, such trading will not enable shareholders to avoid losses. Since positive knowledge will only produce temporal benefits, the incentive to the firm for generating and communicating foreknowledge would be substantially reduced in cases where a disclosure law does not exist. Positive knowledge, being foreknowledge, will become known and inure to the benefit of shareholders anyway.[40] When negative information is already generated as a by-product at zero marginal cost (as in the case of forecasts necessary to make decisions which have to be made anyhow), such negative information will neither be acted upon by shareholders (in view of the law) nor publicly revealed (assuming that the firm will run the risk associated with Rule 10b-5).

In the case of discovery information, the incentive for the firm to produce the information will be provided only through the positive information, since negative information will be suppressed (assuming again that the firm is willing to run the risk associated with Rule 10b-5). Positive information will be immediately made available so as to increase shareholders' wealth as soon as possible. Thus, the disclosure law is likely to exert only a small impact on inhibiting the production of discovery information.[41]

---

[39] Except for the risk associated with not disclosing known negative information due to Rule 10b-5 of Title 240, as explained above.

[40] But the identity of the benefitting shareholders may change between the point of time at which the foreknowledge would otherwise have been generated and the point of time at which it becomes publicly known. In that case, the temporal benefits referred to above and foregone as a result of late generation of the information would include wealth transfer from potential to existing shareholders.

[41] This slightly inhibiting effect results from whatever impact Rule 10b-5 will have on the likelihood that the firm will suppress negative information.

However if, as is likely, most of the insider information is foreknowledge (being results of decisions and actions already taken by a firm), it is highly likely that the net effect of the disclosure law will be to inhibit the processing and communication of insider information. To the extent that inside information has potentially beneficial allocative effects, the net effect of the disclosure law would be harmful since it will not reveal information that improves the allocation of resources. Hence, the consideration of requiring, through regulation or through specification of objectives, that inside information be periodically and systematically processed and communicated may well be worthwhile.

Conclusions

Considering the existing theory and evidence related to efficient markets, the choice among accounting alternatives cannot be determined solely through the examination of market price reactions to accounting information. Explicit formulation of accounting objectives is needed.

Market incentives, even in the absence of present disclosure laws, may not be sufficient to insure the production and communication of economically useful information. The existing disclosure laws aggravate the problem and seem to reduce the incentive to produce and disseminate useful information. To the extent that information has potential allocative effects outside the firm, the existence of a disclosure law may be suboptimal because the firm would lack the incentive to produce information that could make resource allocation more efficient. Thus, present disclosure laws that prohibit the firm from selling information or from benefitting its shareholders vis-à-vis others can destroy the incentive to produce economically useful information.

Presumably, the intent of present disclosure laws is primarily to prevent undesirable redistribution of wealth that could result from monopolistic access to information. In the process, however, the overall magnitude of wealth may be lessened as a result of impeding the production of desirable signals for resource allocation. If the wealth-distribution goal implied in the disclosure law is taken for granted, regulation of what information is to be produced *and disclosed* by a firm is needed to insure that information useful for allocation decisions is produced by a firm.

In other words, if present disclosure laws must continue to exist to satisfy wealth distribution and other goals, *additional* regulation of accounting information by the private and/or governmental sectors seems warranted to nullify the adverse effect that the present laws may have on the production and communication of economically useful accounting information. Moreover, even if present laws are abrogated, market forces still do not seem to provide sufficient incentives for the production of useful information, thus implying that regulation appears necessary. The formulation of accounting objectives, preferably by the accounting profession and other directly involved parties, is a preliminary and a necessary step for such regulation.

A NOTE ON ACCOUNTING ALTERNATIVES AND SOCIAL CHOICE

Joshua Ronen and George H. Sorter

A NOTE ON ACCOUNTING ALTERNATIVES AND SOCIAL CHOICE

Joshua Ronen and George H. Sorter

It has been argued that the selection among accounting alternatives is a problem of social choice and therefore -- within the context of Arrow's (1963) impossibility theorem -- non-feasible. (Beaver & Demski, 1974 and Gonedes and Dopuch, 1974). Arrow demonstrated that it is impossible to specify a social welfare function that induces a single rule or set of rules of choice among alternatives that will maximize social welfare in the Pareto optimal sense without violating certain conditions regarding axiomatic individual choice behavior in a non-dictatorship type of regime. Pareto optimality implies that one cannot reallocate resources so as to enhance any one individual's welfare without diminishing another's. Beaver & Demski (1974) argue that, in order to choose among accounting alternatives, one must make value or ethical judgments and make decisions as to whose well-being should be enhanced, and whose should be diminished.

We agree with Beaver and Demski (1974) that choice among accounting alternatives clearly has social consequences that affect non-users of accounting information as well as users and that may affect different groups and individuals differently. We further agree that these impacts must ultimately be considered in the context of Arrow's impossibility theorem. We disagree however, with Beaver and Demski's implication that the only way of defining the social choice problem is one of attempting to define individuals' preference orderings over accounting alternatives directly. Rather, it seems more appropriate to analyze the social choice problem in two stages: first, the derivation of individuals' preference-orderings over alternative wealth consequences of accounting alternatives, rather than over accounting alternatives directly ; this clearly would be subject to the implications of Arrow's impossibility theorem; second, defining the desired accounting alternatives that maximize aggregate monetary wealth over all. The second stage is not subject to the implication of Arrow's impossibility theorem, and can be analyzed in terms of accounting information that best serves resource-allocative efficiency. In this fashion we still end up with a social choice problem caused by the need to reconcile the maximization of monetary wealth and social welfare, but this time the social choice problem focuses on social policy decisions designed to optimally distribute wealth rather than decisions on choice among accounting alternatives that maximize welfare. Once we have separated the choice problem into the two stages, i.e., into (1) wealth maximization and (2) socially desirable wealth distributions, we can apply the comparative advantage principle and argue that the first stage optimally lies in the domain of the accounting profession and the second lies in the domain of political science, thus allowing for a separation of the function between the profession and elected government. This separation would allow accounting regulators to specify accounting rules and procedures whose objective is efficient resource allocation, and social and political scientists to adopt compensation schemes to reallocate the resulting wealth among individuals and groups in society in a socially-desirable manner. It seems to us that accountants lack the comparative advantage of fulfilling the latter function. A social optimum can be reached if accounting principles can be identified and implemented to achieve socially-desirable wealth distribution. If the compensation principle cannot be implemented in terms of a desirable cost-benefit relationship), then interaction between the accounting regulators and duly-constituted political bodies would be necessary and desirable. In the latter case, i.e., when the compensation principle does not seem to be implementable, it will be the accounting regulator's function to identify as much as possible the impact of alternative accounting procedures considered on different segments of society; this input then can be fed into the political decision-making process in the consideration of alternative policy programs.

Thus, we argue that (1) the choice of accounting alternatives by accounting regulators should not directly deal with social choice issues, but rather, (2) the accounting regulators should analyze the choice of accounting alternatives in terms of the promotion of resource allocative efficiency and leave to elected government and others more qualified in this domain the subsequent social re-distribution choices. The interesting set of questions faced by the accounting regulators now concern whether the choice of accounting alternatives in the context of attaining efficient resource allocation should be based on a normative or a descriptive approach. To this we turn next.

REFERENCES

Arrow, Kenneth, J., Social Choice and Individual Values, (Wiley, 1963).

Beaver, W., and Demski, J., "The Nature of Financial Accounting Objectives: Summary and Synthesis," Studies in Financial Accounting Objectives: 1974, The Journal of Accounting Research, Winter 1974.

Gonedes, N. and Dopuch, N., "Capital Equilibrium, Information Production and Selecting Accounting Techniques--Theoretical Framework and Review of Empirical Work," Studies in Financial Accounting Objectives, Journal of Accounting Research, Winter, 1974.

THE DESCRIPTIVE AND THE NORMATIVE

Joshua Ronen and George H. Sorter

The Descriptive and the Normative

Joshua Ronen and George H. Sorter

Definitions

Prescriptive models are those which are designed to help people make "better" decisions, in the sense of aiding them to behave consistently, with an a priori set of requirements or rules with which they want their choices to conform. These models are "prescriptive" or "normative" insofar as they *prescribe* how one *should* behave; that is, they set ideal norms. Descriptive models, on the other hand, are designed to describe how people actually behave. Both types of models allow for the assessment of expectations or beliefs about the structure of the environment, and about utilities which refer to personal tastes.

In a treatise on the problem of measurement of values and probabilities for the purpose of predicting behavior, Churchman[1] ties together the prescriptive and the descriptive aspects of choice in decision situations, maintaining that prescription should emanate from prediction:

> The present suggestion is to assert that the "ought" in a recommendation can be stated as follows: "X ought to do A in this environment" means "X would do A in the standard environment that defines value measurement." If a scientist states that an executive should follow a certain course of action, he says in effect, "I have measured the values of the executive—or his organization—for the various outcomes that may result from his decisions." These measurements predict what he would do if he were making his decision under the standard conditions of value measurements. When I say he ought to exhibit such-and-such behavior, I mean that this is the behavior he would exhibit if these standard conditions held. Of course, he may not do what he ought to do; that is, the standard conditions may not hold in this environment.

[1] C. W. Churchman, *Prediction and Optimal Decision* (Englewood Cliffs, New Jersey: Prentice-Hall, Inc., 1961), pp. 17-18.

If the prescriptive models were to take into consideration the human capability to process information and the tendency to "simplify" and eliminate part of the stimuli in the environment—then the "prescriptive" model becomes a descriptive model of actual behavior, as Becker and McClintock[2] indicate. They note that "imposing a requirement that a prescriptive model be realistic in its demands upon the users' capabilities tends to make the distinction between prescriptive and descriptive models ambiguous."[3]

The descriptive and the normative models of behavior may require a common set of accounting data. However, they may differ in their input requirements. If so, accounting objectives based on descriptive behavior would require sets of data that are different on occasions from those required for accounting objectives based on normative or prescriptive models of behavior.

Illustrations—Investment Analysis

To illustrate the above, the discussion is restricted to one sub-set of users—security analysts.

Many aspects of investment analysis are viewed as psychological in nature and one of these aspects is certainly the appraisal of man's capabilities for integrating information into a judgment or a decision. The analysts are called upon to make predictions, forecasts, diagnoses and evaluations on the basis of fallible information and with respect to parameters such as expected returns, growth rates, variability and volatility. These tasks are said to be facilitated by means of the statistics discipline. Very often, however, individuals bypass formal statistical procedures when making judgments. When they do this, they are acting as "intuitive statisticians."

The normative aspect of investment analysis relates to decision rules that should be applied to a variety of investment situations taking advantage of theoretically derived or empirically determined quantitative relationships between market factors and security performance. Do security analysts use these normative models as prescribed?

While research in this area is almost nonexistent, related questions have been studied extensively within psychology and other disciplines (primarily medicine). Various techniques from these other disciplines were employed to identify and describe the descriptive models of financial decision-making. Geoffry Clarkson[4] simulated the portfolio selection processes of a bank's trust investment officer. Clarkson studied the officer's verbalized reflections as he was asked to think aloud while reviewing past and present decisions. Using these reflections as a guide, the investment process was translated into a sequential branching computer program. A remarkable correspondence

---

[2] Becker and McClintock, "Behavioral Decision Theory," *Annual Review of Psychology* (1967).

[3] Ibid, p. 241.

[4] G. P. E. Clarkson, *Portfolio Selection: A Simulation of Trust Investment* (Englewood Cliffs, New Jersey: Prentice-Hall, 1962).

was found between the simulated portfolios and the actual future portfolios selected by the trust officer. Similar research plans were used by Cohen, Gilmore, and Singer[5] in simulating the decision processes of bank officers who granted loans. Other attempts to analyze the judgment process in medical diagnosis are described by Kleinmuntz[6] and Rimoldi.[7]

Techniques that are less complex than Clarkson's simulation but more sophisticated than the naïve approach of simply asking the decision-maker how he makes his judgments were developed. These are discussed by Goldberg,[8] Slovic and Lichtenstein,[9] Hoffman,[10] Hammond, Hursch, and Todd.[11] This approach requires making quantitative evaluations of a large number of cases each of which is described by various cue dimensions. Thus the financial analysts could be asked to predict price appreciation for securities that are defined in terms of P/E ratios, earnings, dividend yields, etc. Hoffman and Hammond, Hursch, and Todd suggested fitting a regression equation to analysts' judgments to capture their personal weighting policy, within the framework of a *linear model.*

Also, information processing sometimes utilizes cues in a variety of nonlinear ways (e.g., in curvilinear functions). When analysts associate good investment decisions with complex and interrelated decision rules they probably are thinking in terms of *configural* relationships rather than linear.

Studies of Probabilistic Processing

Some attempts to detect deviations of the descriptive from the normative centered on the prescriptive models of decision theory which assert that opinions about the world should be cast in probabilistic terms. For example, according to the prescriptive model, rather than predicting that a stock will sell at a specific price, we should estimate a probability distribution across a set of possible prices. These probabilities can be used together with the

---

[5] K. J. Cohen, T. C. Gilmore, and F. A. Singer, "Bank Procedures for Analyzing Business Loan Applications," *Analytical Methods in Banking* (Homewood, Illinois: R. D. Irwin, 1966), pp. 218-251.

[6] B. Kleinmuntz, "The Processing of Clinical Information by Man and Machine," *Formal Representation of Human Judgment* (New York: Wiley, 1968), pp. 149-186.

[7] H. J. A. Rimoldi, "Teaching and Analysis of Diagnostic Skills," *The Diagnostic Process* (Ann Arbor: Malloy Lithographing, 1964), pp. 315-346.

[8] L. R. Goldberg, "Simple Models or Simple Processes? Some Research on Clinical Judgments," *American Psychologist* (1968), Vol. 23, pp. 483-496.

[9] P. Slovic and S. Lichtenstein, "Comparison of Bayesian and Regression Approaches to the Study of Information Processing in Judgment," *Organizational Behavior and Human Performance* (in press) and *Human Judgment and Social Interaction* (New York: Holt, Rinehart, & Winston, in press).

[10] P. J. Hoffman, "The Paramorphic Representation of Clinical Judgment," *Psychological Bulletin* (1960), Vol. 57, pp. 116-131.

[11] K. R. Hammond, C. J. Hursch, and F. J. Todd, "Analyzing the Components of Clinical Inference," *Psychological Review* (1964), Vol. 71, pp. 438-456.

information about the payoffs associated with the various decisions and states of the world to satisfy an objective criterion such as the maximization of expected value or expected utility.

When new information is gained the probabilities are revised. The *normative* model that prescribes how such revision is to be made is Bayes' theorem. However, psychologists, led by Ward Edwards and others[12] found experimentally that men are conservative processors of information. While upon receipt of new data, subjects revised their posterior probability estimates in the same direction as prescribed by Bayes' theorem, the revision was typically too small; subjects responded as though the data were less diagnostic than they truly were. Edwards suggested that while they perceive each datum accurately, men are unable to combine its meaning properly with the prior probabilities when revising their opinions.[13]

Assessments of Probability, Variability And Co-variability

The prescriptive portfolio models require that analysts estimate the variances and co-variances of expected returns which are then combined to optimize the investors' utility.[14] For such a model to be actually used, therefore, estimates of probabilities and variances must be provided. But if it is found that the estimation of such parameters is affected by factors that are not specified by the normative models or if they are distorted systematically as a result of intervening psychological variables, then the prescribed portfolio model in which such estimates are to be used may no longer be the optimal model. In this case, modification of the prescriptive model will be required to accommodate the human tendencies. In such a case the information requirements implied by the first normative model may differ from those implied by the modified descriptive model.

Such distortions were indeed found. For example, Tversky and Kahneman[15] identified an "availability bias" in that judgments of an event's probability were found to be determined by the number of instances of that event that are remembered and the ease with which they come into mind. The

---

[12] W. Edwards, "Conservatism in Human Information Processing," *Formal Representation of Human Judgment* (New York: Wiley, 1968), pp. 17-52. W. Edwards, H. Lindman, and L. D. Phillips, "Emerging Technologies for Making Decisions," *New Directions in Psychology: II* (New York: Holt, Rinehart, & Winston, 1965), pp. 261-325. W. Edwards and L. D. Phillips, "Man as a Transducer for Probabilities in Bayesian Command and Control Systems," *Human Judgments and Optimality* (New York: Wiley, 1964), pp. 360-401. W. Edwards, L. D. Phillips, W. L. Hays and B. C. Goodman, "Probabilistic Information Processing Systems: Design and Evaluation," *IEEE Transactions on Systems Science and Cybernetics* (1968), Vol. SSC-4, pp. 248-265.

[13] Edwards, "Conservatism in Human Information Processing," pp. 17-52.

[14] See, for example, William F. Sharpe, *Portfolio Theory and Capital Markets* (New York: McGraw-Hill Book Company, 1970).

[15] A. Tversky and D. Kahneman, "The Judgment of Probability by Retrieval and Construction of Instances," *Oregon Research Institute Research Bulletin* (1971).

availability of instances is affected by such factors as recency, salience, and imaginability—all of which may not be related to the correct probability.

In addition to this distortion, numerous other systematic biases in assessments of probability were found such as misperceiving the probabilities of compound events (Cohen and Chesnick[16] and Slovic[17]). Assessments of variability were found to be affected by the mean of the sequence and its regularity (Lathrop[18]). Thus people somehow judge absolute variability in terms of variability relative to the mean. Also, greater irregularity gives an illusion of greater variability.

In addition to all the above, a great deal of experimental research on risk-taking behavior exists. This research may be relevant for investment decision-making and the information requirements for such decision-making. In this set of research (which is not discussed in this paper), subjects are asked to indicate their preferences and opinions among various gambles. Gambles are studied because they represent in an abstract form important aspects of real-life decisions. They contain elements such as probabilities, incentives and risks which are also the elements of real-life decisions. By using gambles, basic dimensions of risk situations can be manipulated, and hypotheses can be rigorously tested. Whether one can generalize that the results of such experiments simulate real-life decisions under uncertainty must be established by further research.

To illustrate, Slovic[19] found that perceived risk was not a function of the variance of a gamble. Instead riskiness was more likely to be determined by the probability of loss and the amount of loss. This result is congruent with Lorie's[20] complaint that it was absurd to call a stock risky because it went up much faster than the market in some years and only as fast in other years, while a security that never varies in price is not risky at all—if the variance is used to define risk. If indeed descriptive models imply that either the amount of loss or the probability of loss is the main determinant of risk, would it not be concluded that at least from the standpoint of descriptive behavior, accounting information should concentrate on providing estimates for those two parameters?

Summary and Conclusions

In the above analysis, an attempt has been made to illustrate, with a few examples. some of the implications of the vast literature which describes

---

[16] J. Cohen and E. I. Chesnick, "The Doctrine of Psychological Chances," *British Journal of Psychology* (1970), Vol. 61, pp. 323-334.

[17] P. Slovic, "Manipulating the Attractiveness of a Gamble Without Changing Its Expected Value," *Journal of Experimental Psychology* (1969), Vol. 79, pp. 139-145.

[18] R. G. Lathrop, "Perceived Variability," *Journal of Experimental Psychology* (1967), Vol. 73, pp. 498-502.

[19] P. Slovic, "The Relative Influence of Probabilities and Payoffs Upon Perceived Risk of a Gamble," *Psychonomic Science* (1967), Vol. 9, pp. 223-224.

[20] J. H. Lorie, "Some Comments on Recent Quantitative and Formal Research on the Stock Market," *Journal of Business* (1966), Vol. 39, Part II, pp. 107-110.

human behavior in relation to decision models that are actually used. If accounting information is to provide inputs to what people actually use, there is no doubt that a significant amount of research still remains to be conducted.

Normative or prescriptive models are those which should be used, whereas descriptive models are those that are actually used. Given the circumstances underlying the task of the Study Group on the Objectives of Financial Statements, it is believed that an investigation of normative models utilizing accounting information deserves priority.

First, the literature that is relevant to the investigation of descriptive models is both fragmented and indirect. Thus, to gather sufficient evidence that allows the formulation of a unified framework for descriptive models would be both difficult and overly time-consuming, thus placing severe limitations on this approach.

Second, the choice of models that are actually used may also be affected by the set of available information. Thus, to determine what information is required for a specified goal would require identifying the decision model employed; but, at the same time, the information provided to a decision-maker may affect the decision model that is used. The circularity is particularly crucial inasmuch as the Study Group is considering the possibility of enlarging or at least changing the available accounting information. Therefore, the new information may change the descriptive models.

These complexities make the exploration of descriptive models particularly difficult and lengthy. While such an investigation is potentially very useful, it is nevertheless suggested that primary emphasis be devoted to normative models at this stage.

DEVELOPMENT OF A GENERAL FRAMEWORK

AN "EVENTS" APPROACH TO BASIC ACCOUNTING THEORY

George H. Sorter

AN "EVENTS" APPROACH TO BASIC ACCOUNTING THEORY

BY

GEORGE H. SORTER

Reprinted from
The Accounting Review
Vol. **XLIV,** No. 1, **January,** 1969

An "Events" Approach to Basic Accounting Theory

George H. Sorter

In 1966, after two years work, a committee of the American Accounting Association issued *A Statement of Basic Accounting Theory*.[1] Undoubtedly, the most startling recommendations were the sanctioning of current costs and the advocacy of two column (historical and current) reports. To this member of the committee, however, even more startling was that the near unanimous agreement on the recommendations was arrived at by following two very divergent paths originating from two very dissimilar basic concepts about accounting. This split is not confined to committee members but rather seems representative of a more widespread and pervasive difference in the world outside. The majority view of the committee and the predominant faction outside believes in what I here define as the "value" approach to accounting. The minority view, of which I am sometimes the only member, I describe as the "events" approach. This view although implied by some in the past[2] has never to my knowledge been explicitly stated but might have far-reaching implications. This paper seeks to describe and contrast the two schools, present arguments for and illustrate the consequences of an "events" approach to accounting theory; and examine the logic leading to the conclusions embodied in the *Statement of Basic Accounting Theory*. Hopefully, this will provide not only insights and help for the analysis and evaluation of the committee's monograph but perhaps also stimulate discussion and criticism of a new approach and suggest new avenues of research and experimentation to make accounting more responsive to present day conditions.

Two Views — Value and Events

The Value Theory

The "Value" school within the committee, or as they would probably prefer to be termed the "User need" school, assumed that users' needs are known and sufficiently well specified so that accounting theory can deductively arrive at and produce optimal input values for used and useful decision models. Most of the value theorists visualize accounting's purpose as producing optimum income and capital value or values.[3] This leads to the popular sport of proper matching of costs and

[1] American Accounting Association, *A Statement of Basic Accounting Theory*, A Report Prepared by the Committee on Basic Accounting Theory (American Accounting Association, 1966).

[2] This idea, like so many others had its origin primarily in the writings and thought of Professor William J. Vatter who I hasten to absolve from any of its shortcomings.

[3] Not all value theorists are income oriented. Chambers for example can be considered a "value" but certainly not an "income" theorist.

George H. Sorter is Arthur Young Visiting Professor of Accounting at the University of Kansas.

revenue. The assumption is that "proper matching" associates costs and revenue to produce the right income figure or figures—the figure or figures optimal for users' decision models.

Several criticisms may be leveled at this value approach.

1. There are many and varied uses of accounting data and it is therefore impossible to specify input values that are optimal for the wide range of possible uses.
2. For each specified use different users utilize a wide range of different decision models, that they have so far been unable to describe, define, or specify. Further, neither economists nor accountants have been able to advance the theoretically correct decision models.
3. The value theory is unnecessarily restrictive. Thus, events such as leases or commitments have, until recently, tended to be excluded from the accounting universe, partially at least, because they did not affect income or net asset values.

   The orientation of accounting toward producing income and asset values which are nothing but simple attempts to adjust for the lag between cash outflows and cash inflows has impeded the development of more sophisticated lag models made possible by more sophisticated techniques.
4. The value theory is not useful in explaining many current developments in accounting. Income theory, for instance, does not provide a basis for the current sub-aggregates that are utilized in the income statement such as sales, cost of sales, etc. It has also not been helpful in explaining the advocacy of the Fund Statement or in helping the conglomerate and a host of other current problems.

The Events Theory

Proponents of the "Events" theory suggest that the purpose of accounting is to provide information about relevant economic events that might be useful in a variety of possible decision models. They see the function of accounting at one level removed in the decision-making process. Instead of producing input values for unknown and perhaps unknowable decision models directly, accounting provides information about relevant economic events that allows individual users to generate their own input values for their own individual decision models. In other words, given the state of the arts, less rather than more aggregation is appropriate and the user, rather than the accountant, must aggregate, assign weights and values to the data consistent with his forecasts and utility functions. "Events" proponents suggest that the loss of information generated by aggregation and valuation by the accountant is greater than the associated benefit. While they would agree that the accountants' suggested weights and values deserve to be communicated, they would insist that these weights be communicated in disaggregated form so that users always had the nonweighted raw data available as well.

This viewpoint seems particularly appropriate today when little is known about how accounting data is used but may even be preferred when more knowledge about decision models becomes available. It is possible to visualize reasonable decision models that are consistent with an "events" approach rather than a "value" approach. An investor, for instance, attempting to forecast the value of a firm at some future point may utilize two methods: (1) He may base his estimate of future values on the trend, size, and variability of current income or other aggregated values. (2) Alternatively, he may wish to use current accounting data to predict specific future events and then base his estimate of future values on these predicted events. In other words, he may wish to predict income or he may wish to predict sales, cost of sales, taxes, etc. The first model is more consistent with a value approach, the second with an events approach.

The criticism must be met that the "events" approach relies just as heavily upon knowledge of users' models as does the "value" approach. The argument goes as follows. Decisions as to what events are relevant (surely not all events can be recorded) must be made and can only be made with users' needs in mind. Thus, the users' needs must still be known. This is correct. But it seems clear that less need be known about decision models to decide whether or not an event might be relevant for a model than to have to decide how the data fits a specific decision model and what specific weights should be assigned.[4] In the lease example, under an "events" approach, it is only necessary to decide that information about leases, commitments or orders are relevant to a host of decision models for such information to be included in accounting reports. It is unnecessary to justify how, if at all, this information should be weighted in an income valuation model.

To Aggregate or Not to Aggregate

As has been indicated, the real difference between the two schools lies in what level of aggregation and valuation is appropriate in accounting reports and who is to be the aggregator and evaluator. The question as to who is to aggregate or value is not unique to accounting. As Ijiri points out " . . . any aggregation generally involves loss of information in that the resulting total 'value' may be composed of many—possibly infinitely many—different *components*."[5] It is interesting to note that in two widely different areas there have recently been thrusts toward presenting less aggregated data. In modern statistics it is no longer considered good form to merly report confidence intervals. Instead the plea is for full presentation of the underlying data or distributions.[6] Only the user can decide what is or is not significant, given his loss function. In weather forecasts, we are no longer told that it will or will not rain or snow. Instead we are given probability estimates and must ourselves decide whether or not to carry umbrellas or to send out work crews. We are given the underlying raw data and must assign values consistent with our individual utility functions.

Accounting income has variously been thought of as a measure of how much can be spent and still be as well off as before, as a measure of managerial efficiency or as a basis for forecasting future values. But each of these depends on individual expectations, individual preference functions and individual decision models not on some never clearly defined concept of "proper matching of costs and revenues." Unfortunately this attempt to match, the assigning of weights to generate values, the attempt to aggregate into an income figure, destroys potentially useful information about important underlying events and increases possible measurement errors and biases. Every item on an income statement is the result of at least two processes—the underlying event and the accountants' allocation of the event to a particular time period. This allocation has

[4] ". . . a goal which by itself may not be so capable of definition as to determine a single perfect solution may nevertheless be clear enough and important enough to rule out some solutions . . ." from Guido Calabresi, "Fault, Accidents, and the Wonderful World of Blum and Kalven," *Yale Law Journal* (December 1965), p. 222.

[5] Yuji Ijiri. *The Foundations of Accounting Measurement* (Prentice-Hall, Inc., 1967), p. 120.

[6] See Howard Raiffa and Robert Schlaifer, *Applied Statistical Decision Theory* (Harvard University, Division of Research, Graduate School of Business, 1961), p. 68.

the purpose of matching in order to derive a "true" income figure or figures. Lifo and Fifo for example are used in an attempt to produce better income figures. Both, however, destroy information about the consumption event. If either Lifo or Fifo is used consumption of two identical units bought at different prices will necessarily be described differently. A user interested in comparing consumption activity for two periods is unable to distinguish between variations caused by the measurement process, be it Lifo or Fifo, and real differences in the consumption levels.

Deferred taxes attempts to secure proper matching of costs and revenues and thereby destroys information about current tax payments. Conventional absorption costing in an attempt to secure proper matching destroys information about production inputs and outputs since cost of goods sold and inventory become dependent on both the level of production and of sales.

The loss of information due to aggregation also holds for the balance sheet. Necessarily, every balance sheet account is an aggregation of two or more types of events (the events recorded on the debit and credit sides of the account). Very often the events so aggregated vary greatly in type, measureability and variability and therefore destroy much information about specific events. For instance, if current costs or values are used, acquisition and consumption activities as well as environmental changes are combined and the reconstructibility of each specific event is impaired. Acquisitions and amortizations or acquisitions and dispositions are events differing widely in possible measurement error. By combining them in asset and liability accounts information about each is destroyed.

As already indicated, income and capital valuations are attempts to deal with lags between cash outflows and cash inflows. These appear to be unnecessarily crude and primitive given current advances in methodology and measurement technique. The presentation of less aggregated data suggested by the "events" approach might stimulate investigation of more complicated but more useful lag and forecast models that could vary for different industries, firms, time periods, or individuals.

Some Consequences of an Events Approach

This is not the proper medium in which to describe some possible long-range consequences of the "events" approach. In a subsequent manuscript, I intend to speculate on the type of accounting reports appropriate to this approach. Even under the existing accounting framework there are several implications of "events" theory which might help to explain this point of view.

The Balance Sheet

It is currently the fashion to say that the balance sheet or position statement has lost most, if not all, of its significance. But not for event theorists. We view the balance sheet not as a value statement nor as a statement of financial position but rather as an indirect communication of all accounting events that have occurred since the inception of the accounting unit. This indirect communication is provided by summing the effect of all events on the names used in describing these events and then recording the subsequent balances. Inventory, thus, does not report either value or costs but rather describes the acquisition and consumption activities that have occurred. This view has several advantages. It does not purport to report something that is not achieved (i.e., value) and it does facilitate the understanding and analysis of what is described. If the inventory figure, for instance, is visualized as a representation of the inventory, under value theory the accountant must somehow rationalize the particular costs or value figure that he uses. If historical cost is used, the validity of a representation of inventory that ignores value inevitably crops up. If value is used the argument centers about the justification of this rather than some other value. It is certainly difficult to justify either historical costs or any one representation of value. This difficulty does not create so grave a problem for the "event" theorist. Suppose original cost is used. Under an events notion this means simply that acquisition and consumption events, but not environmental changes, are recorded. Original costs need not be justified. One may certainly deplore the absence of information about environmental events (i.e., value changes) but one accepts information about the events that are described (i.e., acquisition and consumption) and uses them in whatever fashion is appropriate.

An "events" approach to the balance sheet could lead to operational rules about balance sheet construction and presentation. The following represents a possible rule. *A balance sheet should be so constructed as to maximize the reconstructability of the events being aggregated.* Various users may thus generate information about particular events they are interested in. One purpose of the balance sheet is to facilitate the preparation of Funds Statements and like reports that provide information about important events.

The Income Statement

For value theorists the purpose of an income statement quite simply is to report income value or values. Under an "events" approach the purpose of the income statement is to provide direct communication concerning the operating events or activities of the firm. Accounting utilizes two forms of communication: an indirect or effect communication of all events (the Balance Sheet) and direct, specific or event communication of certain critical events (Income Statement, Cash Statement, Production Statement, Funds Statement, etc.). The concern of event theorists is not primarily with the final income figure but rather with describing critical operating activities of a firm. The preferred title would be "Statement of Operating Events." Events theory can suggest an operational rule for income statements. For instance, *each event should be described in a manner facilitating the forecasting of that same event in a future time period given exogenous changes.* The deferred tax question would then be resolved by investigating which quantification more reliably forecasts future tax payments. Both Lifo and Fifo would be rejected because they impede the ability to forecast acquisitions and consumptions of inventory in the future.

The "events" school can justify the present organization of the income statement which reports several sub-aggregates such as sales, cost of sales, etc., because these are considered critical operating events. Perhaps this is one instance when an events orientation has already affected the accounting structure.

The Funds Statement

Value theorists, rigidly faithful to their doctrine, have the most difficulty in justifying this statement. They state rather feebly that " . . . the basic purpose of the Funds Statement is to account for the change in working capital during the period covered by the statement."[7] Such a concept certainly underrates the utility of

[7] Perry Mason, "'Cash Flow' Analysis and The Funds Statement," *Accounting Research Study No. 2* (American Institute of Certified Public Accountants, 1961).

this statement and leads to trivial discussions as to the proper definition of working capital. The "events" school thinks of this statement as "A Statement of Financial and Investment Events." The Working Capital account merely represents a useful technique to organize the events and prepare the statement. The important consideration is whether a financing or investment event is relevant and should be reported, not whether working capital is affected by a given event. This again demonstrates the flexibility of an "events" approach. Different financing or investment events may or may not be relevant for specific firms or at specific times. The content of the Funds Statement thus need not remain invariate for all times or for all firms.

"A Statement of Basic Accounting Theory" and the Events Theory

Most of the recommendations contained in *A Statement of Basic Accounting Theory* flow more logically from an "events" rather than from a "value" orientation. Why are standards or guidelines necessary at all if a "value" approach is adopted? If users' needs are in fact well specified then accounting should provide the values that make the decision models operate optimally. The only relevant standard then would be the ability of the data to perform in the model. There would be no need for values to be verifiable or free from bias if they work well in a specified model. If, however, users' needs are not well specified suggesting an "events" approach, then it is necessary to employ standards that limit the range and define the description of relevant events.

The need for two-column reporting under a "value" approach is not clear. Presumably, the need arises because different columns are useful for different users; that is, historical cost data is useful for the stewardship function and current cost data for the investment function. This rather inadequate rationale has led to the assumption that the historical costs column was only advocated as a stop-gap measure until current value could sweep the day. This was not the intent of the committee.

Multi-column reporting seems eminently compatible with an "events" view of accounting. The two column reports advocated by *ASOBAT* is a step in that direction. As the monograph states, "The historical information reflects market transactions, the current cost information reflects market transactions plus 'unrealized' market influences, and the difference shows the effect of unrealized environmental influences."[8] Since the historical cost column includes descriptions of events other than market transactions (i.e., depreciation, amortization, and other significant accruals) and because market transactions and environmental changes are not the only events that have relevance to the firm, the two columns advocated do not go far enough, but they represent a start.

Separate events should be reported in separate columns because (1) they vary in measurability, (2) they vary in controllability, and (3) they vary in importance from period to period. There is no question that market transactions and environmental changes, for instance, vary in measurability. Market transactions can be relatively satisfactorily described by single numbered quantifications (with relatively little measurement error). There is apt to be little variance around that single number. The same, however, cannot be said about environmental changes or forecasts where description by ranges or distributions could be more appropriate and where measurement errors could be material. As long as a single column is used there will be a tendency to continue to

[8] American Accounting Association. *op. cit.*, p. 31.

measure events by a single measurement process which is inappropriate for certain types of events and we shall continue to be faced with troubles in assessing measurement biases or errors.

These events also vary in controllability by the managers of a firm. Clearly, market transactions are more controllable than environmental changes but less controllable than conversions. If accounting reports are to be useful in evaluating management then a separation of events by controllability should help in fulfilling this objective.

Finally, the importance of the different classes of events may vary from period to period. An investor may predict a period of stability where certain environmental changes are expected to be minimal and in order to forecast adequately from accounting data he must then be able to separate the effect of environmental changes from market transactions. This he can do in multi-column reporting. As the importance of different types of events vary, users, according to their estimate of the future, can attach different weights to the different types of events.

At first blush multi-column reporting seems a drastic departure from current practices—but is it really? Presently we use multi-row reporting. We break down the income statement into many sub-aggregates such as sales, cost of sales, S&A expenses, taxes, etc. We break down the balance sheet into many rows by classes of equities and assets. Very little research has been done as to what explains the current level of sub-aggregation and extreme proponents of the "value" school would have a hard time rationalizing the present format of the income statement. Presently the income statement is organized around a functional event structure, and the balance sheet around a functional effect structure. Multi-column reporting would add a "source of events" classification to both reports and instead of accounting reports consisting of a 7 by 1 matrix they would consist of a 7 by 5 matrix. This move from one matrix to another does not seem that revolutionary, and would be facilitated by an events approach.

Conclusion

Admittedly, the above represents only a rough and underdeveloped first approach toward a new orientation for accounting theory. Why, then, is it presented here and now? Only in the hope of encouraging the research activities suggested by this approach and also in the further hope that it might stimulate a reexamination of some essential if rarely expressed implicit tenets of present accounting thought. The areas of possible reseach opportunities indicated by an events approach are many. The following represent a few:

(1) Test whether line by line predictions of events, i.e., the prediction of sales, cost of sales, etc., are more efficient in explaining the future value of a firm than the use of more aggregated figures such as income.

(2) Investigate the present format of accounting reports to see how useful these formats could be, i.e., to what extent do the various subcategories of the income statement and balance sheet covary? To what extent do they provide additional information?

(3) Attempt to develop more sophisticated models to explain the lag between cash outflows and cash inflows, i.e., utilizing fund statements, production statements, and others in an attempt to predict cash flows.

(4) Investigate the information loss due to the aggregations presently used by accountants. How much informa-

tion is lost by aggregating and combining events to produce one income figure or to produce the different balance sheet amounts? A subsequent extension of this would be an investigation of the information loss due to expressing all economic activities in dollar terms.

(5) Construct useful accounting reports based on an events approach.

Ultimately this paper will find its justification if what is presented here as the conclusion will serve as an introduction to the research activities and the reexamination advocated.

A USER ORIENTED DEVELOPMENT OF ACCOUNTING INFORMATION REQUIREMENTS

Joshua Ronen

A User Oriented Development of Accounting Information Requirements

Joshua Ronen

Introduction

Accounting objectives should be based on economies of information, i.e., cost and benefit considerations.[1] If accounting information were a commodity sold at the market clearing price, it could be argued that forces of market equilibrium could insure that accounting information would be produced and communicated at an optimum level consistent with equating the marginal methods and benefits and marginal costs of information. However, accounting information does not constitute a "private good" in the sense of exchangeability at the marketplace; rather, it is provided without charge by the firm to the consumers—in this case, the various users of accounting information.[2] Under these circumstances, the determination of the costs and

[1] Theoretically, the benefit of information is measured by the consequences of decision changes that occur as a result of the information. The cost of information is the value of resources committed to obtaining and communicating it.

[2] The aspects of private goods vs. public goods and the implications of optimal conditions of welfare as well as the underlying factors in determining what constitutes public goods are extensively discussed in the literature. For a good example, see Harold Demsetz, "Some Aspects of Property Rights," *Journal of Law and Economics* (October 1966), pp. 61-70. What makes accounting information in particular a public good is probably the difficulty in guaranteeing exclusive access to the information if it is sold.

It could be argued that accounting information is indirectly sold at the market in that it is used in the determination of stock prices and thus an implicit price is stated through stock price movements. Notice, however, that this process is very indirect (unlike intermediate products which have established market prices) and is influenced by the uncertainty of the resulting benefit that would potentially accrue to the firm through provision of information. By contrast, in respect to private goods, firms are generally price takers in the context of a competitive market, and thus subject to much less uncertainties than in the case of accounting information. More elaborate discussion of this aspect appears later in the paper.

benefits must be made outside the market system.

Although both costs and benefits need to be investigated, it is probably advisable first to identify the benefits of different kinds of information.[3] Even when the cost of some accounting information is prohibitive, the search for alternative means of obtaining the information could be justified if the benefits are large enough. Failure to consider some accounting information merely because its cost is high cannot be justified.

There are various ways to investigate the benefits which could lead to identifying desirable accounting information:

1. The information required by normative decision models of major user groups could be determined.

2. Decision models *actually* used by major user groups could be identified through interviews, controlled experiments, etc., and their information requirements determined. These decision models could either agree with or differ (as a result of universal behavioral tendencies) from the normative models.

3. Preferences of users as to different kinds of accounting information could be identified through interviews and questionnaires.

While all three avenues should be followed[4] primary emphasis should be placed first on information requirements of normative models because:

1. The normative model is the procedure that a rational man follows in making a particular decision in a specified set of circumstances. Consensus among writers regarding the soundness of normative models indicates that a majority of users is likely to follow the normative model. Thus, the benefit of information used in the model would accrue to many users and the sum total of the benefits resulting from providing the information is apt to be large.

2. Normative models can serve as a standard of reference to evaluate actual decision models. If deviations are found to be systematic and universal across many individuals, the deviations could be used to modify the

[3] While there is a lower limit for costs (zero), the upper limit for benefits is indefinite. Thus, while costly information may not be eliminated from consideration (since the benefits could be even larger), information that has small benefit could be eliminated from consideration since the cost is bound to be positive. Starting the investigation with the benefits allows an eventually smaller subset of information to be considered and therefore saves research time and effort.

[4] The implication of the findings of the three avenues to the objectives may be inconsistent. Decisions as to whether (a) the normative model should be modified to accommodate systematic inconsistencies, (b) information should be provided so as to satisfy presently used models without paying attention to normative considerations or (c) individuals should be trained or otherwise influenced to follow the normative models would have to be made. Unless all avenues are followed, however, such inconsistencies may remain unidentified.

normative model. Normative models are selected as a standard of reference since they are consistent with action or behavior that is generally found to be empirically valid.

3. Accounting objectives inferred from expressed preferences of individual users would be varied and would lead to a great number of subobjectives.[5] Criteria would ultimately have to be developed to narrow the resulting multitude of objectives so that the accounting alternatives to be considered would be limited to a feasible subset. The criteria would be implied by prevalent normative decision models. It would be advisable to conduct inquiries into individual preferences in light of the requirements of the normative models.

Benefits Identified Through the Analysis of Normative Decision Models

If it can be determined that many decisions frequently made by more than one user utilize the same piece of information under a relatively large set of circumstances, then the sum total of these benefits may well exceed the cost of providing that information systematically. Thus, it is useful to identify distinct sets of decisions for which information requirements are relatively common and for which the relationships among the information used, the resulting decisions, and the consequences are relatively stable. Once these commonalities are discovered, the benefits would then be compared with the costs of systematically reporting the common information within the accounting system.

Although individual users of accounting information have a multitude of goals and types of decisions, the broad objective of the economy as a whole is defined to be the efficient allocation of resources.[6]

---

[5] For example, consider the set of objectives that can be inferred from the expressed preference of an individual to be provided information on replacement costs. Some objectives that can be induced from this expressed preference and that are consistent with it (to mention only a few): (a) the wish to know the cost of reproducing the firm and its operations, (b) assessing managerial ability to maximize holding gains and minimize holding losses, (c) evaluating the managerial decisions with respect to timing of asset purchases, (d) judging the firm's future ability to finance its operation if it were to replace its existing assets and thus assess its chances for survival, etc. From these objectives numerous higher level objectives could be induced, such as the prediction of future holding gains or losses (inferred from objective (b) above), assessing future managerial ability to maneuver and capitalize on new opportunities (induced from both objectives (b) and (c) above), and evaluating the likelihood of default and material losses as a result of ceasing the firm's operations (inferred from objective (d) above).

[6] This includes the efficient allocation of resources within the firm as one part of the economy, and it thus implies the provision of information to control and motivate actions within the firm to insure efficient allocation of the firm's resources.

When this objective is pursued within a private enterprise system in which it is assumed that individuals seek to maximize their wealth, the accounting objectives must be formulated so that the use of accounting information by individuals to maximize their wealth causes resources to be allocated most efficiently in the economy.[7] Therefore, we need to study decision models used by individuals to maximize their wealth. Inasmuch as it is unrealistic to discuss the multitude of decision models that vary across decisions and individuals, we must attempt to classify decisions into groups that are homogeneous in their information requirements.

There are two primary classes of decisions generally made by individual consumers within the private sector of the economy: consumption decisions and investment decisions. The groups of decisions are interdependent. This discussion assumes a predetermined level of consumption as given and considers investment decisions only. While different groups of decisions may require different information, there are many commonalities in information required for making investment decisions.

Predictability and Comparability. Estimating the future levels of variables relevant to an investment decision is the basis for making the decision. For example, a decision to purchase a machine is based on an estimate of cash flows generated by it. The cash flows from an equity security are the dividends that will be received while the security is held plus the market value of the security when it is sold. Since it is always necessary to predict relevant variables to make investment decisions,[8] one of the primary objectives of accounting is to facilitate the prediction of relevant variables. And indeed this objective has been extensively discussed in the literature in terms of the "predictive ability criterion."[9]

In addition, investment decisions are not made in a void; they usually are made in the context of choice among alternative competing activities. Thus, given a particular level of wealth, the primary decision is how to allocate that wealth among competing investment alternatives. Under these conditions the task is to compare the estimates of future relevant variables of the

---

[7] Whether there are market forces which lead to optimal allocation as a result of individual actions or whether there are possible sub-optimalities that necessitate information regulation is discussed in Joshua Ronen, "The Need for Accounting Objectives in an Efficient Market," contained in this volume, pp. 36-52.

[8] Note that most of the current and noncurrent economic decisions in a firm can be viewed as investment decisions. Thus, an investment in a human resource is expected to generate services and therefore cash flows in the future. Advertising expenses that are related to public relations activities of the firm are no different.

[9] W. H. Beaver, J. W. Kennelly, and W. M. Voss, "Predictive Ability as a Criterion for the Evaluation of Accounting Data," *Accounting Review* (October 1968), pp. 675-683.

investment alternatives and to choose that alternative promising the highest expected benefits. Comparability among the investment alternatives therefore needs to be specified as another important objective for accounting reports.

The Investment Model: Risk and Return. Stating the objectives of predictability and comparability is not sufficient. To make statements about the specific content of accounting reports, we must also specify what objects are to be predicted and compared. For example, predictability of future accounting income may be useful in satisfying the comparability criterion only to the extent that accounting income is the dimension along which different firms or their securities should be compared and ranked.[10]

As the normative investment model most generally used is the one based on portfolio analysis, it can thus be used as a basis to determine desirable accounting output. But the portfolio model should not be viewed narrowly, irrespective of the role of securities in the capital market in efficiently allocating the ownership of the economy's capital stock. Under equilibrium conditions, the savings made available through voluntary decisions on postponement of consumption must be invested in the best combination of securities, i.e., the combinations that produce the highest increment in social wealth (where wealth is understood to incorporate individual preferences of investors).

The Relationship with Economy-Wide Goals. To provide appropriate signals for optimal resource allocation, there must be an environment in which firms can make production and investment decisions and in which investors are able to choose among the securities that represent ownership of the firms' activities on the assumption that security prices "fully reflect" all available information. It is precisely because the empirical research related to the operations of the efficient markets supports the contention that

---

[10] For a discussion of the impropriety of setting merely the predictability of accounting profit as a criterion, see Lawrence Revsine, "Predictive Ability, Market Prices, and Operating Flows," *Accounting Review* (July 1971), pp. 480-489. Any income is an artifact produced by a set of rules or "generally accepted accounting principles." It is quite plausible that accounting income could be a better predictor of future accounting income (which is measured on the basis of the same rules and conventions) than a measure of income reported on the basis of other measurements and rules such as current operating income, exit value income, etc. In fact, two recent studies support this contention. (See John K. Simmons and Jack Gray, "An Investigation of the Effect of Differing Accounting Frameworks on the Prediction of Net Income," *Accounting Review* (October 1969), pp. 757-776, and Frank Werner, "A Study of Predictive Significance of Two Income Measures," *Journal of Accounting Research* (Spring 1969), pp. 123-136.) The real question is whether future accounting income is the proper measure to be forecasted to form the basis of comparison among firms and whether there are other measures either replacing or in addition to the historical accounting income that better serve that purpose.

security prices "fully reflect" available information at any time[11] that the portfolio model is an appropriate basis for determining the objects to be predicted using accounting numbers. This is so because the objects to be predicted from the normative viewpoint must also be utilized to become legitimate objects of accounting.

Since security prices have been found to "reflect fully" all publicly held information and to react unbiasedly to new information, they can be said to reflect the intrinsic or "fundamental" value of the securities.[12] But, for security prices to serve as appropriate signals for optimal resource allocation, the intrinsic value of the stock must coincide with the economic value of the firm, which is defined as the risk-adjusted discounted value of the firm's prospective cash receipts and disbursements.[13] Unless the security's intrinsic value coincides with the economic value of the firm, allocation of resources in the economy is sub-optimal since the marginal cost of capital would not be equal to the marginal expected rate of return. Thus, Pareto optimality conditions are violated.[14]

---

[11] For an extensive review, see the following:

Eugene F. Fama, "Efficient Capital Markets: A Review of Theory and Empirical Work," *Journal of Finance* (May 1970), pp. 383-417; "The Behavior of Stock Market Prices," *Journal of Business* (January 1965), pp. 34-105; and "Random Walks in Stock Market Prices," *Financial Analysts Journal* (September-October 1965), pp. 55-59.

Eugene F. Fama, L. Fisher, M. C. Jensen, and Richard Roll, "The Adjustment of Stock Prices to New Information," *International Economic Review* (February 1969), pp. 1-21.

Benoit Mandelbrot, "The Variation of Certain Speculative Prices," *Journal of Business* (October 1963), pp. 394-419, and "Forecasts of Future Prices, Unbiased Markets and 'Martingale' Models," *Journal of Business* (January 1966), pp. 242-255.

Richard Roll, "The Efficient Market Model Applied to U.S. Treasury Bill Rates" (Unpublished Ph.D. thesis, University of Chicago, 1968).

Paul A. Samuelson, "Proof That Properly Anticipated Prices Fluctuate Randomly," *Industrial Management Review* (Spring 1965), pp. 41-49.

Myron Scholes, "A Test of the Competitive Market Hypothesis: The Market for New Issues and Secondary Offerings" (Unpublished Ph.D. thesis, University of Chicago, 1969).

Roger N. Waud, "Public Interpretation of Discount Rate Changes: Evidence on the 'Announcement Effect'," *Econometrica* (March 1970), pp. 231-250.

[12] As defined in Joshua Ronen and George H. Sorter, "Relevant Accounting," *Journal of Business* (April 1972), pp. 258-282, intrinsic value is the value that encompasses in an unbiased fashion all the relevant determinants of an entity. These intrinsic values depend on the earnings prospects of a company which in turn are related to economic and other factors some of which are peculiar to this company and some of which affect other companies as well (see Fama, "Behavior of Stock Market Prices," p. 36).

[13] See Eugene F. Fama and Merton H. Miller, *The Theory of Finance* (New York: Holt, Rinehart and Winston, 1972), chap. 4, and M. H. Miller and F. Modigliani, "Dividend Policy, Growth and the Valuation of Shares," *Journal of Business* (October 1961), pp. 411-433.

[14] For a discussion of Pareto optimality conditions, see, for example, E. J. Mishan, "A Survey of Welfare Economics, 1939-1959," *Economic Journal* (1960).

If the portfolio model is used in making investment decisions that result in the determination of stock prices, then for optimal resource allocation, the information inputs utilized in the models should best reflect the economic value of the firm, i.e., the prospective cash flows and their risks.[15] Stated another way, assuming that the portfolio model is used by investors and given that (a) security prices should reflect the economic value of the firm and (b) that security prices fully reflect the available information and unbiasedly and instantaneously adjust to new information, the primary objective of accounting emerges as providing information that facilitates the prediction of prospective cash flows and their risks.[16] The derivation of this objective is shown schematically in Figure 1, opposite.

Reliability. Although predictability and comparability are two necessary ingredients (or sub-objectives) of the process of assessing future flows and their uncertainties, predicted and comparable flows and their uncertainties should not and probably will not be used if they are unreliable. Thus, reliability is an objective that is deduced from the higher level objectives in the hierarchy and is presented as a third sub-sub-objective in Figure 1.

Perhaps reliability can best be defined through its elements. Many factors can contribute to the reliability of information. One is whether the information resulted from a consensus about a value or an event that is contestable. The magnitude that results from the consensus would be more reliable than if the consensus involved noncontesting parties. For example, market prices result from the consensus arrived at by buyers and sellers.

---

[15] The informational inputs to the portfolio model (which generally assumes that returns on stock are normally distributed) consists of (a) the one period return on securities which is defined as:

$$r_{jt} = d_{jt}/p_{jt} + (p_{j,\,t+1} - p_{jt})/p_{jt},$$

where r_{jt} is the return on the security during time period t, d_{jt} is the dividend payment during time period t, $p_{j,\,t+1}$ is the price of security at the end of time t, and p_{jt} is its price at the beginning of time t, and (b) the risk associated with the expected return which is generally measured as a standard deviation of the normally distributed return, although other investigators [e.g., see Fama "Behavior of Stock Market Prices," Maurice G. Kendall, "The Analysis of Economic Time-Series, Part I: Prices," *Journal of the Royal Statistical Society,* XCVI (1953), pp. 11-25; Benoit Mandelbrot, "Variation of Certain Speculative Prices"; Arnold Moore, "A Statistical Analysis of Common Stock Prices," (Unpublished Ph.D. thesis, Graduate School of Business, University of Chicago, (1962)); M.F.M. Osborne, "Brownian Motion in the Stock Market," *Operations Research* (March-April, 1959), pp. 145-173; S. James Press, "A Compound Events Model for Security Prices," *Journal of Business* (July 1968), pp. 317-335; and Richard Roll, "Efficient Market Model Applied to U.S. Treasury Bill Rates" (Unpublished Ph.D. thesis, University of Chicago (1968)] tested a broader class of distributions and, in particular, the class of stable Paretian or Pareto-Levy distributions which include the normal distribution as a special case.

[16] Clearly, it can be argued that this information need not necessarily be provided by the firm (either through its accounting system or otherwise). This particular point as well as the interesting question of whether market forces exist that guarantee the provision of this information without the necessity of formulating accounting objectives is discussed by Ronen, "Need for Accounting Objectives in an Efficient Market."

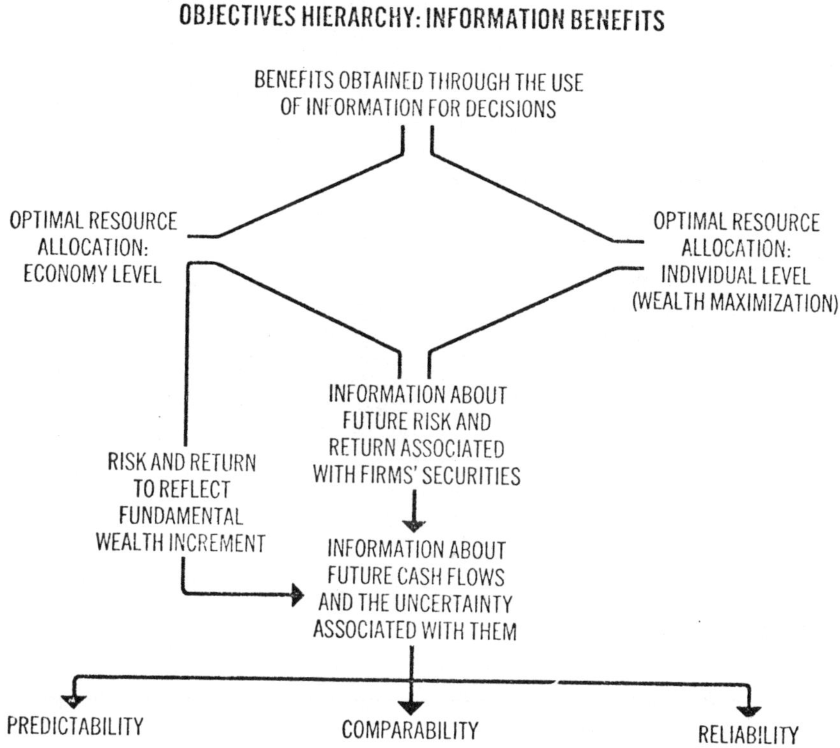

Figure 1

Sellers wish to obtain as high a price as possible for the commodity sold; buyers wish to pay as little as possible. When these contesting parties come to a consensus as reflected in market prices, the market prices can be said to be reliable estimates of the future utility and benefits of the commodity.

The ability to validate information or magnitude of events is another element of reliability. The magnitude of events such as forecasts can be validated through comparing the forecasts with actual occurrences over time. Future forecasts would be considered to be more reliable if the deviations between past forecasts and actual results are small. Information can also be validated through the ability to verify the magnitudes in question. Verifiability can be obtained either through visibility of the magnitudes, for example, through actual cash transactions, or through documentation of the magnitude, as by a legal contract or court decision. The sub-objectives relating to reliability are depicted in Figure 2, page 88.

OBJECTIVES HIERARCHY: INFORMATION BENEFITS

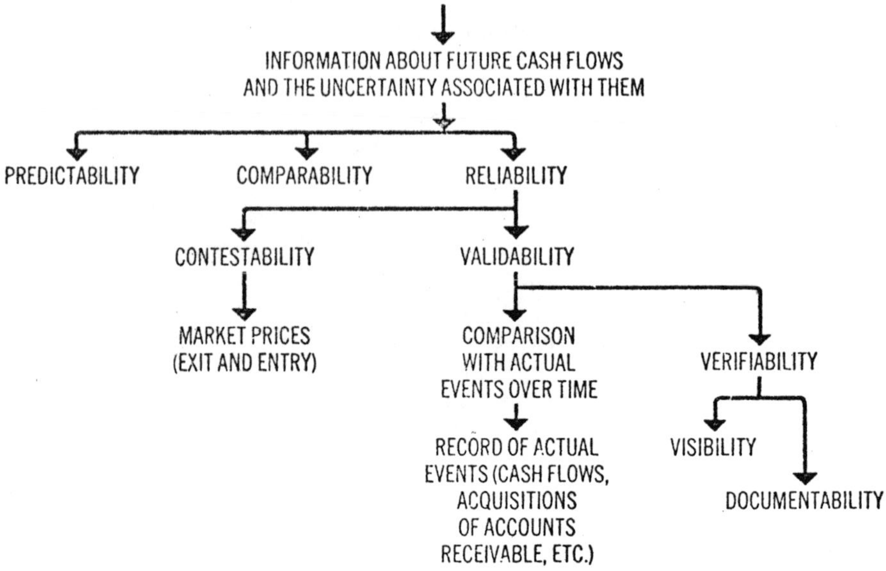

Figure 2

Benefits Obtained Through Actions Made Possible by Steps Required in Providing Information. The process of providing information yields two types of benefits. One type results from using the information; the other results from the actions of individuals motivated by the mere necessity to provide the information. The necessity to provide the information may cause actions that are either beneficial or harmful to the efficient allocation of resources. The mere provision of information may facilitate the control and coordination of factors of production (including the firm's labor force) and goal congruence (conformity of the actions of the firm's personnel with the goal of the firm as a whole). The data required for providing information may also be used to trace the actions of the various employees of the firm and to facilitate control. From the sub-objectives of control, coordination and congruence we can deduce the need for providing forecasts and budgets to coordinate future activities and also the need to keep a record of actual events for comparison with forecasts.

For optimal allocation of the firm's resources, managers and employees need to have profit maximization as a goal. This motivation can be facilitated both by the preparation of budgets and subsequent comparison of results with budgets,[17] and also by compensation of the firm's personnel at amounts that equal their marginal productivity. From this latter objective we again derive the need to record actual events and performance. For the forecasts to be effective in producing desired benefits both within the firm and outside of it, internal and external forecasts should be the same. This aspect of the benefits of providing accounting information is schematically depicted in Figure 3, page 90.

Timeliness and Availability of Accounting Information. To optimize resource allocation, it is also desirable to minimize the time lags between the point at which new information about expected cash flows and their uncertainties first become known and the point at which allocation decisions are made. The faster that new information is made available, the shorter the time lapse until the decision is made and consequently, the shorter the period during which the economy's capital is not optimally allocated. Therefore, information on expected cash flows and their uncertainties should be disseminated as fast as possible once it becomes known. This constitutes the sub-objective of timeliness derived in Figure 4, page 91. How fast information should be disseminated and the frequency of the dissemination depend on the cost/benefit relationships.

To allocate resources optimally, it is also necessary to maximize the number of individuals who possess information on expected cash flows and their uncertainty about different firms. The wider the dissemination of knowledge about alternative combinations of risk and return relative to different securities, the more likely are resources to be channeled to their best use as a result of competitive bids for the more profitable securities. Accordingly the sub-objective of wide public dissemination of accounting information is derived in Figure 4.

Information for Social Goals

Another derivative of the objective of optimally allocating resources within the economy consistent with private maximization of wealth is the need to equate marginal social cost and benefits with marginal private cost and benefits. Loosely speaking, where the actions of the firm affect only its own costs and benefits there would be no divergence between private values (costs and benefits) and social values. In this case, the decision and actions taken in pursuit of the firm's own interests will result in the optimization of both private wealth and the economy's wealth. Where the actions of an individual firm do affect, however, the consequences of other firms' or indi-

[17] Budgets may have a beneficial effect in motivating the work force, but they could also reduce motivation as a result of the manner in which they are generated and their magnitude. The behavioral link between the preparation of budgets and ultimate productivity is complex. For a discussion of this issue, see Joshua Ronen and J. Leslie Livingstone, "An Expectancy Theory Approach to the Motivational Impacts of Budgets" (Unpublished manuscript, The University of Toronto, 1973).

OBJECTIVES HIERARCHY: INFORMATION BENEFITS

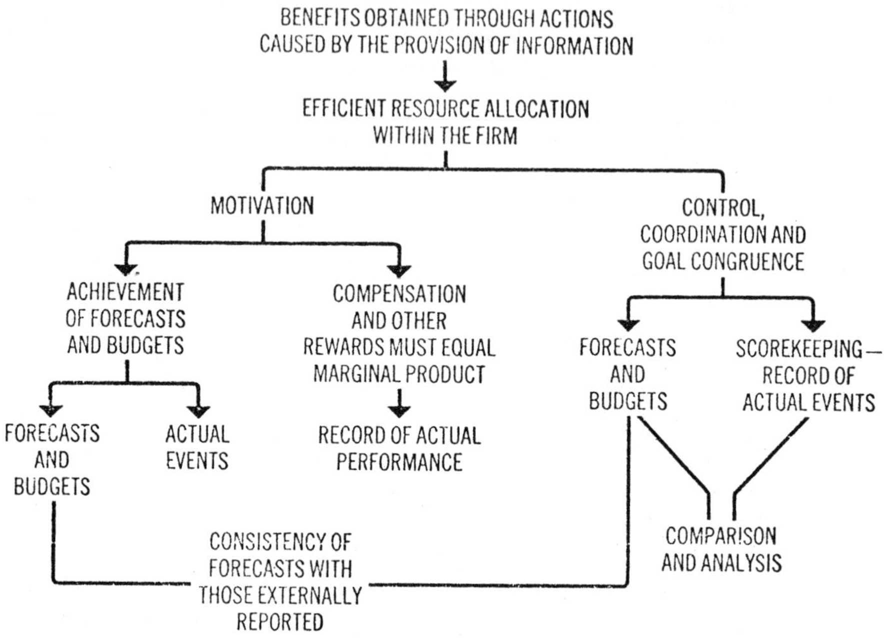

Figure 3

viduals' actions, then pursuing only private benefits *may* not result in the optimization of social benefits or in an efficient allocation of resources. In this case, an accounting objective that is restricted to the consideration of private benefits and costs may require the communication of data that will not meet the social objectives.

It is possible that private profit maximization by a firm will also bring about an efficient allocation of resources, even when the firm's actions directly affect the consequences of other firms' actions. This would be the case when the firm takes into account these effects before it makes its decisions. If the firm is to maximize its profits in the most rigorous sense, it must take into consideration the effect of its actions on other firms or individuals. These effects fall within the normal economic definition of opportunity costs and should therefore be explicitly considered along with other costs in making rational decisions. Reflecting opportunity costs make it possible for accounting report users to properly assess managerial per-

OBJECTIVES HIERARCHY: INFORMATION BENEFITS

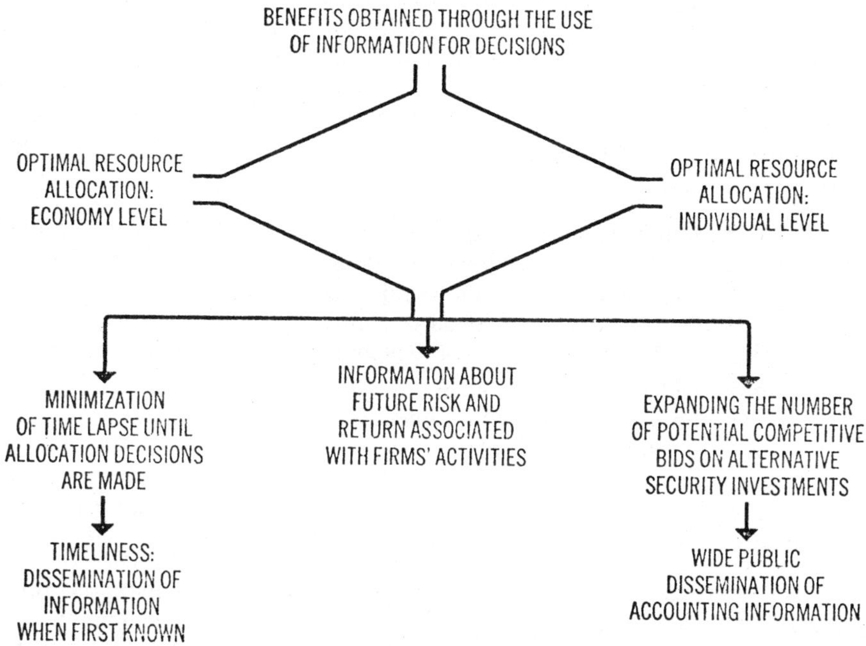

Figure 4

formance. But, in addition, if income figures that result from actual past transactions are deemed to be at all important (both in providing a record of actual past transactions to fulfill the stewardship function of accounting as well as in providing the means to validate past managerial expectations), it is evident that these opportunity costs should be treated in the same manner as other production costs.

The issue becomes more complex when the effect of the firm's actions on others is not or cannot be adequately considered when making decisions within the firm. This would be the case, for example, when the price mechanism of the market, which enables the firm to consider such facts directly in its decisions, either does not exist or is too costly. Operationally, this means that transaction costs such as conducting negotiations, drawing up contracts and inspection are higher than the benefits of adjusting the firm's actions on the basis of the expected effects of these actions on other entities.

In this case, pursuing private interests will not lead the firm to bring about a socially desirable allocation of resources, and governmental intervention, through the legal determination of rights, regulations, and policing, may eventually become necessary.[18] Indeed, because of its power, the government may be able to bring about corrective action at a lower cost than would a private organization. Although the governmental machine may be extremely costly, it may be the alternative to private action. Under these circumstances, the gathering and communication of information about social costs are desirable even in the absence of a potential solution at the private level because:

1. The communication of such information may (subject to the determination that the information is best processed by the firm creating the harmful side activity) lead to a proper kind of governmental intervention that achieves efficient allocation of resources, also indicating that such information should be helpful in determining which of the alternative social arrangements is optimal for dealing with the externality.

2. On the assumption that an efficient market would eventually lead to desirable social action, the communication of information about the cost to the firm that will probably be associated with whatever social arrangement emerges will provide the user of financial statements with better means to appraise the future prospects of the firm.

In Figure 5, opposite, the sub-objective of equating marginal private costs and benefits with marginal social costs and benefits is therefore indicated as a derivative of the optimal resource allocation within the economy, consistent with the optimal allocation at the individual level. Any divergences between marginal private costs and benefits and marginal social costs and benefits need to be reliably predicted and compared among firms. This need is reflected in Figure 6, fold-out, by an arrow connecting the objective of equating the private values with social values to the sub-objectives of predictability, comparability and reliability.

The sub-objectives developed so far from the overall objective of optimal resource allocation (individual and economy-wide levels) can be summarized as follows:

1. Providing information about future risk and return associated with the firm's security: This leads to the requirement of information about future cash flows and their uncertainty.

2. Timeliness: Dissemination of information when first known in order to minimize the time lapse until allocation decisions are made.

---

[18] For a more lucid discussion of this issue, see R. H. Coase, "The Problem of Social Cost," *Journal of Law and Economics* (October 1960). Also, for a more detailed treatment of the accounting implications of social costs and benefits, see Joshua Ronen, "Accounting for Social Costs and Benefits," contained in this volume, pp. 317-340.

OBJECTIVES HIERARCHY: INFORMATION BENEFITS

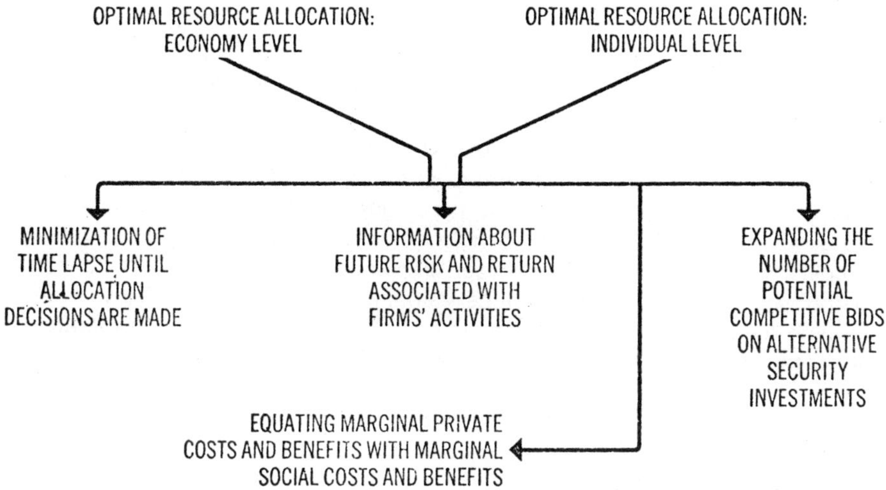

Figure 5

3. Wide dissemination of information to expand the number of competitive bids on alternative security investments.

4. Providing information about divergences between marginal private costs and benefits and marginal social costs and benefits.

From the objective of providing information on future cash flows and uncertainty, the sub-objectives of predictability, comparability and reliability were derived. That is, the accounting objectives so far can be summarized as the timely and wide dissemination of information that enables users to reliably predict and compare expected cash flows and their uncertainty, as well as predicting and comparing divergences between private and social values across firms.

Elements of Predictability and Comparability. Elements of predictability and comparability are diverse and could vary in their degree of importance depending upon the firm's circumstances. However, some general guidelines can be developed as sub-objectives derived from predictability and comparability. Figure 6 which reflects the total hierarchy of objectives and subobjectives (and which incorporates Figures 1 through 5) depicts the development of the predictability and comparability elements.

Prediction can be facilitated if the events that are to be predicted can be associated with other events or dimensions which are either known or more easily predicted.[19] The most obvious information that helps predict future events is a record of the past occurrences of that event. Past occurrences of an event could be extrapolated into the future in accordance with simple rules (at the rudimentary level of analysis) or through use of a more formal and rigorous prediction model (e.g., time series analysis).[20] Thus, we derive the sub-objective of providing information on past cash flows to improve the prediction of expected flows.

Secondly, fluctuations in the firm's volume of output may explain variations in some of the costs. Therefore, knowledge of (or estimate of) future output volume may well facilitate the prediction of future levels of cost with more accuracy than if the nature of the association between volume of output and costs was either not known or not disclosed. Since costs fixed relative to output will occur at about the same magnitude and costs that are variable in relation to output will tend to fluctuate,[21] providing information separately about these fixed and variable costs may make possible a better prediction of future costs.

Certainly, output is not the only dimension or variable with which the movement of costs or any other variables that are to be predicted can be associated. Association can be made with inputs, with activities such as product lines and segments of firms, etc.[22] In addition, present practice

---

[19] This is the primary motivation for the common regression analysis. See, for example, George Benston, "Multiple Regression Analysis of Cost Behavior," *Accounting Review* (October 1966), pp. 657-672, and Robert Jensen, "Multiple Regression Models for Cost Control—Assumptions and Limitations," *Accounting Review* (April 1967), pp. 265-272.

[20] For example, several studies revealed that accounting income could be a better predictor of itself, that is, of accounting income (if the latter is obtained through the same system of rules and measurement as the former) than the other types of income (such as replacement cost income). Also, studies under way explore the statistical properties of time series of events to develop criteria for improving predictions. Thus, providing information about cash flows may help improve the prediction of future cash flows either directly or through the development of such criteria.

[21] See, for example, R. S. Gynther, "Improving Separation of Fixed and Variable Expenses," *NAA Bulletin* (June 1963), pp. 29-39, and National Association of Accountants, Accounting Practice Report No. 10, "Separating and Using Costs as Fixed and Variable," *NAA Bulletin* (June 1960).

[22] The objective of associability leads (when associability is made with product lines) to the separate reporting by product lines and segments that is the subject of much debate now. Clearly, the degree to which such information is to be reported on product lines is the subject of research into the cost of this form of reporting. Part of the cost may be the reduced motivation and ability to generate profits through revealing information beneficial to competitors. This latter occurrence would violate the objective of motivation and the sub-objective of the equality of reward with the individual marginal product that appears elsewhere in the hierarchy as discussed above.

suggests that the associability of costs with manufacturing and selling and administrative functions may motivate the separate reporting of costs by functions. Predictability seems to be the implicit objective that accountants have in mind when they disclose the underlying components such as revenue, cost of sales, and operating expenses, which determine the resulting net income figure. In fact, recent evidence suggests that separate components of the income measurement process may be better forecasted than net income itself which is an algebraic sum of the components. Thus, firms were found to be able to forecast revenues, for example, with more accuracy and precision than net income.[23]

The Time Dimension. One of the major dimensions with which events are generally associated and which is important in prediction is the time dimension. Events that are associated with time are said to be recurring events. Those which are not associated with time are called non-recurring events. The items that are generally grouped as operating expenses and operating revenues tend to be recurring items, whereas the non-recurring items are usually labeled as extraordinary revenue or expense items. Prediction on the basis of a series of past events is made with less errors if the process that generates these events and their measures is well defined and stable. The firm's return is generally the aggregate of many and different processes. When prediction is based on a separate component, each identifiable with a particular generating process, it is apt to be more accurate than when it is based on an aggregate measure that obscures the underlying relationship. Thus, better prediction is presumably made possible by analyzing the time trend of income generated by recurring events more than by analyzing a trend of income that results from both recurring operations and less stable processes. Therefore, disaggregation of events along the dimension of recurrability becomes another criterion that facilitates prediction.

Discriminability Among Information Sources. Associability of events of interest with past events or past dimensions is not the only criterion that may facilitate the improvement of prediction. An important element in facilitating prediction is obtaining estimates (even though subjective) from people who may possess information about the future that makes their own prediction of future relevant events an important input into the predictions of the users of financial statements. The persons who may have some knowledge about the future are likely to be the firm's management.

As indicated earlier, the object of prediction is expected future cash flows and the uncertainty associated with them. But both the cash flows and their uncertainty depend on the specific plans and actions which are affected by and *first* known to the management of firms. Since such plans are de-

---

[23] See R. A. Daily, "The Feasibility of Reporting Forecasted Information," *The Accounting Review* (October 1971), pp. 686-692.

signed to give the firm a competitive edge, they are bound to have significant informational content.[24]

Because a firm's management is the first to know its plans, timely forecasts may prove to be a valuable input to the users of financial statements in predicting future cash flows. Management is in the best position to assess the effects that its specific plans (unknown to others unless communicated) have on future cash flows. It would therefore seem desirable for management to communicate its expectations concerning these cash flows.[25] Managers, however, are not infallible. Expectations based on their plans may diverge from actual results because of the randomness of the underlying events or different interpretations of future events by managers and the market. The difference in interpretation may exist because of two major factors that affect future cash flows: (a) market and industry events that affect all the firms—exogenous factors, and (b) the particular performance of the firm in question, that is, the specific plans or resources, employment decisions made by management, etc. These specific firm decisions are responsible for whether the firm accumulates more or less value than the industry or the market. These are the endogenous factors.

Exogenous factors, contrary to the endogenous, are primarily beyond the firm's control. They may be predicted by relying on the market's expectations as reflected in market prices, but the best source for predicting endogenous factors is probably the firm's management. Thus, the dimension of controllability of events becomes an important criterion in facilitating prediction.[26] The dimension of controllability facilitates prediction not only directly through identifying the source from which expectations are to be obtained—market transactions and market prices for the exogenous factors and management's forecasts for the endogenous factors—but it also facilitates prediction through enabling users to assess managerial performance. Clearly, the past ability of management to forecast, perform and carry out

---

[24] This is generally information that is not currently and systematically made widely available to the market. Some evidence on this is provided by Scholes, "Test of the Competitive Market Hypothesis," who found that corporate insiders often have monopolistic access to information about their firms which if made available would contribute to a better allocation of resources (see Ronen, "Need for Accounting Objectives in an Efficient Market").

[25] Notice that the detailed plans themselves do not have to be made available, only the management expectations concerning cash flows which are contingent on these plans. Consequently, there should be no reluctance by management, out of fear of leakage to competitors, to reflect this information.

[26] A perfectly competitive firm does not possess any particular advantages that allow it to affect its output price by varying its supply and will therefore not earn more than the normal rate of return. It can be said then that the firm's increment in its wealth is determined entirely by exogenous market and industry factors. A monopolistic firm possesses a unique asset (skilled labor force, managerial know-how) that enables it to affect the price of its differentiated product. In this case, the firm can be said to bring its *endogenous* variables to bear on its output price aside from the industry-wide exogenous factors, and it can thus produce higher than a normal rate of return.

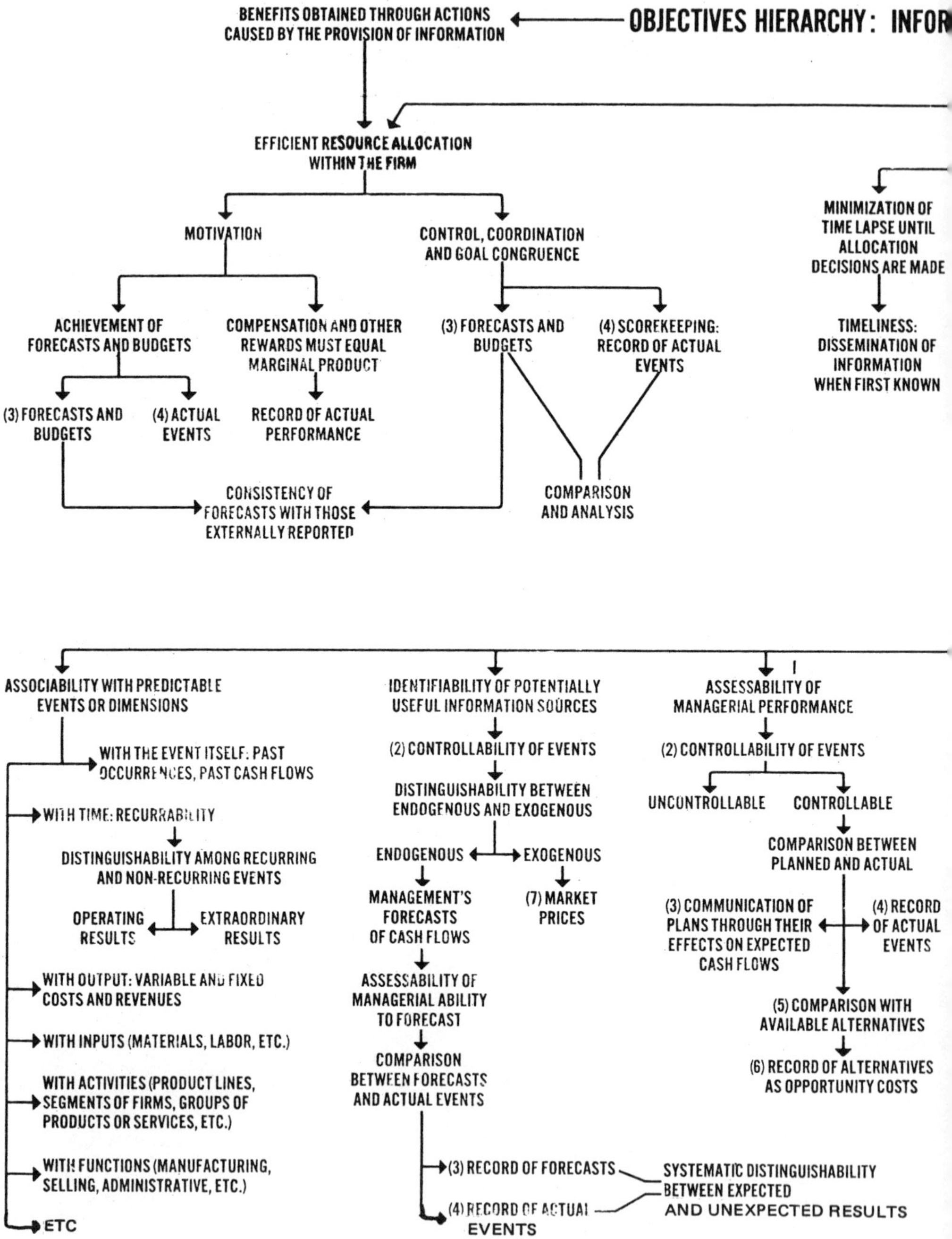
OBJECTIVES HIERARCHY: INFOR
BENEFITS OBTAINED THROUGH ACTIONS CAUSED BY THE PROVISION OF INFORMATION
EFFICIENT RESOURCE ALLOCATION WITHIN THE FIRM
MOTIVATION
CONTROL, COORDINATION AND GOAL CONGRUENCE
ACHIEVEMENT OF FORECASTS AND BUDGETS
COMPENSATION AND OTHER REWARDS MUST EQUAL MARGINAL PRODUCT
(3) FORECASTS AND BUDGETS
(4) SCOREKEEPING: RECORD OF ACTUAL EVENTS
(3) FORECASTS AND BUDGETS
(4) ACTUAL EVENTS
RECORD OF ACTUAL PERFORMANCE
CONSISTENCY OF FORECASTS WITH THOSE EXTERNALLY REPORTED
COMPARISON AND ANALYSIS
MINIMIZATION OF TIME LAPSE UNTIL ALLOCATION DECISIONS ARE MADE
TIMELINESS: DISSEMINATION OF INFORMATION WHEN FIRST KNOWN
ASSOCIABILITY WITH PREDICTABLE EVENTS OR DIMENSIONS
WITH THE EVENT ITSELF: PAST OCCURRENCES, PAST CASH FLOWS
WITH TIME: RECURRABILITY
DISTINGUISHABILITY AMONG RECURRING AND NON-RECURRING EVENTS
OPERATING RESULTS
EXTRAORDINARY RESULTS
WITH OUTPUT: VARIABLE AND FIXED COSTS AND REVENUES
WITH INPUTS (MATERIALS, LABOR, ETC.)
WITH ACTIVITIES (PRODUCT LINES, SEGMENTS OF FIRMS, GROUPS OF PRODUCTS OR SERVICES, ETC.)
WITH FUNCTIONS (MANUFACTURING, SELLING, ADMINISTRATIVE, ETC.)
ETC
IDENTIFIABILITY OF POTENTIALLY USEFUL INFORMATION SOURCES
(2) CONTROLLABILITY OF EVENTS
DISTINGUISHABILITY BETWEEN ENDOGENOUS AND EXOGENOUS
ENDOGENOUS
EXOGENOUS
MANAGEMENT'S FORECASTS OF CASH FLOWS
(7) MARKET PRICES
ASSESSABILITY OF MANAGERIAL ABILITY TO FORECAST
COMPARISON BETWEEN FORECASTS AND ACTUAL EVENTS
(3) RECORD OF FORECASTS
(4) RECORD OF ACTUAL EVENTS
SYSTEMATIC DISTINGUISHABILITY BETWEEN EXPECTED AND UNEXPECTED RESULTS
ASSESSABILITY OF MANAGERIAL PERFORMANCE
(2) CONTROLLABILITY OF EVENTS
UNCONTROLLABLE
CONTROLLABLE
COMPARISON BETWEEN PLANNED AND ACTUAL
(3) COMMUNICATION OF PLANS THROUGH THEIR EFFECTS ON EXPECTED CASH FLOWS
(4) RECORD OF ACTUAL EVENTS
(5) COMPARISON WITH AVAILABLE ALTERNATIVES
(6) RECORD OF ALTERNATIVES AS OPPORTUNITY COSTS

Figure 6

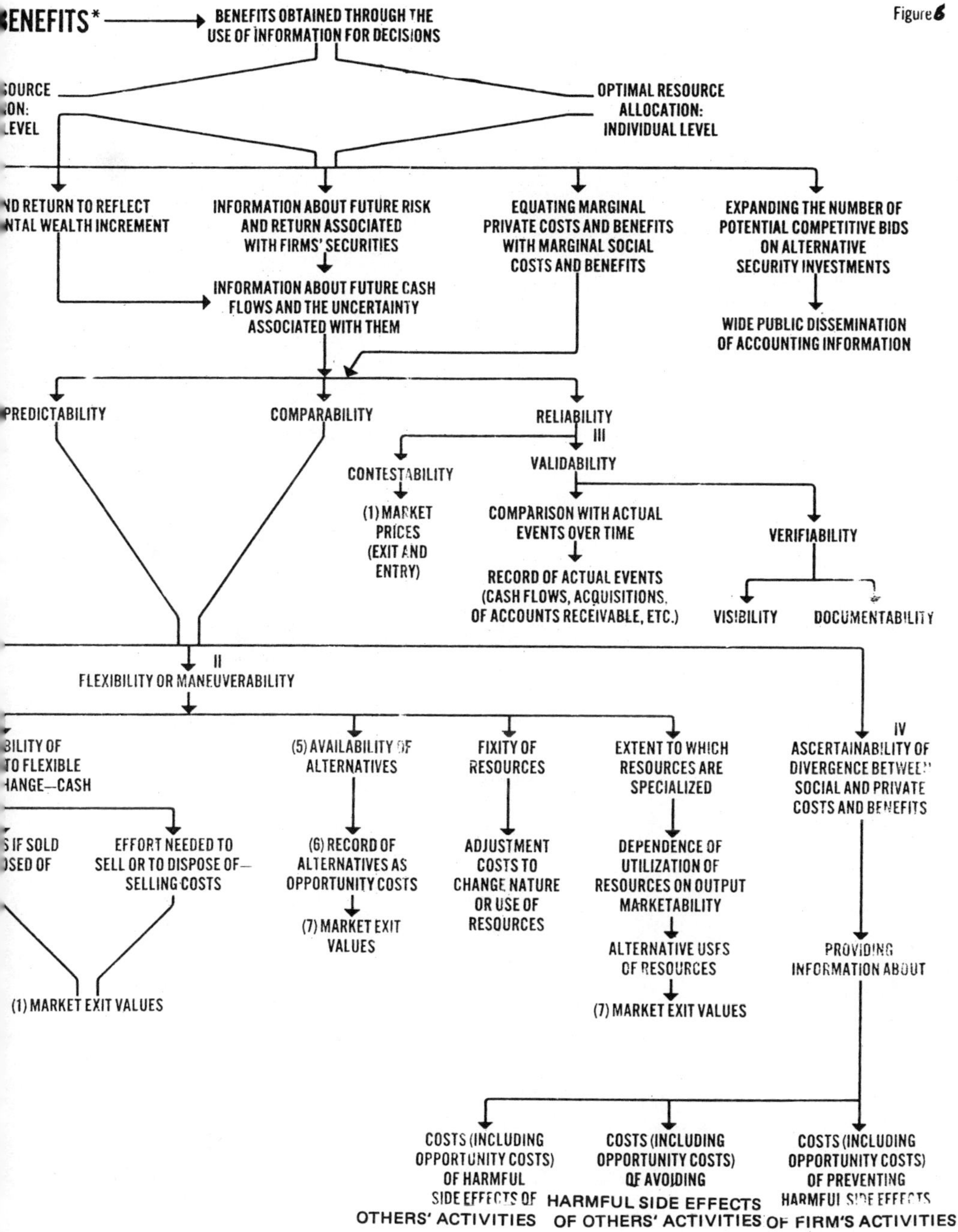

ENEFITS*
BENEFITS OBTAINED THROUGH THE USE OF INFORMATION FOR DECISIONS
OURCE ON: LEVEL
OPTIMAL RESOURCE ALLOCATION: INDIVIDUAL LEVEL
ND RETURN TO REFLECT NTAL WEALTH INCREMENT
INFORMATION ABOUT FUTURE RISK AND RETURN ASSOCIATED WITH FIRMS' SECURITIES
EQUATING MARGINAL PRIVATE COSTS AND BENEFITS WITH MARGINAL SOCIAL COSTS AND BENEFITS
EXPANDING THE NUMBER OF POTENTIAL COMPETITIVE BIDS ON ALTERNATIVE SECURITY INVESTMENTS
INFORMATION ABOUT FUTURE CASH FLOWS AND THE UNCERTAINTY ASSOCIATED WITH THEM
WIDE PUBLIC DISSEMINATION OF ACCOUNTING INFORMATION
PREDICTABILITY
COMPARABILITY
RELIABILITY
III
CONTESTABILITY
VALIDABILITY
(1) MARKET PRICES (EXIT AND ENTRY)
COMPARISON WITH ACTUAL EVENTS OVER TIME
VERIFIABILITY
RECORD OF ACTUAL EVENTS (CASH FLOWS, ACQUISITIONS, OF ACCOUNTS RECEIVABLE, ETC.)
VISIBILITY
DOCUMENTABILITY
II
FLEXIBILITY OR MANEUVERABILITY
BILITY OF TO FLEXIBLE HANGE—CASH
(5) AVAILABILITY OF ALTERNATIVES
FIXITY OF RESOURCES
EXTENT TO WHICH RESOURCES ARE SPECIALIZED
IV
ASCERTAINABILITY OF DIVERGENCE BETWEEN SOCIAL AND PRIVATE COSTS AND BENEFITS
S IF SOLD SED OF
EFFORT NEEDED TO SELL OR TO DISPOSE OF— SELLING COSTS
(6) RECORD OF ALTERNATIVES AS OPPORTUNITY COSTS
ADJUSTMENT COSTS TO CHANGE NATURE OR USE OF RESOURCES
DEPENDENCE OF UTILIZATION OF RESOURCES ON OUTPUT MARKETABILITY
(7) MARKET EXIT VALUES
ALTERNATIVE USES OF RESOURCES
PROVIDING INFORMATION ABOUT
(1) MARKET EXIT VALUES
(7) MARKET EXIT VALUES
COSTS (INCLUDING OPPORTUNITY COSTS) OF HARMFUL SIDE EFFECTS OF OTHERS' ACTIVITIES
COSTS (INCLUDING OPPORTUNITY COSTS) OF AVOIDING HARMFUL SIDE EFFECTS OF OTHERS' ACTIVITIES
COSTS (INCLUDING OPPORTUNITY COSTS) OF PREVENTING HARMFUL SIDE EFFECTS OF FIRM'S ACTIVITIES

plans successfully is an indicator of future performance and therefore represents important input to the prediction process. Further, information about management's particular plans and their results provides insight into risk-taking tendencies of management and, therefore, the future likelihood of engaging in risk-taking activities. Thus, the ability to identify potentially useful information sources can enhance the predictability of relevant events. This is indicated as one of the sub-objectives emanating from the predictability and comparability objectives in the hierarchy shown in Figure 6.

Controllability is only one dimension that could facilitate the identifiability of potentially useful sources (through indicating, for example, that management is potentially a more useful force for predicting the endogenous factors under its control than for predicting the exogenous factors outside its control). Other dimensions may also make identification of the more competent sources for providing information on future events possible. For example, among exogenous factors, different information sources have different degrees of usefulness and competence in providing information about relevant events. Interest rate fluctuations, the money reserve, and credit terms are factors; information concerning them is probably best obtained from the Federal Reserve. Information on the availability of raw materials and future prices, on the other hand, is probably best obtained through observing trends in the supplying industries. However, while other dimensions could be identified, only the controllability dimension is shown in Figure 6 since it serves to indicate a major dichotomy between the exogenous and the endogenous variables.

The distinction between the exogenous and endogenous variables leads (as shown in the hierarchy) to the identification of management as the most competent source for predicting endogenous variables. Since users are interested in expected cash flows and their uncertainty, management forecasts of endogenous variables can be communicated by assessing the endogenous effects on future cash flows accruing to the firm.[27]

[27] While there are many ways for managers to communicate future endogenous events, the forecasts of cash flows by management were chosen in the hierarchy because: (a) such forecasts provide a quantification of the endogenous variables in dollars and (b) since the effects on cash flows will depend on the assumptions implicit in management's forecasts with respect to exogenous factors, such assumptions would be reflected through the forecasts of the total cash flows. These assumptions could also be explicitly stated when management provides its cash flow forecasts. It is important for users to know these assumptions, since if they are considered unrealistic, the quantification of the endogenous effect on the cash flows can then be modified. By communicating future endogenous events via their effects on cash flows, an aggregate measure could be provided if so desired. Provision of management's assessment of endogenous variables through forecasted cash flows certainly does not exclude other ways of communicating this information. Further research is needed to point out the better alternative means. For a recent suggestion to communicate management's probability distribution of forecasts conditioned upon different expectations with respect to exogenous variables, see Amir Barnea and G. Joseph San Miguel, "The Relevance of Earnings Forecasts" (Unpublished manuscript, New York University, 1973).

The best source for predicting the exogenous factors is probably the market itself. It has already been indicated that different sources could be of different competence or reliability in predicting exogenous factors. However, the research on efficient markets indicates that available information in a market (including information affecting exogenous factors relevant to the particular firm) is generally impounded in market prices (whether they are securities or other capital assets). Market prices, therefore, probably best reflect the effects of relevant exogenous factors on the firm. For example, fluctuations in the price of a firm's output reflects anticipated changes in the demand for that output, which is an exogenous factor that is relevant to the firm. Similarly, fluctuations in the market prices of inputs would reflect expectations with respect to changing conditions in the supplying industry and/or the emergence of competing inputs. This leads to the conclusion that market prices should be the source for predicting the exogenous factors that impinge upon the firm's activities, as shown in Figure 6 by the arrow extending from the exogenous branch of the exogenous and endogenous dichotimization.

Proceeding from the endogenous branch and the need for management to communicate its cash flow forecasts, it is necessary for users to assess reliability of the future forecasts. To do this they need to be able to assess management ability to forecast with reasonable accuracy. To assess management ability to forecast, comparison between management forecasts and actual events must be made.[28] Thus, the recording of forecasts *and* actual events (to be compared with forecasts) emerges as a desirable objective. To highlight the deviations of actual events from forecasted events, it is desirable to distinguish between expected and unexpected results of operations in the records. The quantification of unexpected events provides a record of management's "errors" and would be useful in assessing—through the observation of the magnitudes of these errors over an extended period of time—the ability of management to forecast within a reasonable degree of accuracy. Thus, Figure 6 indicates the systematic distinguishability between expected and unexpected results as an objective of accounting.

Assessability of Managerial Performance. Since the firm's progress hinges primarily on management performance, the ability to assess this performance is an important element in facilitating the predictability of the firm's flows and the comparability of these flows across firms. But to facilitate

[28] Thus, it could be argued that in the short run, managers could deceive users by deliberately communicating biased forecasts. But it should be remembered that managers who are likely to do so, when required to communicate forecasts, will probably "volunteer" biased forecasts in the absence of such a requirement. (As is well known, managers presently communicate forecasts in an ad hoc, sporadic fashion.) The requirement to incorporate forecasts systematically and periodically within the accounting system serves at least to deter biasing forecasts since it makes possible the subsequent systematic and periodic comparison of forecasts with actual events.

the assessment of managerial performance, it is essential to distinguish between controllable and uncontrollable events. Thus, the dimension of controllability is important in two respects: one for the identifiability of useful information sources and the other for the assessment of managerial performance. In the hierarchy (Figure 6) several situations are encountered where the same objective is derived from more than one higher level objective. This is indicated by numbers reflected in Figure 6. For controllable events, a comparison needs to be made between management's plans and actual results. The degree of management's success is assessed through both the soundness of their plans and the ability to meet these plans. Furthermore, both management's plans and actual results need to be compared with alternative plans and actions that were available to management. From the need to facilitate such comparison and evaluation can be deduced the objective of providing a record of alternative actions which, for example, could be reflected through the communication of opportunity costs. Thus, from the objective of assessment of managerial performance, two sub-objectives can be deduced which have already been derived through other objectives in the hierarchy. One is the communication of management's forecasts and the effect of specific plans on these forecasts and the record of actual events to be compared with the actual forecasts.

Flexibility or Maneuverability. Of primary importance for predicting the risk associated with the firm's cash flows (but also for assessing return) is the degree of flexibility or maneuverability that the management of the firm possesses in employing its resources. The more numerous the alternatives open to management for utilizing its resources, the greater its resilience to adverse environmental effects such as a decline in demand for its product. A systematic record of the alternative employments of available resources and possibly the resources' opportunity costs will facilitate the assessment of such alternatives. One readily available alternative for the firm's resources is disposal of them. Market exit values of the firm's resources quantify this alternative and are therefore an objective that is derived from the higher level objective of providing information on the availability of alternatives.

Market exit values also satisfy two other sub-objectives that may be derived from the flexibility criterion. These are the convertibility of the resources into flexible means of exchange and the extent to which resources are specialized. Clearly, the more convertible the firm's resources into cash and the greater the magnitude of cash that could be potentially received for them, the more flexible is the firm's management and the higher the degree of maneuverability of the firm's resources. If the market exit values of the firm's resources are small in their relative magnitude, a small number of alternative uses of these resources outside the firm is indicated, and therefore the utilization of the resources within the firm will be highly dependent on the marketability of the firm's specific output. The greater the extent to which these resources are specialized (in the sense of being thus dependent) the lesser is the degree of maneuverability available for management and the less flexible is management in using the assets.

Another factor that affects management flexibility is the degree of fixity of the resources. That is, the extent to which adjustment costs need to be incurred to change the use of the resources. The higher the adjustment costs, that is, the greater the fixity of the resources, the higher are the risks associated with the firm's flows in case adverse environmental effects cause the demand for the firm's output to decline. The flexibility and maneuverability criteria are sub-divided in the hierarchy into four separate (although in effect interrelated) sub-objectives:

1. Convertibility of resources into flexible means of exchange—cash: This sub-objective leads to the objective of providing market exit values as a reflection of the proceeds of resources, if disposed of, less the costs incurred to dispose of the assets.

2. Availability of alternatives: From this can be derived the need to record alternatives, such as opportunity costs. A readily available opportunity cost of the firm's resources is their proceeds. Thus, market exit values are derived again as a sub-objective.

3. Fixity of resources: From this attribute can be derived the need to communicate adjustment costs to change the nature of the use of resources.

4. The extent to which resources are specialized: To reflect the degree of specialization, there must be some indication of the dependence of the utilization of resources on output marketability. Such a dependence could again be reflected through communicating the possible alternative uses of resources, e.g., through use of market exit values.

From the objectives of flexibility and maneuverability two sub-objectives seem important. These are market exit values of the firm's resources and the opportunity costs of such resources, that is, a record of the resources' value in alternative uses. The numbers shown beside some of the sub-objectives in the hierarchy indicate *recurrence* in the hierarchy. In other words, they are derived from more than one objective or sub-objective. While greater recurrence of the sub-objective in the hierarchy does not necessarily indicate that a particular sub-objective is more important, this is likely to be the case.

Ascertainability of Divergences Between Social and Private Costs and Benefits

To make possible the prediction of future divergences between social and private values (costs and benefits) as well as the possible alternative means of dealing with these divergences either at the individual or the governmental level, information must be provided about both past and present divergences between social and private values. The information needs to be provided concerning the following:

1. The actual cost to a firm (including opportunity costs) of harmful side activity engaged in by other firms or entities: Probably, the firm is in the best position to measure and quantify the costs here in the form of direct expenditures or in the form of lost income that it incurs because of harmful externality

(such as pollution, noise, fumes, etc.) caused by another entity. It follows therefore that quantification of these costs for either private action or governmental intervention is best made and communicated by the firm itself, possibly as a part of its accounting system.

2. The costs of avoiding the side effects of others' activities: Certainly if the cost of avoiding the harmful side effects is less than the cost of the harmful side effects if not avoided, the cost of avoidance is relevant quantification of the social costs of the side effects (if the side effects only affect this particular firm). For any governmental action, this cost which can probably be best estimated by the affected firm is a necessary factor in determining the optimal action.

3. Another relevant factor in determining the optimal corrective action is the cost which the firm causing the harmful side effect would incur to prevent it. The magnitude of this cost must be compared to the cost of the side effect to the affected firm as well as to the cost of avoiding that effect by the firm before a decision about the appropriate corrective action can be made.

Summary

Figure 6 shows the hierarchy of objectives and sub-objectives. Each sub-objective was derived from the analysis of information needed to obtain a higher level sub-objective in the hierarchy. While the derivation of objectives and sub-objectives flows in the figure from top to bottom, i.e., from the highest level and the broadest objectives to lower level objectives, the formulation of the high level objectives was at least in part based on how and for what purpose presently provided information is used.

The importance of the framework depicted in Figure 6 lies in the way that objectives or sub-objectives are derived. While both benefit and cost considerations are required to identify objectives, we first concentrate on the identification of the more common benefits to be derived from accounting information. The benefits are based on pervasive normative decision models of major groups of users. Once the overall objectives are formulated, sub-objectives and sub-sub-objectives are derived until different proposed accounting formats and alternatives can be discriminated by assessing and evaluating them in light of the hierarchy of objectives.

ACCOUNTING INCOME AND ECONOMIC INCOME

George H. Sorter

Accounting Income and Economic Income

George H. Sorter

Economic Income

There is general agreement among economists who have written on this subject that income is to be regarded as a measure of the change in "well-being" or "better-offness" occurring in some specific time period irrespective of whether it is measured statically or dynamically and regardless of the measurement bases used.

A change in well-being can result through either immediate satisfaction or increased prospects for future satisfaction. Thus, income has often been defined as consumption plus investment. Consumption corresponds to immediate satisfaction, whereas investment is identified as the postponement of present consumption with increased future consumption or satisfaction as one of its goals.

Economic Income for Individuals

Much of the controversy in defining income for individuals is based on the fact that either current or prospective satisfaction is necessarily subjective and based on individual preferences and the utility assessments of different individuals. A person's satisfaction or consumption may, to a large extent, be nonmonetary. Thus, one person may derive income in the form of personal satisfaction from viewing a painting, whereas another person may not.

The same problem exists in defining investments of individuals. For some persons the ownership of art objects may be an investment over and above their monetary values. For others it may not, and so forth.

Economic Income for Business Entities

These definitional problems are not as acute for business entities. Such organizations (as opposed to individuals who may own the business) should not have utility functions. Their well-being is generally restricted to, and measured by, monetary benefits.

In the case of business entities, consumption is defined strictly as dividends; net investment is defined simply as the change in the value of the firm itself (exclusive of any additional explicit stockholder investments in the firm).[1]

Economic income for a firm is generally defined as the change in the value of the firm plus any dividends paid during the period. Almost unanimous agreement exists among economists that the value of an asset is quantified by the discounted value of the future cash flows attributable to the asset. The value of a firm, which is an asset itself, is also considered to be quantified by the discounted value of the future cash flows attributable to it.

Should the measurement of economic income, or alternatively, an accounting income that corresponds more closely to economic income, be the objective of accounting? A negative response to this question is appropriate for reasons discussed in the next section of this paper.

Economic Income and the Accountant

Users of financial statements would like to know the cash proceeds that they will receive from investments that they make. In terms of equity securities these cash proceeds are measured by the dividends that the stockholder will receive and the market price at which he will be able to sell his shares, that is, his share of the economic income of the firm. This information, however, cannot be supplied by the accountant, at least not presently.

Even in a world of relative certainty where the probabilities of all prospective events affecting a corporation are known, the accountant still could not measure the prospective market values of a firm or its economic income. The price an individual is willing to pay or receive for a security is determined by (1) his expectation concerning future events, and (2) his personal preferences relating to these events. Individuals generally will be willing to pay less for a security which has a 50 per cent probability of returning $100 and a 50 per cent probability of returning 0 than for a security which has a 100 per cent probability of returning $50. Thus, most individuals are risk averse but they are risk averse in differing degrees. The extent to which an individual is risk averse will determine how much less he is willing to pay for the security with a 50 per cent probability of returning $100 and a 50 per cent probability of returning 0. Individuals with different risk preferences will therefore be willing to pay different amounts for securities whose returns are subject to equivalent uncertainties.

The market price of securities reflects a collective consensus of many investors and incorporates their collective risk preferences. Therefore, the accountant, in order to measure prospective market values and economic income, would not only have to know the probability of future events occurring

[1] Many problems of defining income, of course, remain. This definition of income as consumption plus investment can easily be used to analyze such problems as whether the measure of income should reflect deduction for imputed interest on stockholder investment and whether unexpected gains should properly be included in income. Analysis of these problems is not carried further in this paper, however.

but also the collective taste and preferences of investors. In actual fact, of course, he knows neither, and thus the accountant cannot prospectively communicate future market values of a company's shares.

Financial statements can communicate the market value of these shares and the economic income of firms once these have been determined by the market, but this information is adequately communicated through other means, such as the financial press.

It does not seem useful for accountants to describe market values of a firm's securities after the fact. But even if financial statements cannot measure in a prospective sense the market value of a firm's securities, it may be argued that the value of a firm can be described apart from the value of the securities of the firm. However, such an abstract or intrinsic value of a firm apart from the value of the securities does not exist. Value in each and every case represents an assessment by someone. Value as an abstract principle is meaningless. The value of a firm as a whole exists only as it is perceived by others. Value in terms of a dictionary definition of "the relative worth, merit, or importance" or as a useful construct in economics is always relative. Value does not exist in a vacuum; it must always be viewed as value in relation to someone or to some purpose. The "relative worth, merit, or importance" of an object must be defined in terms of the utility of that object in fulfilling goals or desires of individuals. A firm may have value in relation to its stockholders and/or in relation to its managers and/or in relation to its employees. It cannot have value in and of itself apart from these interests. Thus, since the notion of "abstract value" has no meaning, it clearly cannot and should not be measured by accountants.

Even though there is no abstract value of a firm that can be measured by accountants, there are values of individual assets of a firm which may be measured. Aggregation of these asset values may be said to define the value of the firm.

Certainly individual assets of a firm have value, and insofar as these values are known in the market—because of quotations or transactions—these market values could be communicated in financial statements. However, the market value of individual assets of a firm is determined by the utility of those assets as judged by many users with many intended uses. The particular use for which a firm owns an asset is only one of many determinants of value. For example, the market value of an asset will be nil if it is so unique or specific that it can be used only by the firm holding it. No one else will demand the asset if it is of no use to them. Such an asset, however, can have significant value to the firm that owns and is able to use it. Perhaps the best illustration of this point relates to an automobile. It has often been said that an automobile loses one-fourth of its value when it is driven out of the showroom. Such a statement is both true and meaningful, as well as fallacious. If the intended use of an automobile is its sale, then the value of that automobile is in fact reduced when ownership passes from dealer to customer. The dealer generally possesses a comparative economic advantage not enjoyed by the customer, and thus the car is more valuable if sold by the dealer than by the customer. If the intended use of the car, however, relates to its transportation services, then it is fallacious to say that the value has decreased when the car is driven out of the showroom or when ownership passes from dealer to customer.

Market values of individual assets do not always relate directly to their value to the firm holding them. Further, the use value of individual assets of a firm depends to a great degree on their joint use with other assets, and it is difficult to separate value of individual assets from a value of the firm. While market values of individual assets may indeed provide useful information for users of financial statements, the recording of values of individual assets should not be thought of as a fundamental objective of financial statements.

Therefore, income as defined in terms of changes in the market value of individual assets is also not particularly relevant in terms of a specific firm. Income so defined does not measure the progress or attainments of a firm in relation to some specific goal. In fact, it may be argued that a firm cannot have income. If income is indeed a measure of better-offness, can a firm be better-off apart and distinct from the better-offness of stockholders, managers, or employees? People may be better-off but a firm, a fictional entity, cannot be better-off and thus does not have income. In our view, value should always be defined in relation to an individual's goal and not abstractly. Income also should not be defined in the abstract since it relates to the satisfaction of individual goals.

The concept of economic value involves limitations which render it futile, both in terms of implementation and general acceptance, in the context of accounting objectives. Consensus about economic value is properly the function of the market, not accounting. Information provided by the accounting process should be unambiguously characterized and communicated as an *input* to evaluation models; it should give no pretense of being the ultimate *output* or result of evaluation models.

Accounting information of all types, including income statements, balance sheets, funds statements, statements of cash receipts and disbursements, etc., has an important role to play in allowing different users with different tastes, different assumptions, different decision criteria, and especially different risk preferences to evaluate and predict the future cash consequences of the firm. Accountants have long been aware of this and have provided disaggregated information about such items as sales, cost of goods sold and different expenses. Accountants have tried to quantify different assets and liabilities and have provided a funds statement. Had accountants alternatively assumed that their only function was to communicate income and value, this could have been accomplished through a simple process of aggregation. That is, the various operations and events of an entity could have been reported in aggregated form, and only single numbers such as income and value would have been disclosed.

If accounting should provide information useful for prediction, evaluation, and control of certain key variables, rather than reporting the variables or estimates of the variables themselves the following question becomes paramount: Should the objectives of accounting be stated such that accounting information facilitates the prediction, evaluation, and control of cash flows rather than the prediction, evaluation, and control of income? As stated earlier, the notion of income means different things to different people who possess different risk preferences. If the objectives of accounting are stated in terms of income, disagreements concerning proper implementation of accounting may arise due to different and diverse definitions of income. Individual A may argue for method X based on his definition of income, and individual B may argue against method X based on his different definition of income. Thus the argument and analysis concern not method X but the desired and different definition of income. Using the concept of cash flows, which is unambiguous and less abstract, this problem of definition is avoided. Disagreement can and probably will continue to exist, but such disagreement will not revolve around the many ambiguities which result from the many different concepts of income. Use of the concept of cash flows permits the argument, controversy, or analysis concerning the implementation of objectives of accounting to take place on a common ground.

Stating the objectives in terms of the prediction, evaluation, and control of cash flows provides a vehicle for assessing and evaluating all accounting information including income statements, balance sheets, funds statements, and the proper aggregation or disaggregation suitable for such statements. Insurmountable problems related to implementation, communication, and interpretation would result if accounting objectives are defined in terms of accounting income, because methods of assessing and evaluating the worth of different concepts of income are not provided. Thus, no vehicle would exist for making decisions about assets, liabilities, etc.

An example may illustrate this point. Should price level adjusted data be used? If the objective of accounting is to measure income, then the argument can only be joined in terms of whether price level or non-price level adjusted income is superior and whether well-offness should be measured in terms of monetary or "purchasing power" terms. Such an objective, however, would not indicate how this controversy should be resolved.

If, on the other hand, the objective of accounting is to predict, evaluate, and control cash flows, the price level controversy can be resolved, although the solution may differ given varying circumstances.

For instance, accounting income currently describes the relationship between present inflows (revenues) and past and present outflows (cost). This information is useful for evaluating the past and may be useful for predicting future inflow and outflow relationships. It helps answer the question: What inflows will be generated by current and past expenditures for plant and equipment? Should the reporting of past costs be adjusted for price level changes in describing this relationship? The answer should be based on whether adjusted or unadjusted costs are expected to better predict future inflows. This may well depend on whether the past rate of inflation is expected to continue. If it is, then the relationship between current inflows and unadjusted outflows will better predict the future cash inflows in gross dollar terms.

The significance of these dollar inflows will of course be affected by price level changes. The evaluation of the extent of these effects will vary, however, depending on who will realize the cash flows and how they will be utilized. For instance, cash received by stockholders in the form of dividends will probably be spent on "market baskets" different from cash reinvested by corporations. The effect of changes in the general price level will differ to the extent that the usage of cash and preferences for different market baskets differ. This type of assessment is best left to users, since it depends on individual preferences and is necessarily subjective. Yet the method which serves the objective of predicting those cash flows is here capable of objective analysis.

This brief example does not consider aspects of control and evaluation. It helps to illustrate, however, how a controversy like price level adjustments is capable of objective analysis using an objectives framework which relates to cash flows.

THE PARTITIONING DILEMMA

George H. Sorter

The Partitioning Dilemma

George H. Sorter

The events and happenings which affect a firm form the basis for the information found in financial statements and represent a continuum that defies easy partitioning or classification. In like manner, enterprise goals are never finally achieved and cannot be definitively evaluated prior to its dissolution. Nevertheless, evaluations and estimations concerning an entity must be made continually, and information useful for this task needs to be supplied periodically.

The relevant question deals with how to organize, classify, and partition the interrelated and continuous activities of an enterprise so that they can be reported in various financial statements, especially the balance sheet and the income statement. The prevailing view is that all enterprise activity which results in favorable or unfavorable consequences during a given period shall, to the extent that these consequences are recognized, be reported in the income statement. Favorable or unfavorable consequences are described in these statements as increases or decreases in the net assets of the firm. As a result, the income statement presently reports all recognized changes in the net assets of the firm apart from incremental equity investments or disinvestments. Accounting theories and theorists, of course, differ as to what changes in net assets should be recognized—transaction based changes (historical cost), exit value changes, current cost changes, and so forth. But as far as we are aware, all accounting theorists agree that the accounting income of a firm should be the aggregate of all *recognized* value changes. All events that produce recognized value changes, therefore, are reported in the income statement. These same events and these same value changes, as well as events considered neutral in terms of value changes, are also reported in the balance sheet. Sales and cost of goods sold, for example, are part of the income statement and the effect of these events on inventory, receivables, and retained earnings is also reported in the balance sheet. The two statements are said to articulate and thus in some sense are redundant, since all events reported in the income statement are also reported in the balance sheet, although from a different perspective.

In a sense then, events are currently partitioned in terms of their favorable or unfavorable consequences. This is consistent with the economic notion of well-offness. In the period that changes in well-offness are recognized, the events interpreted to have produced such changes are reported in the income statement. These events, as well as events that have not (as yet) produced recognized changes in well-offness, are reported in the balance sheet.

Is this type of partitioning or classification necessarily optimal in terms of financial statement objectives? The answer depends on what user needs are and what information best fulfills these needs. In this paper it is assumed that decision-makers interested in a firm, like decision-makers interested in any economic asset, are essentially concerned with the net cash expected to be generated by that asset. In the case of an asset which has an assumed indefinite life, such as a firm, the primary predictive problem centers around estimating the on-going relationship between cash outflows and resulting cash inflows over an indefinite time horizon. It is this relationship that has been defined elsewhere in this volume as the cash generating ability of a firm. In order to make such predictions, it is also assumed that users essentially

1. Examine the long-run relationships of past cash inflows and outflows.
2. Attempt to identify present factors that would occasion changes in such relationships.
3. Examine future prospects and plans in terms of how these would likely affect future cash flow relationships.

Because of the particular nature of financial statements, it is paradoxical but true that these financial statements are better suited for phases 1 and 3 of the predictive process described above than for phase 2. Financial reports are structured and take time to prepare. They are not the ideal medium for communicating fresh news. By the time financial statements are issued, it is likely that the fresh news will already have been reported via other information channels. Financial statements have a comparative advantage for providing a framework involving relevant past relationships and contemplated future relationships. While this framework enhances the user's ability to evaluate and analyze the significance of current happenings, it does not emphasize either the description or evaluation of fresh news. Financial statements cannot describe fresh news because they are not produced on a timely basis. Financial statements are not suited for evaluations of fresh news because the significance of news is interpreted differently by each user in terms of his own preferences.

The above are only assumptions, but they appear to be logical and to support what has been defined as a cycle approach to the partitioning of economic events in accounting statements. Under this view, cycles of events are classified in terms of whether they are complete, incomplete, or contemplated in terms of cash generation. Separate statements should describe information about each of these cycles. This view essentially envisions partitioning of events on a cash generating project basis. Events that are part of a completed project would be reported in a statement similar to the present income statement; events that are part of an incomplete project would be reported in a statement similar to the present balance sheet, and contemplated projects would be reported in a budget or forecast statement.

Establishing when a project is complete in terms of cash generation is not a simple matter. An enterprise engages in many kinds of projects or investments. These investments vary in duration—some are completed in a few days and some extend over a protracted period of time. Investments also vary in terms of whether the investment goal is directly or indirectly related to cash generation.

The investment in one unit of merchandise inventory is part of a project directly related to cash generation. The project essentially consists of a cash purchase to be followed by a cash sale. At the other end of the spectrum in complexity is the purchase of a building that could be used for manufacturing. The purpose of the building is to house machinery which is employed, along with labor inputs, to convert raw materials to finished goods that are intended to be sold. In this example, many projects are interrelated: the purchase and use of plant, the purchase and use of machinery, the purchase and use of raw materials, the purchase of labor services, the undertaking of an advertising campaign, and many more. In a complex situation of this type, when is a project or series of projects defined to constitute a completed cycle for reporting purposes? It might be suggested that such a cycle is complete only when the longest lived project is complete, that is, when the plant is sold and when all goods produced in the plant have been sold. But at that time, of course, other related projects might be under way, such as machinery purchases, advertising campaigns, the purchase of goods, etc. Therefore, during the life span of the enterprise, all series of projects can be considered incomplete. An extreme conclusion could be reached that no project and no cycle is complete before all projects are considered complete and that the only completed cycle of an enterprise is its total life cycle. According to that view, of course, dissolution of an enterprise would be the only appropriate time for rendering accounting reports based upon completed cycles.

The preceding definition of completed projects would not be very useful. Alternatively, a cycle can be defined as complete whenever a realized sacrifice-benefit relationship is established. This definition is more useful. A cycle is defined as complete whenever an actual or highly probable cash inflow (realized benefit) has occurred and all sacrifices related to that inflow represent either actual or highly probable cash outflows. Essentially then, a cycle is considered complete whenever the cash consequences of a series of activities are predictable with a high degree of confidence.

Obviously this definition of completed cycles is not free from measurement difficulties primarily because of the jointness of sacrifices and/or benefits. Inventory, for instance, is often bought in lots, and a realized sacrifice is made for the lot rather than for individual units. Nevertheless, a cycle is defined as complete whenever a unit is sold, even if others remain unsold.

Similarly, a sacrifice is made for a plant as a whole. The plant, as in the case of an inventory lot, can be considered as a collection of units or assets. Services of the plant during each period may be considered as an individual asset; a cycle is completed when some but not all of these individual assets are utilized. The completed cycle notion, therefore, is not free of measurement and allocation problems. However, it does restrict income statement events to those actions where all cash consequences have occurred or are predictable even though the measurement of these consequences may involve subjectivity and allocation.

The balance sheet, under this partitioning scheme, should report the relationship between actual and potential cash consequences of events that are part of incomplete cycles. Assets should in most instances be described both in terms of the realized sacrifice necessary to obtain the asset and the potential benefit expected to be gained as a result of acquiring the asset. Liabilities should in most instances reflect the past benefit obtained and the future sacrifice demanded as a result of the liability. Some assets and liabilities, however, such as cash and accounts receivable and payable, represent realized rather than potential benefits and sacrifices. These benefits and sacrifices have already been realized because they represent actual or highly probable cash receipts or disbursements. These assets and liabilities nevertheless can be considered as part of incomplete cycles. Continuity of operations implies that realization defines both the end of one cycle and the beginning of the next. The total of net realized liquid assets, to the extent that they are held and not distributed, reflects the start of another incomplete cycle.

If events are partitioned in this manner, the financial statements would not articulate but rather would report distinctly different information. Information about changes in value, prospects or plans, for instance, has no place in the completed cycles statements but would be communicated either in the incomplete or contemplated cycles statement. This is thought to be of more utility than existing partitioning schemes.

The existing partitioning schemes either advocate that all value changes be reflected in accounting income (fair or current value schemes) or they reject the reporting of any value changes except those that result from transactions (historical cost). The fair value approach does not recognize that different kinds of value changes relate in different ways to the assessment of cash generating ability; further, this approach does not provide for structuring the information in terms of pertinent benefit-sacrifice relationships.

Value changes of specific assets impact differently on potential cash generation. The change in the exit value of an asset held for sale, for instance, may be directly related to changes in potential cash generation. Changes, on the other hand, in the exit value of specialized assets held for use may have only a very remote impact, if any, on cash generation. The impact of changes in entry value (current cost) upon cash generation is also complex and will also vary with different assets and different management plans. In any case, these value changes do not directly relate to or describe cash generation. An income statement based on such value changes also does not describe benefit-sacrifice or inflow-outflow relationships. If a firm acquires an asset at a cost of $100 and this asset increases in value to $120 at the end of period 1, the income statement of that period would show $20 income, but would not relate this income to any sacrifice. Therefore, no inflow-outflow or sacrifice-benefit relationship would be described in that period. In year 2, assuming that the asset is sold and that no further value changes occur, the revenue-expense description for that period would be $120-$120 and reflect zero income. Thus, the historical record which describes the relationships between outflows and inflows is masked and obscured, because data which describe potential cash realization are commingled with data which describe realized cash generation. Such commingling of data is not considered to be adequately responsive to users' needs.

The present analysis suggests that it is the historical record which describes the relationships between outflows and inflows for many projects over many successive time periods which is utilized by investors as a basic framework for predicting the return (cash inflow) a firm is likely to experience as the result of making certain investments (cash outflow). The cash inflow-cash outflow relationship for many projects over many successive time periods is apt to provide a better framework for predicting future relationships than one which incorporates different and possibly volatile value changes.

Changes in current values can reflect information about the present, the here and now, that needs to be considered. However, as argued above, such information about the present is not well suited for financial statements. Current values are no longer current by the time they are communicated. On the other hand, the description of completed cash relationships retains utility to the extent that it is considered part of a predictive framework.

The preceding discussion, however, does not imply that a historical record of value changes is not important and should not be reported. Value changes may indeed provide useful evidence concerning the likely prospects for activities presently underway, that is, the likely benefit which will result from the utilization of assets and the discharge of liabilities. By contrasting the sacrifice-expected benefit relationships reported in the balance sheet with the historical sacrifice-benefit relationships in the income statement, the user may be made aware of changed circumstances that he can utilize in his decision-making.

Since value changes do provide useful information, even though they do not represent the totality of all useful information, they should be reported and not excluded from financial reports. Information about value changes that has an indirect impact on the potential cash generation of assets and liabilities currently held is utilized in a different manner from information about completed cash generating cycles. Therefore, the two types of information should not be merged and aggregated in terms of a net income figure. They should be separately reported. If nothing else, defining the income statement in terms of completed cycles will alert users to the fact that not all relevant information about a firm can be impounded in a single-value bottom line figure. Clearly, to make informed judgments about an entity requires more than completed cycle information. On the other hand, attempting to incorporate in the income figure all value changes might give the impression to users that it is possible to make an absolute determination of the change in well-offness of an enterprise for a given period and to adequately quantify such a change by one single-dollar amount.

The preceding analysis suggests the following: The partitioning of events on the basis of a cash generating project basis is necessary for disclosing useful information concerning enterprise earning power. In addition, financial reports should be structured on the basis of nonarticulated statements which separately reflect completed, incomplete and contemplated cycles. This approach highlights appropriate benefit-sacrifice relationships and is therefore optimal in terms of assumed user needs.

ECONOMIC DECISION-MAKING AND THE ROLE OF ACCOUNTING INFORMATION

George H. Sorter
in collaboration with Martin S. Gans, Paul Rosenfield,
R. M. Shannon and Robert G. Streit

Economic Decision-Making and the Role Of Accounting Information

George H. Sorter, Research Director, *in collaboration with Martin S. Gans, Paul Rosenfield, R. M. Shannon and Robert G. Streit*

Individuals and private organizations that control or use economic resources[1] make decisions concerning them. Economic decisions involve production, distribution, exchange, consumption, saving, and investment of economic resources.

Private and Public Goals

Economic decisions are made to serve the goals of individuals and private organizations (private goals) and society as a whole (public goals). Private goals seek to increase present or prospective control and use of economic resources and to reduce uncertainty concerning the control and use of them. Public goals include protecting the economic welfare of individuals and increasing the economic welfare of society as a whole so as to effect an efficient allocation of resources.

In a society such as the United States that emphasizes private enterprise, decisions made to serve private goals are encouraged by laws that define property rights, promote competition, and establish efficient markets. These laws are enacted in the belief that many decisions designed to serve private goals will result in an efficient allocation of resources. However, both private and public goals may change over time. Consequently, laws are modified when economic decisions that are designed to serve private goals conflict with public goals. Resulting changes in laws may either modify or control the ability of individuals and organizations to make economic decisions by transferring such decisions to governmental units. Laws are enacted, for example, to redistribute wealth or income, regulate monopolies, and improve social welfare and the quality of life. The economic decisions of persons

[1] "Economic resources are the scarce means (limited in supply relative to desired uses) available for carrying on economic activities." APB Statement No. 4, paragraph 57.

and organizations are thus made continuously to serve not only private goals but also societal goals to achieve an efficient allocation of resources.

Those who make economic decisions need information to achieve desired goals. Decisions made without adequate information result in the achievement of desired goals only by chance. The need to make informed economic decisions to serve private and public goals and to achieve an efficient allocation of resources identifies the basic goal of financial statements, expressed as follows:

> *Financial statements should provide information useful in making economic decisions that result in an efficient allocation of resources.*

Achieving the Basic Goal

In developing the objectives of financial statements for achieving the basic goal, the economic decisions made in an attempt to achieve private and public goals must be considered. Investigations must be undertaken to determine the information required for the decisions, and characteristics that make information useful for the decisions must be identified. Finally, the portion of the required information that can be best communicated in financial statements must be determined.

Economic decisions are made by individuals and private organizations (private economic decisions) to serve private goals and so to serve public goals. Similar decisions are made by governmental units (public economic decisions) to serve public goals. Information provided by financial statements is required for both private and public economic decisions. Therefore, the objectives of financial statements must be responsive to the needs of decision-makers in both the private and public sectors.

Economic Decisions

Economic decisions are made for the purpose of achieving a variety of goals. In spite of their diversity, all economic decisions have a feature in common: each decision involves benefits and sacrifices. Decision-makers are interested in determining how much they must surrender or give up (sacrifice) in order to receive something else which is presumed to be better (benefit). A benefit is defined as anything received that is considered to be advantageous or for the good of a person or thing; a sacrifice is defined as anything given up or the using up of something that is prized or desirable. Sacrifices and benefits are therefore considered to be anything given or received, respectively, including in each case foregone opportunities. Three dimensions of sacrifices and benefits are considered important for every economic decision, that is, the amount (how much?), the timing (when?), and the uncertainty relating to amount and timing (the risk). Economic decisions continually relate to transformations and trade-offs concerning these dimensions of sacrifices and benefits. When borrowing money, for example, amount is sacrificed in exchange for timing. When lending money, timing and risk are sacrificed in exchange for a greater amount. The insured, in obtaining casualty insurance, sacrifices amount and timing in exchange for reduced risk. By paying premiums before casualties occur, a sacrifice is incurred earlier than by not insuring. Premiums received by the insurance company are anticipated to be larger than the expected amount of the casualty losses by an amount sufficient to cover expenses and contribute toward profit; amount is also sacrificed in this case. The insured, however, receives certainty in exchange.

Estimating Benefits and Sacrifices

An economic decision-maker must explicitly or implicitly estimate the amount, timing, and related uncertainty of benefits and sacrifices affected by decisions. Since part or all of the benefits or sacrifices lies in the future, these variables cannot be known with certainty.

A potential buyer of a security, for example, may know the sacrifice which would be incurred in buying the security, that is, how much money would have to be paid. The potential buyer, however, does not know the amounts, timing, or uncertainty associated with future receipts. A potential seller of a security, on the other hand, may know the benefits that would be received from selling the security, that is, how much money would be received. The potential seller, however, does not know the sacrifice which would be incurred. The sacrifice in selling the security is the benefits which would have been received had the security not been sold. Since the foregone benefits would have been received in the future, the potential seller does not know the amounts, timing, or uncertainty of the foregone benefits. Therefore, information in financial statements should help decision-makers to estimate the economic benefits and sacrifices which result from decisions.

Comparing Benefits and Sacrifices of Alternative Courses of Action

Some economic decisions consist of choosing between only two courses of action. Although only one alternative course of action may have been explicitly selected for evaluation, maintaining the status quo is treated as an alternative in all instances. Most economic decisions, however, involve choosing from among several competing alternative courses of action. Even the explicit consideration of multiple alternatives may result in selection of the status quo as being more desirable. Economic decisions therefore require a comparison of estimated benefits and sacrifices of competing courses of action. Information in financial statements should help decision-makers to compare the estimated benefits and sacrifices associated with alternative courses of action.

Controlling Benefits and Sacrifices

Since some or all of the benefits or sacrifices of a decision may lie in the future, the decision-maker would like to control the outcome of the decision to the extent possible. This is the reason that a creditor, for example, may insist on certain indenture provisions, and why an owner may be concerned with the conformity of enterprise activities with established goals as well as the safeguarding of assets. Various economic decisions provide different opportunities for control. Information in financial statements should help decision-makers to control the sacrifices and benefits that result from their decisions.

Evaluating Past Events

Past results are all that is known with certainty. Since all economic decisions concern the future, conjecture about what may happen is necessarily based in part on information concerning what has happened. That is, knowledge about past events is not sufficient for predicting the future. Also required is an evaluation of past events in terms of the variables relevant for decisions under review. Thus, to facilitate the estimation, comparison, and control of future sacrifice-benefit relationships, information in financial statements should help decision-makers evaluate past sacrifice-benefit relationships.

In summary, the foregoing analysis indicates four general criteria which characterize information considered useful for private economic decisions. Useful information helps a decision-maker to *evaluate* past benefits and sacrifices and to *estimate, compare,* and *control* the amount, timing, and related uncertainty of future benefits and sacrifices which result from decisions. The following important questions remain: (1) What types of information are needed to help the decision-maker to evaluate past benefits and sacrifices and to estimate, compare, and control future benefits and sacrifices? (2) What portion of such information should financial statements provide?

Information Needed to Evaluate, Estimate, Compare, and Control Benefits and Sacrifices

The decision-maker is of course interested in evaluating, estimating, comparing, and controlling benefits and sacrifices. For example, investors and creditors are interested in the amount, timing, and related uncertainty of cash inflows and outflows. However, benefits and sacrifices, as they relate to the achievement of the decision-maker's personal goals, are influenced by activities of the enterprise in which investors (present and potential) have an interest.

Goals of each enterprise are either explicitly stated or implicitly held. They define the purpose and nature of the organization. All managerial decision-making and, in fact, all enterprise actions are directed toward the attainment of its goals. Information that enables users to evaluate enterprise goal attainment and to estimate, compare, and control the prospects for future goal attainment is the essence of all decisions concerning an enterprise. This is true whether these decisions are made internally by management or externally by investors, creditors, donors, or governmental agencies.

It might be argued that external decision-makers are merely concerned with information which relates to their own goals as opposed to information about enterprise goals. Investors might be interested only in the dividends they receive and the market value of the stock they own, evaluated in terms of their own risk and return preferences regardless of the success of the enterprise in terms of its risk and return goals. Similarly, contributors to a university who are primarily interested in educational opportunities for a maximum number of students might look only to the number of students granted or expected to be granted degrees. These contributors may not be interested in the success of the university in terms of its teaching and research goals.

However, the personal goals of external decision-makers are accomplished through enterprise activities aimed at accomplishing enterprise goals. While an enterprise may occasionally, through its actions, succeed in satisfying a decision-maker with divergent goals, this situation is not likely to persist. The external decision-maker must determine whether the achievement or prospective achievement of his goals is causally or accidentally related to enterprise goals. Each decision-maker is interested in the goals of the enterprise and how they relate to his personal goals. Information about past and prospective success of the enterprise in achieving its goals has an important impact on the decision-maker's perception of his personal goal accomplishment.

In summary, information in financial statements should enable users to evaluate, estimate, compare, and control the goal attainment of an enterprise.

Sacrifices and Benefits in Relation to Goal Attainment

The goals of a specific organization define what is considered advantageous or good, prized, or desirable and therefore define the nature of sacrifices and benefits for the organization. What represents a primary benefit or sacrifice for one organization may be a secondary benefit or sacrifice for another. For instance, a hospital which has profit as one of its goals may consider patient receipts as a primary benefit and thus take action aimed at maximizing such receipts. A not-for-profit hospital, for instance, is more willing to perform services for patients who cannot afford to pay. This is not to suggest that a not-for-profit organization is not interested in monetary matters but to indicate that its goals define primary benefits in a different manner.

Given the definition of sacrifices and benefits, goal attainment for any enterprise involves an attempt to maximize benefits and minimize sacrifices. The maximization of benefits—in a broad sense—means increasing the quantity of benefits, accelerating the timing of the benefits, and decreasing the related uncertainty associated with amount and timing. Similarly, the minimization of sacrifices—in a broad sense—means decreasing the quantity of sacrifices, postponing the timing, and decreasing the related uncertainty associated with amount and timing.

Therefore, the assessment of enterprise goal attainment requires information which will facilitate analysis of sacrifice-benefit relationships. All purposeful events of an enterprise, since their primary purpose is to accomplish enterprise goals, have certain sacrifice-benefit objectives. Events having a common sacrifice-benefit objective may be said to constitute an events cycle. For example, both the purchase and sale of inventory are distinct events that generally do not occur simultaneously, but they are clearly related in terms of purpose and consequently constitute part of the same events cycle. Cycles may be classified in terms of the three different stages of sacrifice-benefit relationships: events that are part of a completed sacrifice-benefit relationship, events that are part of an incomplete sacrifice-benefit relationship, and events that are part of a contemplated sacrifice-benefit relationship.

Completed cycles of events. These are cycles of events where all related events have occurred. They represent a completed sacrifice-benefit relationship such as the purchase and subsequent sale of inventory. The sacrifice of having purchased the inventory will yield no future benefits and the benefits realized from the sale of inventory will require no future sacrifices.

Incomplete cycles of events. An incomplete cycle of events represents a chain of events which are all part of an incomplete sacrifice-benefit relationship. A sacrifice may have been incurred, but a related benefit has not yet been realized; a benefit may have been realized, but subsequent sacrifices are required. For example, inventory that is purchased and awaiting sale represents an event which is part of an incomplete cycle.

Contemplated cycles of events. This classification represents sacrifice-benefit relationships which are planned although none of the events, that is, none of the sacrifices or benefits, have occurred.

For purposes of evaluation, estimation, and control, these three cycle classifications must be distinguished. Criteria for evaluating completed cycles must differ from those used for evaluating incomplete or contemplated cycles. Since all related benefits and sacrifices have already occurred, a relatively comprehensive and definitive evaluation of events which are part of a completed cycle is possible.

Incomplete cycles, on the other hand, must be evaluated not only in terms of the events that have occurred, but also by considering the prospective outcome of related future events. Thus, an evaluation of incomplete cycles is much more conditional than in the case of completed cycles.

Contemplated cycles also require evaluation. Since all events, however, are yet to occur, such an evaluation necessarily is more concerned with the planning process underlying the contemplated activities rather than information about the activities themselves.

Information about the different cycles is also utilized differently for estimation purposes. Information about past cycles can only be used inferentially in estimating the future; since the events constituting completed cycles lie wholly in the past and are interpreted to have no future consequences, these events need not be explicitly considered in estimating the future. Rather, information about completed cycles constitutes an important basis for projection after a judgment has been made as to what extent past relationships are considered indicative and relevant for the future.

In contrast to the above, information about incomplete cycles must be explicitly considered in estimating the future. Information about incomplete cycles describes sacrifices that have occurred which are expected to yield benefits in the future and benefits that have been received which will require future sacrifices. In estimating future sacrifices and benefits, therefore, this type of information must be explicitly considered.

Information about contemplated cycles is utilized in another, more different manner for estimation purposes. While information about plans and expectations is clearly relevant for estimation, such information is necessarily subjective and incapable of direct validation. It must therefore be separately analyzed and carefully distinguished from information capable of being partially or completely validated.

Events which are part of a completed cycle, of course, can no longer be controlled. Information about completed cycles plays a role in the control process only to the extent that it indicates areas that might have been managed differently in the past. Such information may thus provide insight into the control of similar events in the future.

Incomplete cycles are partially amenable to control and partially beyond control. Some costs are sunk, but the benefits to be realized from such sunk costs are to an extent controllable. Contemplated cycles are alterable to a much greater degree and thus provide the greatest opportunity for control.[2]

Factual and Interpretive Information

Financial statement users ultimately rely on their own assessment of past and future enterprise goal attainment. Two types of information are useful for enabling the user to make such an assessment. The first type is *factual* information about the occurrence of events which minimizes the judgments and interpretations of the supplier of information. The second type is *interpretive* information that incorporates the judgment of the supplier of information concerning the relationships among events in terms of goal attainment and the implication of past events in terms of future goal attainment.

Factual information is not sufficient because the user is not in the best position to identify and assess the relationships of events in terms of goal attainment. Thus, given only factual information, a user would find it difficult to relate sacrifices made in one period with the related benefits realized in a subsequent period. On the other hand, merely providing interpretive information that relates sacrifices and benefits and indicates contemplated future consequences of past events is not sufficient. If only interpretive information were provided, the user would have no available means for evaluating the interpretations of the preparer in terms of his own preferences and expectations. For example, the amounts presently disclosed on a balance sheet as

[2] The rationale for partitioning enterprise activities in terms of cycles is more fully developed in the paper, "The Partitioning Dilemma," contained in this volume.

plant, buildings, and equipment reveal the portion of past sacrifices that are interpreted by the preparer to result in expected future benefits. Such interpretive information is useful. However, factual information is also useful for describing the acquisition of buildings and equipment; such information is currently provided in funds statements. In conjunction with other information it can be used to validate or revise the judgments of preparers.

Information Generated by the Accounting Process

Accounting encompasses two processes: a data generation process and a data communication process. In generating data, accounting describes certain events or conditions principally in monetary terms using accounting terminology. For example, the purchase of 100 widgets for $1,000 generates accounting data in the form of an inventory increase of $1,000 and a cash decrease of $1,000.

In the past, information communicated in financial statements has tended to be restricted to information generated by the accounting process. However, such a limitation does not adequately serve the goals discussed above. For instance, because of the many uncertainties involved, it may be unsuitable to generate an accounting description in terms of dollar amount of assets of the oil reserves of a particular concern. However, this should not mean that a nonaccounting generated description of oil reserves, such as the number of estimated barrels, should not be included in financial statements if such information is useful for the estimation, evaluation, and control of sacrifice-benefit relationships.

In summary, all decision-makers are interested in achieving their personal goals. Since the accomplishment of these goals is dependent upon the goal accomplishment of the relevant enterprise, decision-makers are interested in the past and prospective goal attainment of the enterprise. Therefore, decision-makers desire information useful for evaluating, estimating, comparing and controlling the amount, timing, and uncertainty of the sacrifices and benefits of an organization. Such information should consist of both factual and interpretive information, should separately describe completed, incomplete, and contemplated cycles of events, and should not be restricted to data generated by the accounting process.

Information to Be Provided in Financial Statements

The preceding section discusses information considered to be relevant for the evaluation, estimation, comparison, and control of benefits and sacrifices. However, financial statements are only one of many different sources of information, and not all information which is relevant can or should be communicated by financial statements.

First, one cannot require that all relevant information be communicated. One must consider cost-benefit criteria. Information may be beneficial for assessing the goal attainment of an enterprise, but the cost of obtaining and disclosing this information may be greater than the potential benefit. Such information should not be required to be reported by any information source. Any attempt to apply these cost-benefit criteria would be particularly bothersome, because the benefits of information may accrue to parties who do not share in their cost. A company, for example, assumes the cost of preparing financial statements that will benefit prospective shareholders and the economy in general. Resolution of these conflicts is a difficult problem which lies with the business community as well as legal and political processes. It is important, however, to stress that information requirements must be subjected to a cost-benefit analysis.

Second, even if the cost-benefit comparison is favorable, such that the information should be reported by some information source, it is not implied that all such information should be reported by financial statements. Information should not be communicated by financial statements if other channels have a comparative advantage in communicating it.

Third, information should be communicated in financial statements only if its credibility is reasonably ascertainable. Users have the expectation that information in financial statements is reliable, impartial, and unbiased. Such expectations provide a useful device for distinguishing financial statement information from other types.

In summary, all information useful for the evaluation, estimation, comparison, and control of enterprise goal attainment should be provided in financial statements unless (1) the cost-benefit criteria are not met, (2) the information can be more advantageously communicated by other media, or (3) the information is such that its credibility is not reasonably establishable.

Although the foregoing requirements are not inconsistent with existing financial statements, they indicate avenues for changing and improving present financial reporting. The present content of the income statement closely approximates, in general, completed cycle activity; the existing balance sheet by and large describes incomplete cycles. In fact, each item on the balance sheet, whether asset or equity, either has a prospective dimension or else it would not be listed. Each asset connotes a future benefit and each liability a future sacrifice. In this sense, the above analysis provides a rationale and justification for the financial statements currently issued.

The analysis also suggests, however, that the utility of the reports lies in highlighting sacrifice-benefit relationships. In the income statement the relationship between past benefits and past sacrifices is disclosed; in the balance sheet the relationship between past sacrifices and prospective benefits (assets) and past benefits and prospective sacrifices (liabilities) is described. By implication, it seems that the balance sheet should disclose both sacrifice and benefit dimensions of assets and liabilities rather than only one or the other as is presently the case. Another implication can be reasonably justified: The relative certainty or uncertainty concerning the prospective benefits and sacrifices should be disclosed, and more detailed information under a separate classification should be provided for highly uncertain items. In addition, assets and liabilities should be grouped in terms of both the controllability of the prospective benefits or sacrifices and the sensitivity of these phenomena to changes in the industry or economy. On the income statement the variability of sacrifice-benefit relationships should be highlighted through a proper grouping of sacrifices and benefits.

The statement of changes in financial position or funds statement is not unlike the required statement presenting factual rather than interpretive information. The preceding analysis, however, provides a rationale for this financial statement; its purpose is explicitly stated as providing factual information concerning events which are expected to influence goal attainment as opposed to mere description of how the events affect working capital.

Conspicuously absent from present financial statements is information concerning contemplated cycles of events. This situation can be explained in many ways, some of which, however, are not appropriate in terms of the foregoing analysis. It is argued that accounting should deal only with history and therefore not deal with plans and forecasts. While the future is indeed the subject matter of forecasts, once formulated they become part of the past, that is, history. If forecasts are communicated, such communication does not imply that the forecasted events will occur, but rather that a plan or forecast concerning such events has taken place. Credibility concerning the occurrence of future events is of course impossible to establish, but it is possible to establish the credibility that a forecast was made and that it was formulated in a specified manner. Related to this issue is the assertion often made that forecasts are too inaccurate to be communicated. But the utility of a forecast as a type of financial statement is established not by the accuracy of the forecast itself, but rather by the accuracy of the resulting estimates made by users of financial statements. The central question is whether the estimates made by such users are more or less satisfactory with or without including forecasts as one of the enterprise financial statements.

The above analysis is applicable to all users and to all organizations, regardless of their specific goals. A brief application of this analysis for economic decisions which involve pecuniary benefits and sacrifices concerning profit-making enterprises follows.

Information Required for Credit and Investment Decisions Concerning Profit-Oriented Enterprises

The primary decisions involving pecuniary benefits and sacrifices are credit and investment decisions.

Credit Decisions

A creditor loans money in exchange for a promise to receive money in the future. He knows his potential sacrifice, that is, the amount he expects to loan. Although he knows the amounts and dates of the promised repayments, he nevertheless does not know what benefits will actually be received. He does not know if the borrower will be able to make the future payments when due. Thus, he is uncertain about both the amount and timing of his future benefits. The borrower in a credit decision similarly knows the amount of money he will receive and the terms of the repayment that he promises, but he is not certain of his future ability to make repayments when due and the potential sacrifices that such repayments will entail.

Since repayments lie in the future, they cannot be known with certainty, and both the lender and the borrower need information useful for evaluating the borrower's past success in meeting such obligations. They both also need information that will allow them to estimate the amounts, timing, and uncertainty concerning the future repayments. The lender needs to compare such information with alternative loan opportunities. The borrower needs information that will allow him to manage his resources and to control his activities such that repayment will be possible, and the lender needs information to determine loan provisions to control the borrower's activity.

Investment Decisions

An investor makes two types of related decisions: whether to buy specific equity securities and whether to sell specific equity securities. His decisions involve choosing from among competing opportunities to buy and sell securities. He knows the sacrifice involved in buying securities, that is, the cost of the securities, but he does not know the benefits from the purchase, that is, the cash dividends he will receive and the proceeds from sale of the securities. Similarly, he knows the benefits from selling securities, that is, the proceeds from the sale, but he does not know the sacrifices involved in the sale, that is, the future cash dividends and selling price foregone. The unknown elements are therefore similar in both buying and selling investment decisions—the future dividends and selling prices of the security. The benefits to be derived from credit or investment decisions, that is, the interest or dividends to be received from a firm and the proceeds to be realized from the sale of an investment, all depend on the cash generating ability of the firm.

The principal goal of profit-oriented concerns is to return to owners of the firm over its life a maximum amount of cash over and above their original contributions. Thus, the attainment of this goal is also dependent upon cash generating ability.[3] Therefore, there is a congruence of goals between creditors and investors and the goals of the firm in terms of maximizing cash generating ability. Consequently, financial statements of profit-oriented concerns should be useful for evaluating, estimating, comparing, and controlling the cash generating ability of a firm. Sacrifices and benefits for such firms must be defined in terms of cash generating ability. Benefits for profit-making concerns are actual or prospective receipts of cash; sacrifices are defined as actual or prospective cash disbursements.

The income statement, or statement of completed cycles, should provide information about cycles of events whose impact on the firm's cash generat-

---

[3] This relationship is more fully discussed in the paper, "Earning Power and Cash Generating Ability," contained in this volume.

ing ability has been determined. Such a statement should report as revenues and expenses those benefits and sacrifices that have been realized in terms of cash generating ability.

A benefit is realized and therefore recognized as revenue when a cash inflow has occurred or is highly probable *and* no further related unrealized sacrifice need be incurred. Similarly a sacrifice is realized and recognized as an expense when a cash outflow has occurred or is highly probable *and* when no further related unrealized benefit is expected. Actual receipt or disbursement of cash is not required for realization, but the cash impact of an event must be determinable with a high degree of probability in order for realization to occur.[4]

The balance sheets of profit-oriented organizations should describe those cycles of events whose impact on the cash generating ability of a firm has not been determined with a high degree of probability. The sacrifice and benefit dimensions of assets and equities shown in such balance sheets should be measured in terms of actual or prospective cash impact. This provides a guideline for the valuation bases to be employed. The prospective dimension of each asset and liability (the benefit dimension of assets and the sacrifice dimension of equities) should be described in terms of the valuation base that most adequately reflects the amount, timing, and uncertainty of the cash impact of the specific asset or liability.

The statement of financial activities (the funds statement) should describe the factual aspects of events having, or expected to have, a significant impact on the cash generating ability of a firm.

Not-for-Profit Organizations

The broad requirements of financial statement information outlined in this paper are equally applicable to not-for-profit organizations. Of course, cash generating ability is not the goal of not-for-profit organizations. Benefits for these entities are not properly definable in terms of cash flows. Nevertheless, they have goals, and there are decision-makers who must evaluate, estimate, compare, and control the goal attainment of such enterprises. Thus, financial statements for such concerns should deal with goal attainment by reporting on completed, incomplete, and contemplated cycles of goal achievement events.

Since the benefits for not-for-profit organizations are largely nonmonetary, while the sacrifices, to a large extent, are monetary, it may not be feasible to produce a dollar (bottom line) figure to describe the impact of completed cycles. It should, however, be possible to describe in nonmonetary terms the benefits realized by a concern's operations and the sacrifices required to produce such benefits. The final reckoning and evaluation of the benefit-sacrifice relationship can properly be left to the user

[4] This concept of realization is more fully explored in the paper, "The Partitioning Dilemma," contained in this volume.

who should be provided with relevant information for making such a judgment. It seems strange and somewhat illogical that financial statements of not-for-profit organizations presently have a greater degree of cash orientation than those for profit-oriented concerns.

Public Economic Decisions

Governmental units operate in a variety of roles while attempting to attain many different goals. In its role as the Department of Defense, for example, the federal government must evaluate, estimate, compare, and control significant amounts of cash receipts and disbursements. In its role as the Securities and Exchange Commission, the federal government must evaluate the information made available by firms for present and potential investors in accordance with specified laws. The federal government also has numerous other information needs when functioning as an employer, investor, creditor or regulator.

For some of those decisions the information detailed in the preceding sections is adequate Governmental fiscal policy involving tax regulation and collection requires information on the cash generating ability of all firms and estimates of resulting cash flows to the government. Such policy decisions are served by the information previously identified.

Relevant information is also required for other governmental decisions. Government has the means to require the format and content of information it desires, while private sector users to a large extent do not have similar means. Nevertheless, describing some dimensions of information requirements of public sector decisions seems useful.

The government must make economic decisions that consider the benefits accruing to and the sacrifices extracted from society as a whole as opposed to private sector decision-makers who consider only their individual benefits and sacrifices.

In some situations, benefits are realized by people other than those bearing the sacrifices, and sacrifices are extracted from people other than those receiving the benefits. Equitable resolution of such situations requires government action and cannot be left to economic decisions between private individuals.

When the benefits or sacrifices received by some persons are not in the best interests of society as a whole, laws are enacted to bring the private benefits and sacrifices more in line with society's goals. In order to determine when legislation is needed, the government, acting on behalf of society as a whole, needs information concerning the social costs and benefits resulting from private economic decisions.

To the extent that social costs or social benefits will have an effect on the cash generating ability of a firm, this information should be reported to facilitate decision-making in the private sector. However, a company may undertake activities which have social consequences that may not affect its cash generating ability in a manner which is easily measurable. This information may be essential for making decisions in the public sector. What, if any, role should financial statements play in providing this information?

The answer may be found in the distinction between interpretive and factual information. There is a need for information concerning a firm's activities which have social consequences. A firm may have a comparative advantage in supplying *factual* information about such events. A firm is in the best position to design its information system to communicate information with social impact such as the number of minority group employees hired or the amount of pollutants produced by its activities. In communicating this information, however, firms are not in a position to evaluate the social consequences of these activities or to measure the achievement of social goals in the aggregate.

As in the private sector, ultimate evaluation and judgment concerning the information should be left to the user—in this case, society and the government. Accordingly, the firm should communicate factual data in its financial statements concerning events having social consequences without attempting to evaluate such data in terms of its social significance.

DEVELOPMENT OF A SPECIFIC FRAMEWORK

RELEVANT ACCOUNTING

Joshua Ronen and George H. Sorter

*Joshua Ronen and George H. Sorter**

Relevant Accounting†

This paper presents a system of external accounting reports which differs significantly from both presently existing financial statements and alternatives thus far suggested in the literature. In the first section of the paper we discuss the measurement inputs required for efficient allocation of resources. We then suggest that accounting, as presently constituted, does not adequately fulfill these informational requirements, and we propose an alternative system to meet these needs. In the third section we illustrate the system by presenting its output—the periodic accounting reports—and analyze these reports in terms of the insights provided for users' needs. In the last section we conclude with implications for future research and for the development of the proposed system.

THE INFORMATIONAL REQUIREMENTS FOR CAPITAL ALLOCATION DECISIONS

The recent literature and research on capital allocation decisions, especially decisions relating to investment in securities,[1] strongly suggest that these decisions are primarily based on prospective returns and prospective risks associated with the returns. The prospective returns and the risks are discussed in the literature primarily within the framework of the portfolio model. Return on investment in securities is defined as the change in the market value of the security plus dividends received during a given period. The risk related to investment in securities is defined as the expected variance of the prospective rate of return of the investors' portfolio. (For rigorous definitions of both return and risk, see the literature cited in n. 1.)

Accordingly, the investor is vitally concerned with prospective market values of securities and fluctuations in these market values, since they are elements affecting both risk and return. The literature on efficient capital markets shows that if an investor desires to predict future movements in market prices, he can do so only by identifying and evaluating the factors determining the "fundamental" value of the security. Thus, Fama states: "The analyst will do better than the in-

* Assistant professor and professor of accounting, University of Chicago.

† This project was sponsored and supported by Touche Ross & Co. The Touche Ross & Co. support extended far beyond finances, and the authors gratefully acknowledge the stimulation, discussion, ideas, help, and encouragement of many Touche partners and staff, especially Robert Kay and Robert Trueblood.

1. See, for example, H. M. Markowitz, *Portfolio Selection: Efficient Diversification of Investments* (New York: John Wiley & Sons, 1959); Eugene F. Fama, "Efficient Capital Markets: A Review of Theory and Empirical Work," *Journal of Finance* (May 1970), pp. 383–417; and William F. Sharpe, *Portfolio Theory and Capital Markets* (New York: McGraw-Hill Book Co., 1970).

vestor who follows a simple buy and hold policy as long as he can more quickly identify situations where there are nonnegligible discrepancies between actual prices and intrinsic [fundamental] values than other analysts and investors and if he is better able to predict the occurrence of important events and evaluate their effect on intrinsic [fundamental] values."[2]

If the capital markets are to perform their role of efficiently allocating the ownership of capital stock among the alternative investments, the fundamental or intrinsic value of the stock mentioned above must coincide with the economic value of the firm. This economic value is defined as the risk-adjusted discounted value of prospective cash flows attributable to the firm.[3] Unless the fundamental value of the security reflects the economic value of the firm, optimal allocation of capital resources in the economy is not obtained. This is so because the marginal cost of capital is then not equated with the marginal expected rate of return as reflected in the fundamental value, and one of the optimality conditions is violated.[4]

Thus, for accounting information to be of optimal utility to individual investors *as well as* to facilitate optimal allocation of capital resources in the economy, it should be useful for estimating the future cash flows of the firm and for identifying the risk associated with these cash flows.[5]

Presently, accounting information does not explicitly deal with expectations about future cash flows. Nor does it explicitly deal with considerations of risk. By and large accounting information today deals

2. See Eugene F. Fama, "Random Walks in Stock Market Prices," *Financial Analyst Journal* 21 (September-October 1965): 58.

3. See Eugene F. Fama and Merton H. Miller, *The Theory of Finance* (New York: Holt, Rinehart & Winston, 1972); Merton H. Miller and Franco Modigliani, "Dividend Policy, Growth and the Valuation of Shares," *Journal of Business* 34, no. 4 (October 1961): 411–32.

4. Indeed, one of the optimality conditions is that the rate of substitution in production is equal at the margin for all products. The same rule applies, of course, to the rate of substitution among capital investments. See E. J. Mishan, "A Survey of Welfare Economics, 1939–1959," *Economics Journal* (June 1960), pp. 197–265.

5. It may be argued that while information about these determinants of economic value is necessary, there is no need for accounting information to reflect these variables. It might be argued that since the efficient-capital-market research indicates that all available information is impounded in a market price, there is no need for accounting to be structured to provide this particular information. Two counterarguments may be offered: (1) Granting the conclusions of the capital-market research, it is possible that by providing this information within the accounting system the total amount of *available* information would be expanded. (2) Even if the total amount of *available* information were not expanded, the cost of providing the information and making it available might well be minimized if the information were communicated systematically and periodically as an integral part of the accounting system. Empirical evidence to either refute or support these counterarguments is presently lacking and cannot in fact be obtained without an accounting system that incorporates the information. We are presently studying this argument and suitable suggestions for empirical testing of these issues, and the results will be presented in a monograph on this topic.

primarily with "realization" and then only when that realization can be conveniently expressed in terms of a single number.

Ideally, accounting should provide the following information: (1) information useful to predict cash flows, (2) information useful for assessing the risks of these cash flows, and (3) information about the realization of expectations.[6] Furthermore, since resource allocation is meaningful only in terms of choices among alternatives, information useful for resource allocation should be expressed in a manner that facilitates comparison.

THE RELEVANT ACCOUNTING SYSTEM

The first major element of our system is to provide information about estimated future cash flows. While estimated future cash flows are determined by many factors such as market forces, industry forces, and the individual firm's own actions, the best source of information about these expectations must be the individual firm itself. Although many sources of information exist for identifying the impact of the market or industry on future cash flows, only the firm itself and its management have current knowledge of its specific decisions and plans. Inasmuch as management for its own planning process must estimate the impact of market and industry forces and because it alone is aware of its plans, we feel that management's estimate of prospective cash flows incorporating its own plans as well as market and industry forces should be communicated through accounting reports.[7]

Management forecasts of expected cash flows should be communicated through a measure that discounts expected cash flows *at a market rate* but not a firm's cost of capital.[8] By using a market rate, expected cash flows are communicated without considering the specific (other than market) risks associated with the cash flows. Risk considerations

6. Information concerning realization of expectations must be provided to allow an assessment of both the reliability of expectations and the quality of managerial performance, as well as to facilitate the improvement of the forecasting process and performance. These issues will be further discussed throughout the paper.

7. That management is the best source of information about its plans is not only intuitively obvious but shown by empirical evidence provided by Scholes, who found that company insiders often have monopolistic access to information about their firms. See Myron Scholes, "A Test of the Competition Market Hypothesis: The Market for New Issues and Secondary Offerings" (Ph.D. thesis, Graduate School of Business, University of Chicago, 1969).

8. Which market rate is selected is of course arbitrary. We did not select the riskless rate, since the market risk rate provides a more relevant standard of comparison for investors in common stock. We suggest using the rate of return attributable to all stocks traded in the New York Stock Exchange. This measure is available and is computed by the Center of Research and Security Prices of the University of Chicago; it is the rate that could be earned on a portfolio of all securities listed in the New York Exchange and therefore is useful as a standard of comparison. It would also be possible to present the estimates of cash flows by presenting a schedule of expectations for each year and not aggregating these expectations through discounting. However, if an aggregate measure is desirable, some discount rates must be used, since the expected cash flows cover different periods.

could of course be reflected by using a risk-adjusted discount rate. High-risk flows would then be discounted at a higher rate and low-risk flows at a lower rate. This method of reflecting risk should be rejected because:

First, the elements that determine risk[9] are manifold and to a great degree subjective; therefore, a single measure reflecting both the amount and the risk of expected cash flows would not be useful, since it is difficult to capture all the determinants of risk through a single modification of the discount rate.

Second, any such modification would inevitably be affected by management's attitudes toward risk, and these may well differ from those held by investors. Also, the attitudes toward risk of different investors would tend to vary.

Third, if a single risk-adjusted rate is used, the financial-statement user would have no readily available mechanism for disassociating the amount of expected flows from risks associated with them.

For those reasons, providing information that allows users to identify the amount of expected cash flows separately from the risk associated with the flows is desirable. Therefore, expected flows should be communicated through discounting at a market (nonfirm-specific) discount rate. We term the resulting amount the market-risk-determined (MRD) value of the firm.

Risk considerations, however, are an important determinant of economic value, and accounting must present information to facilitate risk assessment.

Useful insights into the aspects of risk can be gained by comparing the MRD value of a firm with the exit value of a firm's net assets and of its equity. The exit value of an asset is defined as the net proceeds (after transaction costs) that can be realized by severing the assets from the firm. The exit value of a liability and of the stock equity is the amount necessary to redeem it. The exit value of net assets is the difference between the exit values of assets and those of liabilities. The difference between the firm's MRD value and the sum of the exit values of the firm's net assets is defined as the *specific advantage* of that firm. The difference between the firm's MRD value and the exit values of its equities is defined as the *specific residual*. The specific advantage of the

9. Risk depends on the following major elements: (1) Probabilities associated with expected cash flows; (2) the covariance of the expected cash flows with the alternative cash flows available to information users (see, for example, Fama, "Efficient Capital Markets"); (3) the degree of uncertainty associated with the realization of the expected flows (while the degree of uncertainty may manifest itself in the variability of cash flows, there are advantages to considering these elements separately, in the absence of explicit knowledge about the extent to which such uncertainty effects the probability distributions). Another element of risk associated with the above but which deserves to be separately identified is (4) the extent to which the realization of these expected cash flows is within the firm's control. For instance, cash flows expected through the collection of accounts receivable are generally more within the firm's control and less under the influence of others than the cash flows expected through the sale of most products. The more controllable the realization of flows, the less risk may be associated with these flows.

firm reflects that part of the expected flows that cannot be realized unless the firm continues its specific operations and continues to assume the risks associated with these operations. Exit values of the firm's net assets represent the cash flows that could be realized if the firm does not continue its specific operations, and are independent of uncertainties associated with the specific operations.

The specific residual reflects that portion of the expected flows that have not yet been captured by the market value of the firm's securities either (1) because the market assigned a risk factor that is higher than the market general risk to the firm's expectations, (2) because the market does not accept the magnitude of the future cash flows as reflected in the firm's expectations, or (3) through a combination of these two.

All of the elements of risk we have discussed are related to both the above differences. The larger the specific advantage, the larger the uncertainties that may be associated with realization of the firm's expectations. First, consider what happens if none of the firm's expectations materializes. Two firms with equal MRD value, but where one firm has zero exit values (specific-advantage firm) and the other firm has net exit values equal to the MRD (exit-value firm), will significantly differ in the potential loss that could ensue if their expectations fail to materialize. If the expected demand for the firm's products fails to materialize, a total loss would ensue for the specific-advantage firm but no loss would ensue for the exit-value firm, since its individual assets could then be sold separately. Exit values could also decline as a result of the firm's expectations failing to materialize, but this decline is likely to be smaller than the potential decline in the firm's MRD value. A smaller decline in the exit values is probable because the existence of exit values demonstrates that there must be other users for the firm's assets. These other users may demand the assets not only for producing the same products and services that the particular firm produces but also for providing other products and services. Thus, even if the demand for a firm's specific product declines, it is less likely that a similar decline will occur in the assets' exit values, which may be derived from other uses and other products and services. If a decline in exit values comparable with a decline in MRD value is to occur, it is necessary not only that the demand for the output of the particular firm decline but that the demand for the output of other like firms also decline; further, if the assets can be used for other services, a decline of the demand for these other services must occur as well. Thus, the higher the proportion of specific advantage to the firm's MRD value, the higher the firm's exposure to a potential decline in its value. More of its future would depend on the market's acceptance of the firm's particular service or products. The larger an asset's exit value, the more flexible is the firm in employing its resources and the less dependent it is on its specific plans and operations. The specific-advantage firm is restricted in its alternatives, since its assets have zero exit values.

This potential loss represents just one aspect of the uncertainty associated with the firm's cash flows. Other aspects of uncertainty are also related to the magnitude (both absolute and relative) of the specific advantage. The specific-advantage firm has expectations (1) that may not be shared by anybody else, (2) that may not have been validated by anybody else, and (3) the realization of which is less under the firm's control than for exit-value firms. If the firm's expectations are not accompanied by exit values of its assets, the expectations may be held only by the firm. The existence of exit values must mean that some other unit or units have expectations concerning the employment of these assets, the magnitude of which is reflected in the exit value. Thus, while the MRD value may reflect only one firm's expectation, the asset's exit values necessarily represent the mean expectation of more than one entity. The exit value of the firm's assets is the price agreed upon by buyer and seller in the marketplace. The variance associated with exit values—representing the mean of expectations held by more than one—is presumably smaller than that associated with expectations held by one.

Not only does the existence of exit value imply *shared* expectations, it also provides evidence for the market validation of the expectations. Exit values represent a market's consensus that has already been established about expected cash flows obtainable from the assets independent of their specific utilization by the firm.[10] All the firm needs to do to realize exit values is to sell the assets. However, to realize the portion of the firm's value that is not reflected in the exit value of the assets requires the existence of a future market for which no evidence may yet exist and which will be determined by factors that may not be under the firm's control.

For all these reasons, the larger the specific advantage of the firm, the larger is the risk that can be associated with that firm's cash flows.[11]

The Specific Residual

Additional information about potential risk can be gained by comparing the exit value of the stock equity with the firm's MRD value. The exit value of the stock equity reflects the capital market's evaluation of both the magnitude and the risks attached to the firm's expected flows. If investors accept management's forecasts and if they feel that the risks

10. Indeed all assets of the firm have both a universal and a specific or use value. The specific value is determined by the asset's marginal contribution in producing the firm's specific cash flows. The universal value is determined by the proceeds that the asset can generate when not part of the specific bundle of assets that defines a particular firm. The universal values are the exit values of assets. The exit value of an asset can be separately realized. The use value cannot.

11. We have not discussed the relationship that may exit between the specific advantage and the covariance of the firm's expected cash flows with other expected flows. Although we defer the discussion of this interesting question to our monograph, our preliminary investigation indicates that the relative magnitude of the specific advantage may provide helpful insights into the assessment of the expected covariance.

associated with these forecasted flows are correctly expressed through discounting by a market discount rate, then the exit value of the stock equity will be equal to the MRD value of the firm. If the MRD value of the firm exceeds the exit value of the stock, this implies that either the market does not fully accept the magnitude of the firm's expectations or that the investors attach a greater than market risk to these expectations. The larger the specific residual, the larger the risk that attaches to the firm's flows regardless of which of these factors produced the divergence between MRD value and the exit value of the stock equity.[12]

Both the specific advantage and the specific residual provide separate insights into aspects of risks and need not necessarily coincide. A firm with a large specific advantage relative to its MRD value, for example, could at the same time have a small specific residual (relative to the MRD value). Established oligopolistic firms like IBM, for instance, may well fall into this category. The large specific advantage indicates that if the demand for IBM products fails to materialize, their options are few. On the other hand, the small specific residual indicates that the market shares IBM's forecasts and has validated them as reflected by the market price of the securities. Thus, in this case, while the exit values of assets do not reflect a market consensus on the firm's expectations, the close correspondence between the MRD value and the exit value of securities does.

It is necessary to communicate both the expectations of the firm as reflected in the MRD value and the exit values of its assets and its equities. Ideally, both values should be communicated in a probabilistic manner; that is, a probability distribution of each should be provided. Both exit values and discounted expectations cover a range of values and cannot be adequately reflected through a single number. Probabilistic measures, however, represent a dramatic and drastic departure from current practice. More research on both the behavioral and other implications of probabilistic measures should be conducted before their adoption is advocated. Single numbers should be used to describe these values only provisionally until this further research can be accomplished.

Retrospective Data

The reporting of prospective cash flows and exit values alone would not represent adequate reporting for either investors or management. To evaluate, audit, and improve predictions of prospective cash flows, it is necessary not only to communicate expectations but also to communicate events that have occurred. Communication of past events is necessary to allow information users to evaluate management's performance and predictions, as well as to better predict and control future management performance, actions, and policy.

12. If the market does not accept the magnitude of expected flows, this represents a disagreement about these expectations and therefore larger uncertainty. Larger uncertainty is clearly also implied if the market attaches a higher than market risk to the firm's expected flows.

Accountants, of course, have always reported retrospective data. In the system that we advocate, this reporting of past events must, however, differ from current practice. Past transaction data should be separated into expected and unexpected elements. Only in this manner are these data useful for validating and evaluating the forecasts that have been reported in earlier periods, as well as for evaluating the effectiveness of management. In addition, past events must be described not solely in terms of historical cost but also through their effect on exit values. Since exit values are an important part of the relevant accounting system, changes in them should be communicated when they occur.

Relevant Accounting Reports

The basic elements of the relevant accounting system consist of the reporting of expectations about cash flows, the reporting of exit values, and the reporting of retrospective data. These elements are communicated through two basic reports—the balance sheet and the cost and benefit statement. The cost and benefit statement, which is a new statement, is supported by two detailed statements—an income statement, which reports changes in the MRD value of the firm, and a realization and derealization statement, which reflects changes in risk elements of the firm as reflected in changes in the composition of assets and liabilities.

The Balance Sheet

Table 1 illustrates the balance sheet. It contains three columns for both the assets and the liabilities and equities. These columns describe the historical costs, the specific advantage, and the exit value of the assets and liabilities and the specific residual of the firm. We distinguish among major groups of assets. These are cash assets (cash, marketable securities, and accounts receivable), other current assets including inventories and supplies, and fixed assets. There are no figures in the Specific Advantage column for specific assets or liabilities because the specific advantage of the firm results from the joint operations of assets. While it might be possible to attribute incremental specific advantages to individual assets and liabilities, this poses severe measurement problems and the incremental advantages would not be additive. The benefit and cost of reporting incremental specific advantages for individual assets is a subject for further study. To indicate that it might be desirable at a later stage to show incremental specific advantages, a specific advantage column is provided.

Specific amounts are shown, however, for individual assets under the Exit Value column. The firm's assets could, of course, be sold either individually or in various combinations. More than one exit value can be attached to an asset. One is the exit value of that asset if sold individually, another is a portion of the proceeds if the asset is sold in combination with other assets. In the latter case, an attempt could be made to measure the incremental contribution of an asset to the joint proceeds. Alternatively, exit values could be shown for groups of assets

Table 1

Comparative Balance Sheet as of 12/31/00 and 12/31/01: Liabilities and Equity

Assets	Historical Cost		Exit Values		Specific Advantage*		Total Economic Value	
	12/31/00	12/31/01	12/31/00	12/31/01	12/31/00	12/31/01	12/31/00	12/31/01
Cash assets:								
Cash	2,100	2,600	2,100	2,600				
Marketable securities	150	150	200	200				
Accounts receivable (net)	3,320	2,820	3,300	2,800				
	5,570	5,570	5,600	5,600			5,600	5,600
Other current assets:								
Raw materials	700	1,000	650	1,130				
Work in process	800	2,250	300	3,050				
Finished goods	1,000	0	1,200	0				
Supplies	150	100	50	30				
	2,650	3,350	2,200	4,210			2,200	4,210
Fixed (net):								
Building	10,000	9,700	9,950	10,050				
Machinery and equipment	20,000	24,100	20,250	23,750				
	30,000	33,800	30,200	33,800			30,200	33,800
Firm's specific advantage					11,000	12,875	11,000	12,875
Total	38,220	42,720					49,000	56,485

Table 1 (cont.)

Liabilities and Stockholders' Equity	Historical Cost		Exit Values		Specific Advantage*		Total Economic Value	
	12/31/00	12/31/01	12/31/00	12/31/01	12/31/00	12/31/01	12/31/00	12/31/01
Liabilities:								
Current:								
Accounts payable	1,500	5,580	1,500	5,580				
Short term	300	300	300	300				
Other	150	150	150	150				
	1,950	6,030	1,950	6,030				
Long term:								
Bonds	17,000	17,000	18,000	18,000				
Other	7,000	7,000	7,000	7,000				
	24,000	24,000	25,000	25,000				
Total liabilities	25,950	30,030	26,950	31,030			26,950	31,030
Equity:								
Stock:								
Contributed capital	10,000	10,000	13,050	15,000				
Retained earnings	2,270	2,690						
	12,270	12,690	13,050	15,000			13,050	15,000
Specific residual					9,000	10,455	9,000	10,455
Total	38,220	42,720					49,000	56,485

* Incremental specific advantages associated with individual assets and liabilities are not provided (see text).

rather than for individual assets. At the theoretical level, the exit value of a firm's assets should reflect that amount that could be obtained through selling the assets in combinations that maximize the sales proceeds. However, to indicate that the disaggregation problem for exit values is apt to be less difficult than for specific advantage, exit values for each group of specific assets are shown.

The exit values of assets may be either higher or lower than their historical cost. Historical cost is not always more conservative than exit valuation. Lower exit values primarily result from the particularization of purchased assets.[13] Work in process, raw materials, and other supplies may therefore have historical cost in excess of exit values. The relationship between the exit value of fixed assets and their historical costs is harder to predict. The particularization of fixed assets will produce exit values which are below historical cost at the date of purchase. But this may well be offset later by fluctuations in exit values. The more unstable the environment and the older the assets, the more difficult it is to predict the relationship between exit values and historical costs. This ambiguity is indicated in the balance sheet by reporting exit values for fixed assets that are slightly higher in the first year and equal to the historical costs in the second year.

For cash assets, the exit values closely approximate historical cost. Any difference in valuation for these assets is only attributable to the difference between historical cost and exit value of marketable securities and accounts receivable. The difference in accounts receivable is due to the uncollectability associated with the receivables. This illustrates the acceptance of exit valuation in present accounting practice.

No additional comments are necessary to explain the liabilities in the balance sheets. Two comments are appropriate concerning the equity section. The market value of the stock,. that is, its exit value, reflects both contributed capital and retained earnings, and no separation between these two is possible in the Exit Value column. The specific residual reflects that portion of the firm's MRD value that has not been validated by market consensus and reflected in the market value.

The Cost and Benefit Statement

Traditionally, the benefits that accrue to a firm have been identified as the income of a firm. Neither economic income nor accounting income, however, captures all the benefits associated with the operations of the firm. The two major determinants of a firm's value are the return or magnitude of expected cash flows and the risk or uncertainty associated with these. Thus, the benefits accruing to a firm should reflect both these dimensions. The benefits may accrue to a firm either through an increase in the size of expectations (due to either the passage of time or the

13. A particularization of an asset is putting it to a specific use within the firm other than sales. In that case the exit value is apt to be lower than the purchase price.

revision of expectations) or through a reduction in the risk or uncertainty associated with the expectations. Similarly, the cost to a firm represents either a reduction of the magnitude of expectations or an increase in risk, or both. This dual nature of benefits and costs is not adequately described through either economic or accounting income. Economic income represents changes in the wealth of the firm. Since wealth is the present value of the firm's expectations, economic income does reflect changes in these expectations, that is, changes in the magnitude and in the timing of expected cash flows. Economic income reflects changes in risk only through changes in the discount rate used. This does not give an adequate, explicit representation of changes in risk. Additionally, economic income does not explicitly differentiate among the varying uncertainties associated with the varying composition of assets. Thus for purposes of economic income it makes no difference whether cash flows are expected to result from assets not yet held, from inventory that has been manufactured, or from accounts receivable that have not yet been collected. But the certainty of realizing cash flows from these different assets differs.

Economic income is deficient in the sense that although it reflects changes in expectations, it does not explicitly reflect changes in realization; accounting income errs in the other direction. By and large, accounting income is affected only to a minor degree by expectations and changes in expectations and deals almost exclusively with realizations. Generally, accounting income is recognized only when expected cash flows are realized through the generation of cash or accounts receivable. Both economic income and accounting income describe different aspects of the benefits that accrue to the firm. Neither of them fully describes all the benefits. A more complete description of the benefits should reflect both expectations and changes in expectations as well as the realization pattern and changes in this pattern. In relevant accounting, the benefits accruing to a firm are described as (1) the change in expectations, that is, the change in the MRD value of a firm, and (2) changes in realization as evidenced by a change in the assets composition from more specific and therefore more risky assets to relatively less specific and therefore less risky assets.

This can perhaps be best illustrated in discussing the conversion of inputs to outputs. If these conversions were expected, the MRD value of the firm remains unchanged. This conversion does represent, however, a stage of realization. Other things being equal, this is a benefit to the firm. This is substantiated by the fact that the exit value of finished goods, for instance, would generally be larger than the sum of the exit values of the inputs, and this benefit is reported in the cost and benefit statement as an increase of exit values. The uncertainty associated with realizing the expectations based on selling output that has already been manufactured is less than that associated with expectations requiring both manufacturing and selling.[14] All persons interested in the firm are concerned

14. The subsequent conversion of output to cash—the sale event—represents

with both changes in economic income (expectations) *and* changes in the realization pattern.

Under our measurement system, the increase in the value of the firm due to increased expectations is quantified by the economic income. The second benefit resulting from a change in the asset composition of the firm from a greater to a lesser level of risk is communicated through changes in exit values and their composition. If increases in exit values are unexpected, they may also lead to a change in the MRD value of the firm, which would be shown as revisions of expectations in item 7 of the cost and benefit statement (table 2). These increases in exit values are

Table 2

Statement of Costs and Benefits

Costs:		
1. Decline in exit values	$1,800	
2. Purchase loss	120	$1,920
3. Imputed interest on exit values (net)		1,105
Benefits:		
4. Increase in exit values		
a. Appreciation of exit values		1,250
b. Value added (excluding depreciation)		2,200
		3,450
5. Purchase gain		0
		3,450
6. Time growth of expectations: imputed interest on total net assets (including specific advantage)		2,205
7. Revision of expectations		1,200

broken down into purchase gains, which in this case are zero; into value added, which reflects increase in exit values resulting from the operating activities of the firm; and into the residual change in exit values. These three elements are added to produce the gross increase in exit values of assets of $3,450. Notice that both declines and increases in exit value are measured at their gross amount. Thus some assets increased in exit value and others declined, and these are shown separately.

Items 6 and 7 represent benefits attributable to the size of expected cash flows. Item 6 quantifies the time growth of expectations. The time growth of expectations, that is, the change in expectations due to the passage of time, is quantified by the imputed interest on the MRD value of the firm. Item 7 quantifies the net revision of expectations as of the year end. This revision would obviously be based on information gained

the final stage of realization. For this reason we separately report the exit values of cash assets and other assets and show this conversion in the realization and derealization statement. As discussed later, in the cost and benefits statement only realizations affecting the magnitude of exit values are shown.

during the year. A major source of information for this revision would very likely be the unexpected events shown in the detailed statements.

Under costs are shown the decrease in exit value of the assets that declined in value (the increase in exit value of assets whose value appreciated is shown under benefits). This decline may or may not be associated with a decline in the total value of the firm. Whether or not it is, it always represents a cost in the sense of the increasing uncertainty associated with the cash flows.[15] If the decline in exit values was expected, that implies the total value of the firm remained unchanged and therefore the decline in exit values is offset by an equal increase in the specific advantage. Since, more uncertainty attaches to specific advantage than to exit values, this represents an increased risk. If a decline in exit values was unexpected, it may lead to a revision of expectations regarding future cash flows and therefore to changes in the value of the firm which would affect item 7 of the cost and benefit statement. The second item under costs, the purchase loss, also reflects a decline in exit values but is separately reported to reflect the increasing uncertainty directly caused by the purchasing activities of the firm. Thus items 1 and 2 together present declines in exit values that can be added to produce the gross total decline of $1,920. The next item of cost cannot be added to these figures. It represents the imputed interest on the exit value of net assets. This amount of $1,105 represents opportunity costs and must be interpreted differently from the change in uncertainty described by items 1 and 2. This is a component of the returns foregone as a result of having held the assets.

So far we have discussed three nonadditive elements of cost: (1) the decline in exit values, representing increased uncertainty; (2) possible unfavorable revision of expectations, which will be described in item 7; and (3) foregone benefits. All three, however, represent costs even if nonadditive.

The events giving rise to costs and benefits listed above are reported in more detail in two statements: the income statement and the statement of realizations and derealizations. The income statement describes events affecting the MRD value of the firm, while the statement of realizations and derealizations describes events affecting the composition of the firm's assets and liabilities, which in turn affect the uncertainty facing the firm.

The Income Statement

The income statement (table 3) details events affecting the value of the firm. Columns are provided for both historical cost income and economic income. The Historical Income columns show the changes in the historical cost value of the firm, while the Economic Income columns show the change of the MRD value of the firm. Expected and Unexpected columns

15. An idea similar to this, i.e., that reduction in risk is identical with reduction in costs, is discussed by E. J. Mishan in "Welfare Criteria for External Effects," *American Economic Review* (September 1971).

Table 3
Income Statement (Changes in the Value of the Firm

	Historical Income		Economic Income	
Sales	Expected	Unexpected	Expected	Unexpected
Inflows	5,000	200	5,000	200
Outflows:				
Values of goods sold:				
On conversion:				
Inputs	3,000	100	2,000	200
Value added			1,800	
On sales:				
Additional inputs	700		800	
Value added			400	
	(3,700)	(100)	(5,000)	(200)
	1,300	100	0	0
Interest revenue	20		4,900	
Interest expense	(1,000)		(2,695)	
	(980)		2,205	0
Revision of expectations				1,200
Total	320	100	2,205	1,200
Interest appropriation			2,205	

are provided for both historical cost income and economic income. This allows users to validate management's expectations and to assess and evaluate past managerial performance. Historical income is communicated essentially in the same manner as reported today with the exception that expected and unexpected components are identified and separately reported. Historical cost income is reported as a record of market transactions useful for discharging part of the traditional stewardship function of accounting.

The data provided in the Economic Income columns differ greatly from those shown under the Historical Income columns. Under the Economic Income columns, operating income, that is, income realized by sales, is zero. This is necessarily so because the output of goods and services is valued at their exit value (i.e., the selling price less transaction costs incurred in the selling process). These transaction costs are incurred on the date of sale and are shown as a part of the outflow; thus, the inflow and outflow must now equal each other. Despite this equality the outflows and inflows are separately described because the disaggregation of these events provides insight into the operations of the firm. Users are interested in the total amount of sales inflow and in the various components of the sales outflow. The sales outflow is decomposed into two components: the exit value of the output recognized at the time of conversion and the increments in exit value up to the time of sales. For each of these two components we further distinguish between the value of the inputs and the value added. Inputs merely represent the transformation of other assets into the goods and services provided by the firm. Value added represents that portion of the exit value of the output that is attributable to the specific operations of the firm.

For historical cost income, interest revenue is merely the interest earned on interest-bearing assets. The interest expense represents the interest accrued or paid on interest-bearing obligations. For economic income, interest revenue represents the market rate of return imputed on the total assets of the firm (including specific advantage). The interest expense represents the market rate of interest imputed on the liabilities of the firm. The net amount of $2,205 thus represents the market rate of interest imputed on the MRD value of the firm, and it reflects the growth of the MRD value of the firm as a result of the passage of time.

Revision of expectations only affects economic income, not historical income.

Realizations and Derealizations Statement

As previously stated, there are two aspects to the benefits and costs associated with a firm or an investment—the magnitude of the flows and the uncertainty associated with the flows. The income statement presented costs and benefits with respect to the magnitude of the flows. Table 4 details events causing changes in the assets composition which result in changes in uncertainty. This statement reports the "realization events," that is, events that result in conversion from more risky assets to less risky assets. These are conversions from specific advantage to exit values and conversions from exit values of noncash assets to exit value of cash assets.[16] The derealization events are those which cause shifts from less risky assets to more risky assets. These events include conversion from exit value of cash assets to exit values of noncash assets and from noncash assets to specific advantage. By and large, conversion from exit value of noncash assets to exit value of cash assets represents sales of assets and services, while conversion from exit value of cash assets to exit value of noncash assets represents purchases of assets and services.

Realization due to the conversion of specific advantage to exit values may be due to three factors. One of these factors is the change in exit value due to the fulfillment of the firm's function; this represents the value added. The second factor is the change in exit values resulting from holding of assets by the firm; this "holding gain" could be broken down to reflect the growth of the exit value due to the passage of time, and the changes due to general or specific price level changes. A third change in exit values, which our sample firm did not experience, may be

16. Since cash assets are traditionally the means of exchange, less uncertainty is associated with their realization. Their value is recognized by all parties, and thus a consensus about their exit value is more readily available than for other assets. The exchange of cash assets for cash is either guaranteed or required by law. This is not generally so for other assets, such as inventory, where the conversion to cash depends on events partially controlled by others.

Table 4
Statement of Realizations and Derealizations

	Net Cash Assets		Other (Net)		Specific Advantage	
	Expected	Unexpected	Expected	Unexpected	Expected	Unexpected
Realizations:						
From exit values—noncash to exit values—cash:						
Sales	5,000	200	(5,000)	(200)		
Interest revenue	20		(20)			
	5,020	200	(5,020)	(200)		
From specific advantage to exit values:						
Value added			2,200		(2,200)	
Changes in exit values of net current assets:						
On conversion			300		(300)	
At year end			150		(150)	
			2,650		(2,650)	
Derealizations:						
From net cash assets to exit values:						
Purchases:						
Current assets	(3,200)	(400)	3,200	400		
Fixed assets	(5,000)	300	5,000	(300)		
Interest expense	(1,000)		1,000			
	(9,200)	(100)	9,200	100		
From exit values to specific advantage:						
Purchase loss			(100)	(20)	100	20
Changes in exit value of fixed assets (net)			(1,000)		1,000	
			(1,100)	(20)	1,100	20
Total realizations	5,020	200	(2,370)	(200)	(2,650)	
Total derealizations	(9,200)	(100)	8,100	80	1,100	20
Net	(4,180)	100	5,730	(120)	(1,550)	20
Net change in assets	(4,080)		5,610		(1,530)	
From the income statement:						
Imputed interest					2,205	
Revisions of expectations					1,200	
Net change in specific advantage					1,875	

due to purchase gains. Thus the realizations due to the operating activities, the holding activities, and the purchasing activities of the firm are separately reported in this statement.

The conversion from exit values to specific advantage represents derealization events. These are broken down into the purchase loss attributable to the purchasing activities of the firm and other decreases in exit value due to the holding activities of the firm.

None of these events changes the MRD value of the firm unless they cause a revision of expectations. Thus all represent conversions of specific advantage to exit values and vice versa. This is not to say that realization and derealization events, especially if unexpected, may not affect the value of the firm, but they do so only through a revision of expectations, which is separately reported.[17]

The last two items in the statement, the imputed interest and the revision of expectations, are also shown in the income statement. While these are not realization and derealization events, they are added to the Specific Advantage column so that all the changes in assets' composition and values from one balance sheet date to the next are reflected in this statement. The statement therefore articulates with the comparative balance sheets presented in table 1.[18]

The Utility of Relevant Accounting Reports

The relevant accounting reports described can provide many useful standards of comparison. Accounting reports have traditionally provided only one standard of comparison: last year's figures compared with this year's figures. The need for relevant standards for comparison appears obvious, since all decisions are essentially concerned with choices among alternatives. The communication of both expectations (MRD value) and exit values in our reports provides information useful to the assessment of risk and affords the means for highlighting opportunity costs of both the entity and the investors. At any given point of time the exit value of the assets represents a universal opportunity cost[19] of holding these assets. The exit value of the stock equity represents the opportunity cost to investors of holding their securities. In each case, the exit values represent

17. The level of disaggregation of events reflected in the statement is, of course, not the only possible level of disaggregation. The events shown in the statement may be shown in more or less detail depending on the informational needs of the users.

18. The firm had no capital contributions or distributions. Had there been some, these events would properly not have been reflected in any of the statements except the balance sheet. Thus they would have to be added to obtain complete articulation with the balance sheet.

19. We choose the universal opportunity costs because they represent the lower limit of specific opportunity costs. The specific opportunity cost of using an asset is generally defined as the alternative benefit from using the asset in the next best employment. This specific opportunity cost depends on particular available alternatives for managers and stockholders at a given point of time. Clearly, the identification of these particular and time-specific alternatives creates great difficulties. We record the universal opportunity costs because these are independent of the particular managers' and stockholders' decision alternatives and because they are independently quantifiable. The specific opportunity costs can be measured only in conjunction with the utilization of other assets of the firm or of the stockholders. It is only the universal opportunity cost which can be uniquely associated with the specific asset or share.

the foregone proceeds of severing the assets or selling the securities. Through communicating the exit values the balance sheet gives an indication of the static opportunity cost to both the investors and the firm. By communicating the MRD value, these static opportunity costs can be compared with the expected benefits, that is, the level of expectations.

Not only are opportunity costs of holding the assets (or securities) identified, but the opportunity costs of continuing to operate or having operated the assets for any given time are also measured in a dynamic sense. This dynamic opportunity cost can be broken down into two elements: (1) the interest or the alternative return that could have been achieved had the assets been severed from the firm, or the securities disposed of by investors; (2) the decline in exit values of the assets (securities) over the time period. Had the assets been sold initially, the imputed interest on the exit values could have been earned; further, the decline in exit values that occurred would have been avoided. Thus, the opportunity cost of holding the assets over any given time period is the foregone interest plus the decline in exit values.

These avoidable opportunity costs can be compared with the benefits of having operated the firm, which consist of both realization benefits and increments in value. The statement showing these opportunity costs and specific benefits for our sample firm is presented below:

Statement of Avoidable Opportunity Costs and Unique Benefits

Avoidable opportunity costs	
Decline in exit values	$1,800
Less: increase in exit values	1,250
Net decline in exit values	550
Add: foregone interest on exit values (net)	1,105
Net avoidable costs of having held the assets and continued as a firm	$1,655
Unique benefits of having operated as a firm	
1. Realization benefits:	
Purchase gain	$ —
Less: purchase loss	120
	(120)
Add: value added (excluding depreciation)	2,200
	$2,080
2. Increments in value:	
a. Time growth	2,205
b. Revision of expectations	1,200
	$3,405

It may also be useful to compare some of the elements in the above statement separately. Thus, the economic income or increment in value which the firm has achieved (part of the benefit) can be contrasted with the alternative returns that could have been realized had the firm disbanded (see the statement below).

Statement of Increase in the Value of the Firm and Alternative Returns

Economic income	
Imputed interest on total net assets (including specific advantage)	$2,205
Revision of expectations	1,200
	$3,405
Alternative returns	
Imputed interest on exit value (net)	$1,105

In this comparison, the risk consideration is not included in the benefits. The economic income is merely the increase in the MRD value of a firm. It consists of the interest imputed on the MRD value of the firm plus a revision of expectations, and it totals $3,405. This is contrasted with the alternative return, which is imputed interest computed on the net exit value of the firm's assets and is taken from the cost and benefit statement.

Also, meaningful comparisons can be made with alternatives available to the stockholders of the firm, as shown in the next statement:

Avoidable Opportunity Costs for Stockholders

1. Imputed interest on stock	$1,305
2. Decrease in exit value of stocks	0
	$1,305

Specific Benefits of Having Continued to Invest in the Firm—Appropriation of the Increase in the Firm's Value[20]

Economic income	
1. Increase in exit value of stocks	$1,950
2. Increases in specific residual	1,455
	$3,405

This shows the avoidable opportunity cost of the stockholders continuing to be associated with the firm; this cost consists of the market rate of interest computed on the beginning stock value plus the decline in the value of the stock during the period, if any. This is compared with the specific benefits of having continued to invest in the firm; these benefits are the economic income or the change in the MRD value of the firm, which must be reflected as an increase in the exit value of stock and/or as an increase in specific residual.

The specific residual describes the portion of the MRD value of a firm that has so far not been captured by the market value of a security. Therefore, as already stated, the higher the proportion of the specific residual to the MRD value, the larger is the uncertainty for stockholders of realizing their flows. Therefore, other things being equal, an increase in the exit value of the stock with an equal decrease in the specific

20. In addition to size benefits, i.e., increase in the MRD value of the firm, stockholders receive a realization benefit when part of their share in the MRD value of the firm is converted to a cash asset in the form of dividends. Thus dividends represent a realization benefit but not a size or income benefit.

residual represents an increasing acceptance of the firm's expected cash flows and the assessment of the risks associated with them, and a greater degree of reliability can be attached to these forecasts.

The above report represents some of the relevant comparisons that can easily be made through information provided by relevant accounting. In addition, the separation of all events into expected and unexpected components provides another important standard of comparison.

Comparison of expected events with past events generates data that improves the ability of investors and managers to assess the reliability of future forecasts, as well as to evaluate past performance and predict future performance. A major objective of accounting reports has long been the evaluation of the success of a firm and its management. To a large extent, this success is due to proper planning and successful accomplishment of plans. The relevant accounting system communicates both the plans and the degree to which they have been accomplished. Reporting forecasts and the subsequent validation of forecasts makes possible a more realistic assessment of the firm's progress to date. It also provides a helpful basis for evaluating the firm's subsequent forecasts. Comparisons between forecasts and actual occurrences for one firm over time will make it possible to judge the reliability of these forecasts. Reporting the differences between forecasts and actual occurrences for *all* firms makes it possible to judge the comparative forecasting ability of the different firms. These comparisons would indicate to investors the extent to which they can rely on different firms' forecasts and will provide managers with valuable feedback for improving their future forecasts and plans.

If forecasts and achievement of forecasts are communicated for all firms, investors will be able to contrast the variability and measure the covariability of a given firm's flows and expectations with the flows and expectations of other firms. The extent of this covariability is an important element for efficient investment strategies, and its measurement can be facilitated by this feature of the relevant accounting system.

DATA REQUIREMENTS

The foregoing discussion of the relevant accounting system has, we trust, indicated its potential usefulness.

An objection may be raised that it requires unobtainable or unauditable figures. Worry may be expressed that management of firms would be harmed by revealing their expectations and that auditors of firms would be sued because they have included subjective quantifications in accounting reports. An analysis of the data requirement of the relevant accounting system suggests that these worries are not necessarily well founded. The relevant accounting system requires the following data: (1) forecasts of cash flows and the market rate of interest to obtain the MRD value of the firm; (2) measurement of the exit values of the firm's assets and equities at various points of time, and forecasts of prospective changes in exit values;[21] and (3) measurement of past transactions.

Predicted Cash Flows

Cash flow forecasts are now made by firms, since they are required for managerial plans and daily decisions. But these forecasts are communicated only in an ad hoc fashion through press releases and presentations before financial analysts' societies, etc. If these forecasts are made, they should be communicated within the framework of systematic accounting reports and thus be made available for systematic validation. This would provide a realistic measure that could be used by investors and other interested parties to evaluate subsequent forecasts. Although the forecasts are not auditable when they are made, they become auditable as subsequent events occur. The firm is responsible for providing a monitoring system for validation of forecasts. Since forecasts presently exist and since they are not systematically communicated to outsiders, information they contain is probably obtained by some but not all interested parties. Relevant accounting requires that this information be communicated to all interested parties and therefore reduces the possibility of gains from inside information.

The horizon over which forecasts are presently made varies from firm to firm. Although someday it may be desirable to establish a mandatory horizon, no single horizon should now be required. No firm should be required to make forecasts. All firms would be required to communicate forecasts if they were made. The only requirement consists of communicating forecasts if they are made. The MRD value of a firm that did not make forecasts would consist only of exit values; thus the firm would be identified either as a conservative firm or as a conservatively reporting firm.[22] A conservatively reporting firm would pay the price of reporting only the exit values of its assets. If the specific advantage were informative and valuable for investors, the market would penalize firms that did not make and report forecasts. Under relevant accounting, competitive pressures would be created to induce firms that have not hitherto made forecasts to start doing so in order to provide more relevant information about their potential prospects. Indirectly, the firms would benefit through the improved decision making made possible by explicitly considering forecasts. Today some firms are more conserva-

21. Forecasts of expected changes in exit values are necessary at a minimum for calculating the terminal values at the end of the forecast horizon. They are also useful for assessment of risk. This topic is more fully developed in the subsequent monograph.

22. It is possible to have a firm with a negative specific advantage, such as a bond investment mutual fund. This comes about because the interest on bond (expected cash flows) is discounted at the market rate of interest, which is larger than the bond rate. The negative specific advantage indicates that the firm faces less than market risk.

tive than others in their accounting practices. This conservatism is not readily apparent to users. Under our system, a firm which is conservative in accounting treatment would be identified as such.

The objection may be raised that communicating forecasts would adversely affect the position of the firm through the communication of confidential information. Forecasts, however, may be communicated at various levels of aggregation. Under relevant accounting they are aggregated into one value—the MRD value of the firm. Detailed forecasts are only reported retrospectively when actual events have occurred and when they are separately reported as expected or unexpected. At that point the forecasts are past history, and it is hard to see how this would decrease the competitive advantage of the firm. Requiring detailed forecasts to be reported prospectively might be desirable, but research into the cost (including competitive disadvantage) and benefit of doing so must be undertaken before a particular level of disaggregation is recommended.

Exit Values

Actual exit values are required by the relevant accounting system. If a distinction between expected and unexpected changes in exit values is to be made, exit values as of year-end will have to be forecasted. In addition, exit values must be estimated as of the end of a forecast horizon if that horizon does not coincide with the termination of the firm. This is necessary because terminal values must be provided whenever the forecast horizon ends. These terminal values are surrogates for any discounted cash value attributable to events subsequent to the end of the horizon.

The estimation of prospective exit values provides useful inputs to the relevant accounting system. However, as with the forecast of cash flows, it should not be mandatory. A firm cannot be forced to estimate, but, as with forecasted cash flows, investors' pressure may induce firms to provide such forecasts and thus allow expectations to become a part of the accounting systems.

The measurement of actual exit values, however, should be required. Measuring and auditing exit values is possible. The more material the exit values of any assets, the more readily quantifiable such exit values are likely to be. The more specific an asset, the less is its exit value in relation to its use value. The more universal an asset, the greater is its exit value in relation to its use value. For universal assets, it is likely that an established market will provide satisfactory evidence for the quantification of the exit value, such as wholesale prices for the firm's inventory. In fact, auditors are presently required to consider these exit values to quantify inventory at "cost or market, whichever is lower." Calculating exit values of cash, accounts receivable, and marketable securities is even less difficult and is presently required by every audit program.

Obtaining exit values for fixed assets, services, and intangibles is more difficult. For some of these assets a relatively well-structured second-hand market exists, for example, cars, machine tools, and like assets. Even if a second-hand market does not exist, mortgage values may be obtainable and may represent a reasonable floor for the exit values. When direct methods such as the above are not suitable, indirect methods may be employed to estimate exit values by relating the exit values to available surrogates.[23] Whatever the difficulties in quantifying these exit values, measures for quantifying exit values are apt to be available for assets whose exit values are material.

Many intangibles and services have zero exit value. This is not to say that these assets have no value. They possess use value but generally no separable value. Realization of these values depends on the continued operation of the firm. For example, human capital (except for baseball teams and similar organizations) generally has zero exit value. Cash flows and other actual transactions are presently reported and do not represent additional data requirements.

The data requirements of relevant accounting consist of (1) data presently available and communicated, such as historical cost and transactions; (2) forecasts that exist but are not presently communicated in systematic fashion; and (3) exit values. Exit values represent the only new measurement that must be made, and the cost of obtaining these measurements should not be prohibitive.

CONCLUSIONS AND IMPLICATIONS

Our system provides a host of measures such as cash values, historical cost values, exit values, and use values. It provides measures to identify and predict flows of benefits both in terms of the size of the benefits and in terms of their certainty. It does not provide a single measure for the value of an asset or for the benefits that can be associated with a firm. This is unfortunate but necessary. We can understand the desire to have a single figure such as a point estimate of income that captures all that is significant about a firm. But the complexities and multidimensional aspects of economic activity cannot be captured by such a single figure.

One of the objections that is sure to be raised against our system is that it would increase the vulnerability of the firm and of its auditors to law suits. This is probably not so. The reason behind much of the frustration that sometimes erupts in a law suit is occasioned by describing complex activities in a simplistic manner that is neither appropriate nor decision relevant. Providing more information, even though subjective, may well lessen rather than increase the dissatisfaction and frustration with current accounting and therefore the exposure to liability suits.

The information we provide is more complex, more multidimen-

23. See, for example, James C. McKeown, "An Empirical Test of a Model Proposed by Chambers," *Accounting Review* 46 (January 1971): 12–29.

sional, and therefore possibly more difficult for investors to use. The investor may complain about the difficulty inherent in using this information, but at least the information is provided. It is even more difficult to use information that is necessary but not provided.

By combining exit values and the MRD value of the firm, some of the deficiencies inherent in each measure, if used separately, are eliminated. The following objection has been justifiably raised against exit values: Why record the value of an asset at its disposal value when disposal is an alternative rarely resorted to? This objection is valid if only exit values are communicated. However, in relevant accounting, while the exit value reflects *a* value, it is not *the* value. And exit values are communicated not only for valuation purposes but also to provide a standard of comparison to facilitate the evaluation of risk and alternative returns. Thus exit values are surrogates for many attributes relevant to information users in addition to their use for valuation.

Objections to discounted cash flow values primarily center on the necessarily subjective nature of these estimates. But these objections are lessened through also providing objective data that place the subjective estimates in proper perspective. Our system provides this perspective through communicating the MRD value of a firm only in conjunction with exit values and historical measures.

Much research remains to be done. First the system must be implemented and applied to an actual firm. It will also be necessary to evaluate different methods of quantifying expected cash flows and the other essential elements of the relevant accounting system. The feasibility of incorporating probabilistic information and the optional levels of aggregation and disaggregation, etc., must be assessed.

These alternative forms of processing and communicating relevant information must be evaluated in terms of their costs and benefits. How frequently forecasts should be made and over what horizon they should extend must also be investigated. Users' reactions to information of this type must be explored so that the communication process can be improved. We are presently working on these and other problems and hope to present the case study and some of the results in a monograph.

This paper represents the initial effort to identify and describe the relevant accounting system. Our hope is that relevant accounting and subsequent research will be able to explicitly relate accounting variables to economically relevant decision variables.

DISCOUNTED CASH FLOW ACCOUNTING

Joshua Ronen

CONCEPTUAL PAPERS

Discounted Cash Flow Accounting

Joshua Ronen

Discounted cash flow accounting is an attempt to measure the wealth of a firm at a particular point in time and the changes in wealth over time, that is, economic income. The economic income concept is viewed as a change in state of wealth that occurred in the past, knowledge of which may be useful for decisions of users of financial statements, but is not necessarily derived from their decision-making requirements. According to this view, there exists an underlying "true" state of the world and changes therein. The construct called "income" is supposed to denote an aspect of the changes in the "true" state of the world. The concept of economic income, however, could also be useful in satisfying the decision-making requirements of users of financial statements.

Traditionally, economists referred to the changes in the "true" state of the world as changes in well-being during a given period.[1] Whether this view of the underlying state of the world implies that income measurement is the process of describing only past occurrences or whether the measurement process also necessarily reflects the measurer's beliefs concerning future occurrences depends on the definition of well-being. Broadly, well-being can be understood to reflect the overall "happiness" or "felicity" or "utility" of the organism or entity whose income is measured. In a descriptive sense, this view of well-being would include attitudes, satisfaction levels, and other psychology-related states of felicity in addition to wealth. In the normative sense and in the absence of formalized methods of quantifying psychological states of felicity, the well-being of the holder of a firm's stock derives from the "wealth" or "value" of that firm and the risk associated with that value,

[1] Thus, J. R. Hicks defined a man's income for a week as being "the maximum value which he can consume during the week and still expect to be as well off at the end of the week as he was at the beginning." *Value and Capital,* 2nd ed. (Oxford, 1946), p. 176. This concept, originally developed relative to a person's income, has been adopted by some writers as the concept of business income. Edgar O. Edwards and Philip W. Bell, *The Theory and Measurement of Business Income* (Berkeley: University of California Press, 1961).

where the value of the firm is understood to be the present value of its expected net cash flows.

The Case of Certainty

Indeed, it has been repeatedly shown that, irrespective of the utility preferences of individual consumers and investors, if they are to be able to maximize their utility in a world of certainty and in a perfect capital market, the firm's objectives should be to maximize the market value of their equity in the firm, that is, the discounted value of future cash flows.[2] This corresponds to the ordinary theory of production in economics where the decision variables are determined on the basis of the market prices for the alternative outputs, the costs of the various factor inputs, and the technological possibilities of production. Once a production scheme has been determined so as to maximize the owners' equity value, they can spend their shares of the proceeds on whatever pattern of consumption possibilities appeals to them most at various points in time.

The maximization of wealth or the value of equity to owners is identical to the maximization, as of a given point in time, of net returns or profits. That is, there is no conflict between the stock and flow forms of the criterion of wealth maximization. The value of the firm is the weighted sum of the returns per period, the weights being the discount rates applied to these returns. The only situation in which the criteria of maximizing profit and maximizing market value of the firm conflict is when increases in returns for some periods involve reductions in other periods. In this case the universally applicable market value criterion should be used.[3]

In a world of certainty and perfect capital markets, the value of the firm is the present value of its expected net cash flows or the present value of the expected stream of dividends to stockholders. The discount rate in a world of certainty would be the market rate of interest which is assumed, through the arbitrage system, to be unique and common for all investments in the capital market.

For example, a valuation model based on dividends would stipulate the total value of the firm at time period zero (t_0) to be

$$(1) \quad v(o) = n(o)p(o) = \sum_{t=1}^{\infty} \frac{n(o)\ d(t)}{(1+r)^t}$$

Where: p(o) = the market price per share at the start of period O.
v(o) = the total value of all shares outstanding at the start of period O.

---

[2] See, for example, Eugene F. Fama and Merton N. Miller, *The Theory of Finance* (New York: Holt, Rinehart and Winston, 1972) for a lucid and elaborate proof of this rule.

[3] We do not get into the controversy about whether management will in fact act in the best interest of the firm's owners or rather in its own best interests. It is usually argued that incentive and sanction systems work to bring management to identify stockholders' goals as its own.

n(o) = number of shares outstanding at the start of period O.
d(t) = dividend per share at the beginning of period t, assumed to be paid only to holders of record as of the start of period t-1.
r = the one-period market rate of interest.

That is, the present value of the total dividends to be paid in future periods on the shares outstanding at the beginning of period zero.

Alternatively, we can emphasize the stream of cash earnings generated within the firm as

$$(2) \qquad v(o) = \sum_{t=1}^{\infty} \frac{R(t) - W(t) - I(t)}{(1+r)^t}$$

Where: R(t) = the firm's receipts at t from operations.
W(t) = wages and similar outlays for the services of factors of production not owned by the firm.
I(t) = outlays on capital account at t.

Thus, R(t) — W(t) — I(t) = net cash flow at t.

To express the present value of the shares currently outstanding in terms of the stream of "net cash flows" generated in the firm, we define X(t) [identical to R(t) minus W(t)] as the "net operating cash flow" at period t. We then have

$$(3) \qquad v(o) = \sum_{t=1}^{\infty} \frac{X(t) - I(t)}{(1+r)^t}$$

as the basic formula for the current market value of the firm.[4]

This equation for the firm's value can be expressed in terms of accounting earnings as follows: If we let Z(t) equal the depreciation estimate at period t, A(t) equal R(t) minus W(t) minus Z(t), i.e., the accounting earnings, and N(t) equal I(t) minus Z(t) (which is net investment in the sense of net change in the accounting book value of the assets), then we can express the above equation as

$$(4) \qquad v(o) = \sum_{t=1}^{\infty} \frac{A(t) - N(t)}{(1+r)^t}.$$

An equation for the valuation of the firm using accounting earnings is therefore equivalent to an equation using the net cash flows, provided the proper elements are incorporated.

Moreover, the returns to stockholders (i.e., dividends plus capital gains) are equivalent in any period to the total cash earnings of the firm, provided the firm has no special growth opportunities in the sense of investing at a rate of return, r^*, that is higher than the market interest rate, r. Thus, if G(t+1) is the total capital gain during period t to stockholders of record as of the start of t and D(t+1) is the total dividend at t+1, it can be shown that[5]

$$D(t+1) + G(t+1) = X(t+1)\left[\frac{r(1-k)}{r-kr^*}\right]$$

[4] See Fama and Miller, *Theory of Finance*, pp. 86-98.

[5] Ibid., pp. 96-97.

where r^* is the rate earned on internal investments and k is a constant proportion of total cash earnings that is invested so that

$$Xk(t+1) = I(t+1).$$

Now, if $r^* = r$, the stockholders' returns equal $X(t+1)$, the total cash earnings. Otherwise, if the firm has special growth opportunities, the returns are greater than the cash earnings by a factor of $\left[\frac{r(1-k)}{r-kr^*}\right]$, which is greater than unity. If we concentrate on capital gains, $G(t+1)$, we find that $G(t+1) = k_rX(t+1) + kX(t+1)\left[\frac{r^*-r}{r-kr^*}\right]$ where the term $k_rX(t+1)$ is retained cash earnings at $t+1$. That is, capital gains are equal to retained earnings when the firm has no growth opportunities $(r^*=r)$. However, when $r^* > r$, capital gains exceed retained earnings by the quantity $kX(t+1)\ (r^*-r)\ /\ (r-kr^*)$ which is the interest on the total market value at t of the firm's future investment opportunities.[6]

Notice that all these generalizations apply only to the case of perfect markets and a world of certainty. Once the assumption of perfect markets is abandoned, we can no longer use maximization of the firm's market value as a proxy for maximization of the utility of owners. In an imperfect market, without explicit assumptions as to the stockholders' tastes and how they are comprised, we cannot identify a unique investment pattern for the firm which maximizes the welfare of all stockholders. We can only make the weak statement that the preferred position lies within a certain range of such investment pattern.

However, when perfect capital markets are assumed, the maximization of current value as a proxy for the maximization of owner's utility also implies that, given the pattern of investments selected by the firm, the market value of the firm and thus the shareholders' wealth is independent of the firm's dividend and financing decisions; thus, operating and financing decisions can be made independently. This principle, in turn, implies that appreciation in the price of stock is equivalent, for the investor, to a dividend payment. In other words, if a stock appreciates in price, regardless of whether the investor actually sells the stock, for him this appreciation is equivalent to a cash receipt since he always has the opportunity of selling the stock for its cash equivalent. This appreciation is an opportunity cash receipt in the sense that, had the investor not decided that keeping his funds in the firm is more profitable than selling it, he could have sold the stock and received the market appreciation in cash.[7]

---

[6] See Fama and Miller, *Theory of Finance*, p. 97.

[7] For example, Fama and Miller, *Theory of Finance*, p. 84, in refuting the bird-in-the-hand argument emphasize that ". . . the independence proposition does not require stockholders to be indifferent as between a present dividend and a future dividend or capital gains. It says, rather, that once management is committed to undertake and finance a given investment program, an increase in the dividends in any period will simply lead to a corresponding reduction in the ex-dividend value of the shares in the same period. . . ."

Having thus shown that the value to a stockholder of his holding is identical to the present value of his expected stream of dividends *or* to the present value of the firm's cash earnings, it is now relevant to ask whether accounting should quantify this value. After all it could be argued that, if such identity exists, the value of the firm is already quantified through the market mechanism in the price of the stock. Thus, there would be no need to quantify it in the accounting report.

The Case of Uncertainty

However, if the assumption of a world of certainty is relaxed, the market value of the stock reflects not only the present value of expected dividends or cash flows to the firm but also the uncertainty associated with the flows. In other words, the uncertainty and the degree of risk associated with the occurrence of the expected cash flows are considered by transactors in the marketplace when they determine the market value of capital instruments through supply and demand.

In a world of uncertainty, the expectation of the firm's management with respect to both the magnitude of cash flows and their uncertainty may differ from that of transactors in the general marketplace. As a result, the market value of the securities will not necessarily be identical to the present value of cash flows as expected by the firm's management. But management expectations regarding future cash flows and their uncertainty may represent useful information which enables market transactors to predict cash flows and their associated uncertainty. Transactors must make these predictions in order to facilitate their own decision-making.

Both the future cash flows and their uncertainty depend on the specific plans and actions that are implemented by, and first known to, the firm's management. Since such plans are designed to give the firm a competitive edge, they are bound to have significant informational content. Because the firm's management is the first to know its plans, timely forecasts by management with respect to future cash flows may prove to be a valuable input to the users of financial statements in their predictions of future cash flows. Management is in the best position to assess the effects of its specific plans on cash flows. The question is, are there market forces that would make these plans and the cash flows derived from them known to the market in the absence of a requirement for forecasts to be published by management? This question is discussed in detail in the paper entitled "The Need for Accounting Objectives in an Efficient Market," pages 36-52, where it was concluded that there is a need for management to communicate its forecast of cash flows.

Cash Flow Expectations. Generally, cash flows that a firm generates are influenced by two major factors:

1. Market and industry events that affect all firms, i.e., exogenous factors.
2. The particular performance of the firm in question, i.e., the specific plans and decisions made by management. These firm-specific decisions are

responsible for whether the firm accumulates more or less value than the industry or the market. These are the endogenous factors.

It is of particular importance that management communicate the cash flows contingent on its plans.[8] Since these plans are under management control, any deviation from them would reflect on management ability to predict and/or to perform. Exogenous factors, contrary to the endogenous, are primarily beyond the firm's control and may be predicted by relying on market expectations as a whole as reflected in market prices. However, the best source for predicting endogenous factors is probably the firm's management itself. As indicated, by obtaining management predictions of endogenous cash flows, users can assess management predictive ability and possibly performance. Also, information about management's particular plans and the actual results provides insights into risk-taking tendencies of management and therefore its future likelihood of engaging in risk-taking activities. However, since cash flows are a joint result of both endogenous and exogenous factors, management can only communicate its forecasts of the total cash flows resulting from both factors; but at the same time it could, and perhaps should, explicitly state its assumptions relative to the exogenous factors. In fact, management could provide forecasts of cash flows that are conditional on different assumptions regarding the exogenous factors. By doing this, users can evaluate these assumptions and make adjustments, if necessary, in the forecasts for their own decision-making purposes.

It is suggested that management communicate its forecasts of cash flows separate from its consideration of uncertainty associated with them. The primary reason for the separation is that users' preferences *and* their assessments of the risk inherent in future events (both exogenous and endogenous) may differ from management's. If management's prediction of the magnitude of cash flows is disclosed separate from its judgment concerning risk and uncertainty, users will be able to combine the components to fit their own judgments and preferences toward risk. Users cannot do this if they are given only one value, that is, the magnitude of cash flows combined with the risk and uncertainty perceived by the firm's management.

Management is thus potentially a more useful source for predicting the endogenous factors under its control than for predicting exogenous factors. For example, with respect to exogenous factors, different information sources have different degrees of usefulness and competence in providing information about relevant events. Interest rate fluctuations, the money supply, and credit terms are factors, information on which is probably best obtained from the Federal Reserve; whereas, information on the availability of raw materials and future prices is probably best obtained through observing trends in the supplying industries. With respect to some events, the best source for pre-

[8] Since the detailed plans do not have to be made available, but only the management's expectation of cash flows that are contingent on the plans, there should be no reluctance on management's part to communicate this information out of fear of leakage to competitors.

dicting the exogenous factors is probably the market itself. The research on efficient markets indicates that available information in a market[9] (including information about exogenous factors relevant to the particular firm) is generally impounded in market prices of securities or other capital assets. Market prices therefore best reflect the effects of relevant exogenous factors on the firm (although publicly available endogenous information would also be reflected). For example, fluctuations in the price of a firm's output reflect anticipated change in demand, which is a relevant exogenous factor affecting the firm. Similarly, fluctuations in the market prices of inputs would reflect expectations with respect to changing conditions in the supplying industry and in the industries of competing inputs.

Reporting Both Discounted Cash Flows And Exit Values

In a frictionless market, prices are unique; that is, entry and exit values are identical. But they may differ in a market in which transaction costs exist. Since we also wish to provide measures of risk separately from expected magnitudes of cash flows, it seems reasonable to provide market prices at exit values of firm's assets rather than at entry values. Exit values of assets reflect not only the opportunity costs of holding assets within a firm[10] but also the potential cash proceeds that are available to the firm in case of unfavorable market conditions. Consequently, both management forecasts of expected cash flows and the exit values of the firm's assets and liabilities should be communicated.[11]

Ronen and Sorter[12] provide a detailed discussion of the advantages of such combined reporting and recommend the accounting reports to be communicated. Ingredients of this system consist not only of expected cash flows and exit values but also actual transactions. The latter will enable users to assess the reliability of future forecasts by comparing management forecasts and actual events. Expected and unexpected results of operations are also distinguished to highlight the deviation of actual events from forecasted events. The quantification of unexpected events provides a record of man-

---

[9] See, for example, Joshua Ronen, "The Need for Accounting Objectives in an Efficient Market," pp. 36-52, and Eugene F. Fama, "Efficient Capital Markets: A Review of Theory and Empirical Work," *Journal of Finance* (May 1970), pp. 383-417.

[10] The marginal cost of capital services per unit equals $rp_b + (p_b - p_e)$ where p_b and p_e are the prices per unit of capital at the beginning and end of the period respectively, and r is the one-period rate of return. The optimal investment of an asset is found at the point at which this cost is equated with the marginal cash flow that can be generated by the asset (see, for example, Fama and Miller, *Theory of Finance*, p. 117).

[11] Exit values are also discounted cash flows. But these reflect the *consensus* expectations of market transactors with respect to both the magnitude of cash flows and the risk associated with them, as discussed below.

[12] Joshua Ronen and George H. Sorter, "Relevant Accounting," *Journal of Business* (April 1972), pp. 258-282.

agement's "errors" and would be useful in assessing—through the observation of the magnitude of the errors over an extended period of time—the ability of management to forecast within a reasonable range of accuracy.

Summary and Discussion of Some Benefits of the System

By separately communicating economic return and risk, this system reflects aspects of both benefits and costs that accrue to a firm: the changes in the magnitude of expected cash flows and the changes in the uncertainty associated with the realization of these flows. Corresponding to these two elements of benefits are two elements of costs. The actual costs that are incurred by a firm to obtain the said benefits include both the decline in the magnitude of expected cash flows and the unfavorable shift in their time pattern as well as a shift in the asset's composition from less risky assets to more risky assets. If these elements are provided separately, investors and other users of financial reports are better able to evaluate the performance of one firm relative to other firms and thus to evaluate the attractiveness of one investment vis-à-vis other investments.[20] Moreover, these costs and benefits are also provided in a relativistic setting in the sense that a measure of opportunity costs is provided as a standard of comparison against which the particular value of the firm, its expected cash flows, and its actual cash flows, can be contrasted. At any point in time, the exit value of the firm's assets represents the universal opportunity costs of holding these assets to which the particular benefit of holding and employing these assets—the MRD value of the firm—can be compared. Over a period of time, the benefit of the firm can be contrasted with the period opportunity cost of continuing to operate the assets. This is measured by the interest that could have been earned by severing the assets from the firm initially plus the decline in the exit value of the assets over the time period. The period opportunity cost may be measured both ex post and ex ante. The ex post information is provided by applying the market rate of interest to the assets' exit values and communicating changes in exit values during the period. The ex ante measure consists of estimates of expected changes in exit values plus imputed interest.

The ex post and ex ante measures of opportunity cost can be compared with ex post and ex ante measures of benefits. Ex post benefits include the changes in expectations and the pattern of realizations. Ex ante, the benefits are expected realizations plus the time growth of expectations. Furthermore, the opportunity costs can be disclosed to both the firm and the stockholders.

By separating events into expected and unexpected components, the system allows the assessment of the reliability of past forecasts. Both management's plans and the degree to which these plans have been accomplished are communicated. Comparison of expected flows and actual flows provides variance or measures of deviation that should, over time, be useful

---

[20] Examples of such a cost and benefit statement and other financial statements highlighting different aspects of concern to investors are provided and elaborately discussed in Ronen and Sorter, "Relevant Accounting."

in assessing the success of the firm and of its management. When such deviations are reported for all firms as a result of wide adoption of the system, comparative measures of deviation will thus be provided making it possible to evaluate the performance and the capability of managements of different firms. Also, the general adoption of the system will allow investors to contrast and measure the covariability of the given firm's flows and expectations with the flows and expectations of other firms.[21]

Appendix

Reconciliation with Valuation Models

The purpose of this Appendix is to reconcile the cash earnings for any one period with the accounting income generated in the discounted cash flow (DCF) system. Alternatively, is the system consistent with valuation models of the firm? Since it was demonstrated in the literature that a dividends valuation approach is identical to a cash earnings valuation approach, it would be sufficient to show that the proposed system is consistent with one of these valuation models: The cash earnings model is chosen for this analysis.

To show that the one-period accounting income that was suggested is consistent with a cash earnings approach to valuation, note that equation (3) can be rewritten as follows:

$$(5) \qquad v(o) = \frac{X(1) - I(1)}{1 + r} + \sum_{t=2}^{\infty} \frac{X(t) - I(t)}{(1 + r)^t}$$

But I(1), which is the outlay on investments in period 1 (assumed to occur at the end of the period), is equal in equilibrium[22] to the asset's exit value and to the discounted value of net cash flows that the asset is expected to generate. That is,

$$(6) \qquad I(1) = \text{exit value} = \sum_{t=2}^{\infty} \frac{NF(t)_{I(1)}}{(1+r)^{t-1}}$$

where $NF(t)_{I(1)}$ is the net cash flow generated in period t from investments in period 1. But these net cash flows are simply the revenue resulting from employing these investments minus the outlays associated with operating the

[21] A conceptual reconciliation of the system with the firm's valuation models is provided in the Appendix.

[22] The condition of equilibrium will be relaxed later to show that the consistency of the accounting income with the cash earnings valuation model is also maintained when I $\neq$ exit value $\neq$ discounted net cash flows, which is the more realistic case. Also, this model assumes certainty; consequently, it is assumed that the capital budgeting decision is based on known cash flows, disregarding the issue of variability and correlatedness with other streams of income.

investments, and they can be described as $R(t)_{I(1)} - W(t)_{I(1)}$ or $X(t)_{I(1)}$. Thus (6) can be rewritten as

$$(7) \qquad I(1) = \frac{X(2)_{I(1)}}{1+r} + \left(\sum_{t=3}^{\infty} \frac{X(t)_{I(1)}}{(1+r)^{t-2}} \right) \frac{1}{1+r} = \frac{X(2)_{I(1)}}{1+r} + \frac{At(2)}{1+r},$$

where At(2) is the value of assets acquired in period 1 [I(1)] as of the beginning of period 2 or, equivalently, the exit value of period 1 investment as of the end of period 1.

Similarly, with respect to investments made at the beginning of period 0 the following can be formulated:

$$(8) \qquad I(o) = \frac{X(1)_{I(0)}}{1+r} + \left(\sum_{t=2}^{\infty} \frac{X(t)_{I(0)}}{(1+r)^{t-1}} \right) \frac{1}{1+r} = \frac{X(1)_{I(0)}}{1+r} + \frac{At(1)}{1+r},$$

where At(1) is the value of assets acquired in period 0 [I(0)] as of the beginning of period 1, or, equivalently, the exit value of period 0 investment as of the end of period 0.

But $X(t)_{I(0)}$ is included in the total cash flows from operation for period t_1. Therefore, we can decompose X(t) into X′(t), the net cash flows resulting from assets excluding investments in period 0 [I(o)], and $X(t)_{I(0)}$, which is the period t cash flows resulting directly and specifically from assets acquired in period 0. Thus, (5) can be rewritten as

$$(9) \qquad v(o) = \frac{X(1) - I(1)}{1+r} + \sum_{t=2}^{\infty} \frac{X'(t) + X(t)_{I(o)} - I(t)}{(1+r)^t}$$

The following equation results after rearranging:

$$(10) \qquad v(o) = \frac{X(1)}{1+r} + \left(\sum_{t=2}^{\infty} \frac{X(t)_{I(o)}}{(1+r)^{t-1}} \right) \frac{1}{1+r} - \frac{I(1)}{1+r} + \sum_{t=2}^{\infty} \frac{X(t) - I(t)}{(1+r)^t}$$

But since

$$\left(\sum_{t=2}^{\infty} \frac{X(t)_{I(o)}}{(1+r)^{t-1}} \right) \frac{1}{1+r} = \frac{At(1)}{1+r},$$

equation (10) reduces to

$$(11) \qquad v(o) = \frac{X(1)}{1+r} + \frac{At(1)}{1+r} - \frac{I(1)}{1+r} + \sum_{t=2}^{\infty} \frac{X'(t) - I(t)}{(1+r)^t}$$

According to (6),

$$I(1) = \sum_{t=2}^{\infty} \frac{X(t)_{I(1)}}{(1+r)^{t-1}}.$$

Therefore:

$$(12) \qquad \frac{I(1)}{1+r} = \sum_{t=2}^{\infty} \frac{X(t)_{I(1)}}{(1+r)^t}.$$

Since $X(t)_{I(t)}$ is included in X′(t), X′(t) can be decomposed to X″(t), the net cash flows resulting from assets excluding investments in periods 0 and 1, and $X(t)_{I(1)}$, which is the period t net cash flows resulting directly and specifically from assets acquired in period 1. Thus, (11) can be rewritten as

$$(13)\qquad v(o) = \frac{X(1)}{1+r} + \frac{At(1)}{1+r} - \frac{I(1)}{1+r} + \sum_{t=2}^{\infty} \frac{X(t)_{I(1)}}{(1+r)^t} + \sum_{t=2}^{\infty} \frac{X''(t) - I(t)}{(1+r)^t}$$

By combining (13) and (12) the following equation is obtained:

$$(14)\qquad v(o) = \frac{X(1)}{1+r} + \frac{At(1)}{1+r} + \sum_{t=2}^{\infty} \frac{X''(t) - I(t)}{(1+r)^t}.$$

But by reiterating the above manipulation, it can be shown that the summation term on the far right in equation (14) finally vanishes, and the following results:

$$(15)\qquad v(o) = \frac{X(1)}{1+r} + \frac{At(1)}{1+r}.$$

In other words, the value of the firm at the beginning of period 0 is the net cash flows received at the beginning of period 1 plus the value of the firm or the value of all its assets, at the beginning of period 1, both discounted back one period at the one-period market rate of return.

But v(o), the value of the firm at the beginning of period 0, is the total value of its assets at the beginning of period 0. That is, v(o) = I(o). Thus, we can write

$$(16)\qquad I(o) = \frac{X(1)}{1+r} + \frac{At(1)}{1+r},$$

or,

$$I(o)(1+r) = X(1) + At(1)\,,$$

and the income which is the value of the firm multiplied by the one-period market rate of return is

$$(17)\qquad I(o)r = X(1) + At(1) - I(o)\,.$$

That is, the income for period 0 is the net cash flow X(1) plus the difference between the discounted cash value of the firm's assets at period 1 and 0.[23]

The fact that income is not identical to the one-period cash flows results from the necessity of explicitly taking into account the future cash flows emanating from the current period's assets.

Note that the income in (17) may also be interpreted to be the net cash flows minus depreciation (Z):

$$(18)\qquad I(o)r = X(1) - Z$$

where

$$(19)\qquad Z = I(o) - At(1)$$

or,

$$Z = \sum_{t=1}^{\infty} \frac{X(t)_{I(o)}}{(1+r)^t} - \sum_{t=2}^{\infty} \frac{X(t)_{I(o)}}{(1+r)^{t-1}}.$$

---

[23] It can be similarly shown that when investments are made during the period, the discounted cash value of these investments at the time of purchase should be similarly subtracted to obtain the period's income.

Thus, under conditions of equilibrium, when the discounted cash value, the exit value, and the entry value are all identical, the accounting income based on entry value or replacement costs will provide flows which are consistent with the firm's valuation models.

When the assumption of certainty is relaxed, allowance must be made for possible changes in the expectations of cash flows. In this case, both the exit values and the capitalized economic advantages as of the end of period t may be different when expected as of the end of t from their value when expected as of the beginning of period t. Thus from (3),

(20) $$V(t) = \sum_{i=t+1}^{\infty} \frac{X(i) - I(i)}{(1 + r)^{i-t}}$$

where both X(i) and I(i) are the net cash flows from operations and the capital outlays respectively, as envisioned at the beginning of the tth period. Also,

(21) $$V(t + 1) = \sum_{i=t+2}^{\infty} \frac{[X(i) - I(i)] + \Delta[X(i) - I(i)]}{(1 + r)^{i-(t+1)}} + [X(t + 1) - I(t + 1)] + \Delta[X(t + 1) - I(t + 1)].$$

Where $\Delta[X(i) - I(i)]$ represents the change in the originally anticipated i^{th} period net cash flow now envisioned from the beginning of the period t + 1 and $\Delta[X(t + 1) - I(t + 1)]$ is the change in the previously anticipated net cash flow as of the beginning of period t + 1. Subtracting (20) from (21) yields the period t's economic income (hence Y):

(22) $$Y = \sum_{i=t+2}^{\infty} \frac{[X(i) - I(i)]}{(1 + r)^{i-(t+1)}} - \sum_{i=t+1}^{\infty} \frac{X(i) - I(i)}{(1 + r)^{i-t}} + [X(t + 1) - I(t + 1)] + \Delta[X(t + 1) - I(t + 1)] + \sum_{i=t+2}^{\infty} \frac{\Delta[X(i) - I(i)]}{(1 + r)^{i-(t+1)}}.$$

Now the following definitions can be presented:

$$Ye \equiv \text{expected income} \equiv \sum_{i=t+2}^{\infty} \frac{[X(i) - I(i)]}{(1 + r)^{i-(t+1)}} - \sum_{i=t+1}^{\infty} \frac{X(i) - I(i)}{(1 + r)^{i-t}} + [X(t + 1) - I(t + 1)],$$

Yue ≡ the portion of unexpected income relating to the current period cash flows ≡ $\Delta[X(t + 1) - I(t + 1)]$,

and

Yuf ≡ the portion of unexpected income relating to future cash flows

$$\equiv \sum_{i=t+2}^{\infty} \frac{\Delta[X(i) - I(i)]}{(1 + r)^{i-(t+1)}}.$$

Thus Y is broken down into three components

(23) $$Y = Ye + Yue + Yuf.$$

It should be noted that the expression for Ye is equivalent to the operating current cash flows X(t + 1) less the economic depreciation which equals

$$\sum_{i=t+2}^{\infty} \frac{[X(i) - I(i)]}{(1 + r)^{i-(t+1)}} - \sum_{i=t+1}^{\infty} \frac{X(i) - I(i)}{(1 + r)^{i-t}} - I(t + 1)$$

where according to the previous notation,

$$\sum_{i=t+2}^{\infty} \frac{[X(i) - I(i)]}{(1 + r)^{i-(t+1)}} \equiv At(t + 1);$$

$$\sum_{i=t+1}^{\infty} \frac{X(i) - I(i)}{(1 + r)^{i-t}} \equiv At(t)$$

and so the expression for depreciation would be: Z = At(t + 1) − At(t) − I(t + 1) where in this case At(t + 1) includes not only the original assets At(t) but also the additional assets acquired at [I(t + 1)].

But the expression for Ye can be rewritten, after performing the indicated subtraction, as follows:

$$\text{(24)} \qquad Ye = \sum_{i=t+2}^{\infty} \frac{[X(i) - I(i)]\,(1 + r) - [X(i) - I(i)]}{(i + r)^{i-t}}$$

$$- \frac{X(t + 1) - I(t + 1)}{1 + r} + [X(t + 1) - I(t + 1)]$$

$$= \sum_{i=t+2}^{\infty} \frac{[X(i) - I(i)]r}{(1 + r)^{i-t}} - \frac{X(t + 1) - I(t + 1)}{1 + r} + [X(t + 1) - I(t + 1)]$$

$$= \sum_{i=t+1}^{\infty} \frac{[X(i) - I(i)]r}{(1 + r)^{i-t}} = r \sum_{i=t+1}^{\infty} \frac{X(i) - I(i)}{(1 + r)^{i-t}} = V(t)r$$

by equation (20).

Thus it is found that Ye = V(t) • r, that is, expected income equals the value of the firm as of the beginning of the period multiplied by the one-period market rate of return.

From (17) and (24) is obtained

$$\text{(25)} \qquad Ye = V(t) \cdot r = X(t + 1) + At(t + 1) - At(t)$$

if I(t + 1) = 0 and

$$\text{(26)} \qquad Ye = V(t) \cdot r = X(t + 1) + At(t + 1) - At(t) - I(t + 1)$$

in the more general case where $I(t + 1) \neq 0$.

A TEST OF THE FEASIBILITY OF PREPARING DISCOUNTED CASH FLOW ACCOUNTING STATEMENTS

Joshua Ronen

A Test of the Feasibility of Preparing Discounted Cash Flow Accounting Statements

Joshua Ronen

This paper examines the feasibility of applying the discounted cash flow system of accounting to an actual firm. In particular, it attempts to provide some insight into the time and effort required to implement such a system. In this sense, valuable information will be gained relative to the cost of implementing the system.

Brief Description of the Discounted Cash Flow (DCF) Accounting System

The DCF system quantifies the firm's value (or wealth) by discounting its expected net cash flows over a specified time period. The total value of a firm would thus be communicated in the annual report as the present value of cash flows as of the report date; this value may be separated into specific assets and liabilities reflecting for each asset and liability the present value of their expected contributions to the cash flows of the firm. Nevertheless, a separate communication of their relative contributions to cash flows is considered useful for evaluating management performance in relation to the individual assets and liabilities. The discounted cash flow accounting system is most useful when the discounted value of *both* the firm and its individual assets and liabilities are communicated along with the exit values of the assets and the liabilities. An elaborate description of such a combined system is provided in the preceding conceptual paper, "Discounted Cash Flow Accounting," pages 143-160. The exit-value system (without DCF) has been investigated by another researcher in "A Test of the Feasibility of Preparing Exit-Value Accounting Statements"; the financial data presented in this paper, therefore, relates to discounted cash flows only.

Future cash flows are discounted at a rate which reflects average market risk. In this case average market risk was approximated by the average industrial rate of return for the period 1953-1970. This discount rate, though in a sense arbitrary, causes the discounted value to reflect the average market risk and thus to constitute a standard against which firms characterized by different levels of risk can be compared. The discount rate is applied to expected cash flows over whatever time period the firm chooses for its own planning purposes. Clearly, the longer the period, the more the specific nature of the firm's particular operations is reflected in the resulting value. To approximate the expected flows beyond the firm's period, the exit value of the firm's assets less its liabilities is used as a surrogate for the present value of future flows expected beyond the period. These exit values constitute the market consensus of the expected flows attributable to the net assets.

As indicated, in addition to the total net value of the firm, management can estimate the net cash flows attributable to specific assets or groups of assets. The attributable flows are the net incremental cash flows which can be related to owning and operating the assets. They are measured as the difference in the cash flows generated by the firm *without* the particular asset or group of assets and the cash flows generated *with* the asset or the group of assets. For the purpose of discounting, cash flows estimated for one-year periods can be assumed to fall at the middle of each year. The availability of data and the specific assumptions made in the preparation of the DCF accounting statements for the test firm are described below.

Data Availability

The firm recently prepared forecasts of financial statements on an annual basis for a three-year period. Prior to December 1971, forecasts were not explicitly made with respect to either cash flows or any other accounting data. The forecasts, which are based on product lines and plants, were available for the years ending December 31, 1972, 1973, and 1974. They include the following: (1) projected results of operations (which include sales, gross profit, pre-tax income or loss, and net income or loss), (2) projected balance sheets and (3) projected source and application of funds for three years.

Preparation of Discounted Cash Flow Accounting Statements

The methods of forecasting the income statement and balance sheet items and the cash flows were as follows:

Income Statement Items. A moderate growth in sales was projected in order to determine the sales figure. No formal forecasting method was used. Rather, past sales were extrapolated in a rather simple and straightforward manner. The projections for 1972 were based on existing orders plus specific orders expected to be received during the year. Forecasts for 1973 and 1974 were made without reference to specific orders. The sales forecast reflected the differential rates of growth for different plants and departments. Gross profit and pre-tax income were based on fixed estimated percentages of sales: 55 per cent and 10 per cent, respectively. (Notice that the estimate for the pre-tax income was not derived from the gross profit previously estimated, but was based on the original sales estimate.) The 10 per cent estimate of pre-tax income is admittedly on the conservative side. Also, no separate budgets for purchases and production were derived from the sales budget. Rather, as indicated, fixed percentages of gross profit and pre-tax income to sales were assumed.

Balance Sheet Items. Most of the current assets were primarily projected with reference to sales. Based on past experience, accounts receivable were forecast at the level of 120 days of average daily sales. Similarly, inventory was determined to be 50 per cent of annual sales computed on a quarterly basis, i.e., the inventory at year-end was estimated at an amount equal to total sales of the past two quarters. This percentage is presumably based on a turnover ratio of two. For the other current assets a constant growth was projected at $40,000 a year, based on historical increases.

For the fixed assets, no specific projections were made relative to particular assets. The forecasts were made only in the aggregate. According to the company's officers, no retirements were expected during the three-year horizon except for insignificant assets approximating $25,000 in total. All expected increases are therefore new purchases of equipment (buildings were not expected to be increased).[1] Thus, the expected equipment increases were $100,000 in 1972, $200,000 in 1973, and $200,000 in 1974. Since information about the useful life of separate assets was not readily available it was not feasible to forecast increments in fixed assets by examining the retirement age of specific assets. The group depreciation procedure is employed by the test company. The annual group depreciation rate is 10 per cent for equipment and 2 per cent for buildings (on a straight-line basis). Other assets which traditionally include patents, capitalized research and development costs and goodwill, were written off in 1971. The forecast, consequently, does not include amounts for these elements of cost.

The projected accounts payable were determined to reflect an amount which approximates 45 days of the average daily direct costs (primarily raw materials), excluding labor, involved in the manufacture of products. This estimation procedure is also based on past experience. The current portion of long-term debt is determined by reference to the contracts. The bank debt was projected according to the estimated need to draw on an open credit line of $2.5 million.

The Discounting Procedure. Since forecasts are available for only three years through December 31, 1974, surrogate figures are needed to approximate the cash flows after that date. As surrogates, estimates of the exit values of assets and liabilities as of December 31, 1974 (and as of December 31, 1973 for comparative purposes) were made. The estimates were based on the exit values as of December 31, 1971 as computed for the purpose of preparing the exit value accounting statements. Certain adjustments were

[1] No growth was expected in the buildings although at the time of preparation of the forecasts, the possible addition of a new building was discussed by management.

made as explained below. Since the methods of computing the exit values of assets and liabilities as of December 31, 1971 are discussed elsewhere in this volume, this paper only describes how these values were adjusted to arrive at an estimate for exit values as of December 31, 1974 (and December 31, 1973).

Estimated Exit Values. Exhibits 1, pages 205-206, and 2, pages 207-208, show the forecasted balance sheet items at both their book value according to historical cost accounting and their estimated exit values as of December 31, 1973 and December 31, 1974, respectively. As can be seen from the exhibits, the exit values of accounts receivable and other current assets were

Exhibit 1

Test-Firm
Forecasted Balance Sheets
at Historical Cost and Exit Value
as of December 31, 1973

			Historical Cost ($000)	*Exit Value* ($000)
Assets				
Current Assets.				
Cash			$2,081	$2,081
Accounts receivable			1,715	1,715
Inventory			2,384	2,393
Other			210	210
Total current assets			6,390	6,399
Fixed Assets:				
Land		$100		
Building	$1,022			
Less: Accumulated depreciation	131	891	991	952*
Equipment	700			
Less: Accumulated depreciation	249		451	284*
Total fixed assets			1,442	1,236
Total assets			$7,832	$7,635

Figures reported are net of tax liability (refund) which would arise from sale:

Land and building	248
Equipment	(14)

Exhibit 1—continued

	Historical Cost ($000)	*Exit Value* ($000)
Liabilities and Stockholders' Equity		
Current Liabilities		
Accounts payable	$ 690	$ 690
Accrued expenses	170	170
Accrued taxes	50	50
Current portion of long-term notes payable	150	150
Total current liabilities	1,060	1,060
Long-term Liabilities:		
Notes payable	242	242
Stockholders' (Residual) Equity:		
Preferred stock	1,500	
Common stock	390	
Additional paid-in capital	2,397	
Retained earnings	2,243	
Net exit value (assets less liabilities)		6,333
	6,530	6,333
Total liabilities and stockholders' equity	$7,832	$7,635

assumed to be identical to their conventional book values. The inventory at historical cost was adjusted to its estimated exit value by applying to it the ratio of the estimated exit value to the historical cost of inventory as of December 31, 1971 (as computed and shown in the separate paper on the exit value method).[2] The exit values of land and buildings were assumed to be (both at December 31, 1973 and December 31, 1974) identical to the exit value as of December 31, 1971, that is, $1,200,000 less the tax liability that will be incurred if the land and buildings are sold at the corresponding balance sheet dates for $1,200,000. Note that it was assumed that no additional buildings will be acquired although, as indicated earlier, such an acquisition may take place. (See footnote 1 above.)

In estimating the exit value of equipment as of December 31, 1973, and 1974, it was assumed that (1) gross equipment purchases during 1972, 1973, and 1974 are composed of the same proportions of different kinds of equipment as the stock of equipment as of December 31, 1971; (2) no equipment will be retired during the forecast horizon; and (3) the exit value of equipment

[2] The company's personnel do not expect either the inventory's composition in terms of product lines or its cost and market-value relationships to change significantly in the future.

as of the forecasted balance sheet dates bears the same ratio to their costs as their estimated exit value bears to gross costs as of December 31, 1971, with appropriate adjustments for age.

Liabilities, both current and long-term, were assumed to have the same exit value as their conventional book value. The difference between the exit value of the assets and the exit value of the liabilities constitutes the net exit value of the firm's assets.

Computation of the Discounted Value. Exhibit 3, page 209, shows the discounting procedure. This Exhibit shows the net cash inflows forecasted for fiscal years 1971, 1972, 1973, and 1974. As indicated, the net cash inflow for any year was assumed to fall on June 30 of that year (at the year's mid-

Exhibit 2

Test-Firm
Forecasted Balance Sheets
at Historical Cost and Exit Value
as of December 31, 1974

			Historical Cost ($000)	*Exit Value* ($000)
Assets				
Current Assets:				
Cash			$2,375	$2,375
Accounts receivable			1,715	1,715
Tax refund			335	335
Inventory			2,384	2,393
Other			230	230
Total current assets			7,039	7,048
Fixed Assets:				
Land and building				
Land		$100		
Building	$1,022			
Less: Accumulated depreciation	151	871	971	928*
Equipment	900			
Less: Accumulated depreciation	324		576	374*
Total fixed assets			1,547	1,302
Total assets			$8,586	$8,350

*Figures reported are net of tax liability (refund) which would arise from sale:

Land and building	272
Equipment	(2)

Exhibit 2—continued

	Historical Cost ($000)	Exit Value ($000)
Liabilities and Stockholders' Equity		
Current Liabilities:		
Accounts payable	$ 690	$ 690
Accrued expenses	230	230
Current portion of long-term notes payable	369	369
Total current liabilities	1,289	1,289
Long-term Liabilities:		
Notes payable	986	986
Stockholders' (Residual) Equity:		
Preferred stock	1,500	
Common stock	390	
Additional paid-in capital	2,397	
Retained earnings	2,024	
Net exit value (assets less liabilities)		6,075
	6,311	6,075
Total liabilities and stockholders' equity	$8,586	$8,350

point). These net cash inflows are then discounted for the period indicated to their present value at December 31, 1971. The discount rate applied was 12 per cent (the average rate of return earned on industrial stock traded on the New York and the American Stock Exchanges for the period 1953 through 1970.) To the discounted value of these net cash inflows is added the present value of the net exit value of the firm's assets. When we add to these resulting figures the net cash balances as of December 31, 1970, and December 31, 1971, respectively, we obtain the total discounted cash value of the firm.

No separate cash inflow estimates were obtained for land, buildings, and equipment. The net cash inflow attributable to current assets and liabilities are probably identical to their exit values. (See the balance sheet in Exhibit 4, page 210.) The reason that separate estimates were not obtained for land, buildings, and equipment was not the infeasibility of obtaining such estimates. The firm's personnel were capable of making these estimates; time constraints precluded them from doing so while this empirical investigation was being undertaken.

Discussion and Conclusion

While the forecasts prepared by the firm were not based on complex mathematical models, they reflect the best estimates of the future cash flows.

To that extent the resulting discounted value reflects management's expectations with respect to the firm's future performance. While the forecasting horizon only extends to three years, the results are different from either the conventional valuation or the exit valuation. Of particular interest is the comparison of the discounted cash value of the firm with either the net exit value of its assets or the conventional book value of its equity. The DCF value for December 31, 1970 of $4.975 million is significantly less than either the conventional net asset value of $6.262 million or the net exit value of $5.789 million. (See the exit-value empirical paper contained in this volume.) The discounted cash flow approach suggests that, had the same forecasts been available as of December 31, 1970, the firm may have been better off to sell its assets and cease operations or to take an alternative course of action. For December 31, 1971, the DCF value ($4.921 million) exceeds both the conventional net asset value ($4.529 million) and the net exit value ($4.593 million), indicating that the firm should continue its operations.

Note that there is no inconsistency in the different indications for the two dates. Given that the firm has already incurred a large loss for 1971, it is no longer better off by ceasing its operations at the end of that year since the exit value has decreased (reflecting the loss) to an extent that makes the continuation of operations the better option. The important thing is that, overall, the firm may have been better off if the forecasts had been available as of December 31, 1970, and a decision had been made to cease operations or to pursue an alternative course of action. This result can be explained in a different way by looking at the changes in the DCF value of the firm during

Exhibit 3

Test-Firm
Computation of Discounted Cash Flows
as of December 31, 1970 and 1971

	Net Cash Inflow	Present Value as of December 31, 1970		Present Value as of December 31, 1971	
Year	($000)	Years	($000)	Years	($000)
1971	$1,922	½	$1,816		
1972	40	1½	34	½	$ 38
1973	83	2½	63	1½	70
1974	294			2½	221
Total discounted cash flows			1,913		329
Add: Cash as of Balance Sheet date			36		1,958
Present value of net exit values (assets, excluding cash, less liabilities):					
as of December 31, 1973 ($4,252)			3,026		
as of December 31, 1974 ($3,700)					2,634
Total discounted value of the firm			$4,975		$4,921

1971, as reflected in the income statement (Exhibit 5, opposite). The firm incurred a net decrease of $54,000 in its DCF value ($4.975 million—$4.921 million). But the loss is really greater than that since normally the firm would expect to earn 12 per cent (the discount rate) on its initial value of $4.975 million or $597,000 to reach a total value as of December 31, 1971 of $5.572 million. Compared with the DCF value of $4.921 million, a net loss of $651,000 is indicated. It must be noted that for December 31, 1970 the horizon was assumed to extend only through 1973, i.e., a constant three-year horizon was assumed. Thus, actual cash flows of 1971 were assumed to be accurately forecasted as of December 31, 1970. On the other hand, the projection for 1974 was assumed not to be known until December 31,

Exhibit 4

Test-Firm
Comparative Discounted Cash Flow
Balance Sheet

	December 31, 1970 ($000)	*December 31, 1971* ($000)
Assets:		
Current Assets:		
Cash	$ 36	$1,958
Accounts receivable	3,584	1,761
Tax refund	—	1,296
Inventory	2,549	3,097
Prepaid Expense	*	*
Fixed Assets:		
Land and building	*	*
Equipment	*	*
Other	*	*
Liabilities and Stockholders' Equity:		
Current Liabilities:		
Accounts payable	1,103	1,361
Taxes	268	—
Current portion of long-term debt	—	37
Short-term note payable	—	2,750
Other	175	31
Long-term Liability:		
Note payable	—	759
Total Discounted Value of the Firm	$4,975	$4,921

* As explained in the text, no separate estimates were obtained for the incremental cash flows attributable to these assets; the total DCF value of the firm need not equal the sum of DCF value of individual assets less liabilities had these DCF values been obtainable.

Exhibit 5

Test-Firm
Income Statement
Change in the Value of the Firm

	($000)
Imputed return on the DCF value of the Firm[1]	$597
Opportunity Cost[2]	(116)
Revision of expectations[3]	535
Net loss	($ 54)

[1] This is the discount rate of 12 percent applied to the DCF value of the firm as of December 31, 1970 ($4,975).

[2] This is imputed interest on $1,922 for one half year ($112) and on $36 (beginning cash balance) for 1 year ($4); it reflects the interest-equivalent earnings foregone as a result of not having reinvested the year's cash flows at the market rate of return.

[3] This is the difference between $5.572 million, the DCF value of the firm that would have resulted from the passage of one year and the receipt of cash inflows during 1971 had there been no changes in expectations, and $4.921 million, the DCF computed as of December 31, 1971, less the opportunity cost of $116—the earnings foregone for 1971. In this case, the revision of expectations results from the addition, as of December 31, 1971, of one year (1974) to the horizon. See also the explanation included in the foregoing analysis.

1971. In this sense, the addition of the projections for 1974 into the DCF value for December 31, 1971 (and moving the expected net exit value one year further to December 31, 1974), constitutes, by construction, a revision of expectations by the firm's management.

The market value of the stock as of December 31, 1970 (the average January 2 quote was applied) amounted to $17.752 million, much above the DCF value, indicating higher expectations by the market as compared to the firm's expectations.[3] And, indeed, as of December 31, 1971, the market value of the stock declined to $10.870 million, significantly closing the gap.

The researcher's time and involvement approximated 40 hours.[4] Since the forecasts were already available, only minimal time was required on the part of the firm's personnel. It is believed that estimates of cash flows attributable to specific assets or groups of assets could be obtained at a relatively small amount of time and cost, especially if the system were to be widely and systematically applied by many firms.

As to auditing discounted cash flow statements, it should be noted that only the methods of forecasting need to be assessed and evaluated by the auditor. Auditors should clearly have no responsibility in relation to the cash flow estimates. Such cash flow estimates should reflect management's ex-

[3] Note that the firm's expectations extend to only a three-year horizon. The market's horizon may be longer.

[4] The exit values as of December 31, 1971 were already estimated by another researcher, and time to compute them is not included in this estimate.

pectations to be validated and assessed as a result of comparison with actual cash flows. The auditor's function would be restricted to expressing an opinion on the forecasting methods and whether the same methods were applied in internal and external reports. The difficulties that can be encountered in auditing predictions of future exit values are somewhat similar to those encountered in estimating present exit values; the latter are discussed in the "Exit Value" empirical paper, pages 213-228, contained in this volume.

PROVIDING RELEVANT FINANCIAL STATEMENT INFORMATION

Joshua Ronen and George H. Sorter

Providing Relevant Financial Statement Information In a Period of Changing Prices

by

J. Ronen and G.H. Sorter

The unusual strains on capital markets in recent years, a period of widely fluctuating prices, have critically tested the ability of enterprises to attract private savings. It is now more essential than ever for management to give investors information that will enable them to channel their savings to their greatest advantage and result in the efficient allocation of resources. Efficiency of resource allocation is best promoted by information that enables investors to make unbiased estimates of the anticipated cash return on investments.[1]

To allow users to make such assessments, corporations should provide information that aids in predicting the amount, timing, and uncertainty of net cash flows. This in effect is an explicit objective stated in the Trueblood Report issued by the American Institute of Certified Public Accountants (AICPA) in 1974. (Objective No. 4 of the report). The purpose of this paper is to analyze the various valuation or quantification methods that are currently proposed for use in financial statements (such as, the FASB's, the Sandiland's Committee reports and the SEC) in terms of their utility in making such estimates.

[1] By allowing individual investors, in assessing the desirability of alternative investments, to equate their cost of capital with the best possible estimate of the return, this information will likewise make possible the satisfaction of Pareto optimality conditions.

There are various ways of obtaining information that assists the prediction of cash flows. The market value of a corporate security is one source, because it reflects a consensus of investors regarding future cash flows and their uncertainty. Management's own internal forecasts of cash flows, even though subjective in nature, may also prove to be valuable information to users of financial statements in making predictions. Management is in the best position to assess the effects of its specific actions on cash flows. These actions, which are first known to management, and the forecasts required to decide on them, are bound to have significant meaning for investors. If managers are arriving at these decisions with the possibilities of inflation fully in mind, as they should be, then this information will be valuable to investors even if they have differing forecasts of price changes. Thus management's expected net cash flows, separately disclosing the timing and risk dimensions in order to allow users of financial reports to apply their own risk preferences, are clearly the ideal starting point in generating forecasts.

Unfortunately, forecasting cash flows is not now part of accepted accounting practices, with or without specific assumptions about inflation, and the evolutionary process required to make such methods acceptable will undoubtedly be very slow at best. Consequently, users of financial statements must make their own predictions of cash flows de novo and accounting information helpful for this purpose should be provided.

The Implied Objectives of Suggested Proposals:

As explicitly stated at times and as otherwise implied, the FASB, SEC, and the Sandilands Committee and other proposals are designed to help users make decisions in a period of changing prices and help assess and evaluate the firm's progress, past and future. An integral part of such assessment is the evaluation of management performance. Two primary objectives thus emerge from careful analysis of the proposals:

1. To allow users of financial statements to more efficiently predict the future earning power of the firm and

2. To allow users to more effectively assess managerial performance.

In assessing the performance of management, one should distinguish between two components: 1) the ability to actually perform, i.e., making efficient operating decisions and 2) the ability to predict future events relevant to the firm's operations. Both components are aspects of managerial ability to enhance the earning power of the firm and both should therefore be assessed.

Financial statements to meet these objectives should preferably provide information that helps users predict the ability of the corporation to generate future cash and to assess the uncertainty surrounding the cash flows. Also, it should facilitate the assessment of managerial ability to perform as gauged in terms of the generation of cash and enhancement of future cash generating ability of the firm. It is clear that no single measure will accomplish this. Without much further thought and research, it can be safely concluded that we are in need of a multi-dimensional system where different measures can best be combined by the users themselves for the purpose of predictions and assessments.

The question of interest is, what are the dimensions which, from a cost-benefit standpoint, are most usefully included in the financial reporting system? Since our purpose is to accomplish the aforementioned objectives, we should concentrate our efforts on searching for approaches that provide measures useful for prediction and performance assessment, and that simultaneously are feasible and least costly. Ideally, we should search for approaches that are implementable in phases where we can gain information from early phases about the desirability of implementing subsequent phases. Before discussing our suggested approaches, we review the strengths and weaknesses of existing proposals for valuation.

Strengths and Weaknesses of Existing Proposals

The first method is historical cost (HC), the accepted method of valuation. This is essentially a quantified record of actual cash or near-cash inflows and the actual cash outlays that were required to produce the cash inflows.

The second method is current cost or replacement cost valuation (CC). This substitutes for the actual (or historical) expenditures the outlays that would have to be made at today's prices for equivalent assets.

The third method is general-price-level adjusted historical cost (GP). Here the actual historical costs are adjusted for movements in the general price level.

The fourth method is exit values (EV). This values assets in terms of how much these assets could be sold for, in normal nondistress sale. Both CC and EV are generally referred to as "current values."

All too commonly, as in the suggestion of the SEC and the FASB, the proponents of different methods of determining current values have made it seem that these systems are mutually exclusive. It is assumed, for example, that replacement cost must prevail over exit value or vice versa. Nor has there been a serious attempt up to now to assess the benefits of these methods in terms of specific criteria--specifically, in terms of facilitating prediction and evaluation of earning power, i.e., cash generating ability.

We also submit that, even if management's own forecasts were to be reported in financial statements, these alternative methods of valuation would still be extremely useful in assessing the validity of published management forecasts. They would yield insights into the premises underlying discounted cash flow valuation (DCF), the standard technique used in arriving at decisions regarding capital expenditure. For example, management's forecast might represent an extrapolation of past trends developed through historical cost quantification, or it might significantly differ from these trends. Different questions would be raised in either case. Again, forecasts of increased cash flows would be assessed very differently if a firm's exit values or replacement costs were declining or increasing at the time the forecast was made.

Each of the valuation methods has a role to play in helping to assess the validity of prediction and in assessing performance in periods of volatile prices. This even applies to historical cost valuation. Though it is often asserted that historical cost data assume a stable price level--i.e., a zero rate of inflation--this is not true. Rather, the prediction model utilizing historical cost assumes a continuation of the past trend of inflation, a trend that might have been zero or some other rate. To the extent that the future duplicates the past, historical cost data therefore will be good predictions of future cash generation.

This is illustrated by the following example:

Suppose that a firm buys a product at the beginning of the year when the cost of the product is $5.00 and the selling price is $10.00. This product is then sold at the end of the year when price and cost have both increased by 10 percent. Then, under historical cost quantification, sales are shown as $11.00 and costs as $5.00. This prediction model would assert that costs of $5.00 today would yield $11.00 a year from now, or in other words that a current cost of X will result in a cash inflow of 220 percent of X one year from now. This will, in fact, be the case if inflation continues at the rate of 10 percent a year. A purchase of one unit at $5.50 today will indeed generate $12.10 when sold a year from now if the selling price then has increased by 10 percent over today's price. Thus, the relationship of revenue as 220 percent of cost would continue.

To be sure, the real value to the firm of the $12.10 just cited will not be the same a year from now as today. But the first purpose of financial statements is to facilitate the prediction of the <u>nominal</u> amount of cash to be generated, leaving to others the interpretation of the significance or value of such cash amounts. Presumably, the impact of inflation will be best accounted for not by changing the amount of cash predicted, but rather by using a higher discount rate for discounting the value of the cash expected to be generated. This, in fact, is what seems to occur as we witness the higher interest rates and lower price-earnings ratios during periods of anticipated inflation. If the impact of inflation is allowed to affect the numerator of the prediction model, then discounting with prevailing interest rates that have anticipated inflation built in will double-count the effects of inflation and gravely distort the resulting measure.

Historical cost prediction thus assumes a continuation of past relationships and trends rather than an unchanging environment. If past trends are not continuing, the prediction model is of course, defective. Much the same may be said of simple prediction models based on current cost or replacement cost valuation. Under replacement cost accounting, cost of goods sold will be quantified not in terms of the cost of actual purchases but rather in terms of the "current cost" of the inputs consumed in the manufacturing and selling process. This does not quantify the prospective purchases to be made to maintain inventory levels unless there is no further change in the cost of goods. Thus, these quantifications do not allow an efficient prediction of future expenditures necessary to replace the assets consumed. In fact, if the assets have already been replaced, a LIFO method of valuation would adequately describe the expenditure necessary to maintain capital.

Moreover, this method does not allow users to predict the price and quantity relationship between input and output. The problem arises because the change in the input price of an asset will undoubtedly change the quantity of the asset demanded by a firm unless there is a corresponding change in the output price. Using the example just given, the current cost or replacement cost model will be valid for predicting cash flow relationships only if the output price remains at $11.00. Only then will the current replacement cost of $5.50 adequately measure the input-output relationship. But in that case, the firm probably will change its investment in inventories or assets in general. The assumptions built into the current cost replacement prediction models are stable prices from here on and no change in the mix of assets. To the extent that these assumptions are unrealistic, the prediction model itself is unrealistic. This problem is even aggravated further in the case of longer life assets where the implied prediction of no change in prices is even less realistic than in the case of current assets.

Note that from a balance sheet perspective, the weaknesses of replacement cost accounting loom even larger. If existing assets cost more to replace than their original acquisition cost, an "unrealized gain" results under replacement cost accounting. It is at best difficult to see how a higher projected cash outflow to replace existing assets results in a gain, realized or unrealized.

An alternative to the current cost method is the adjustment of historical costs by changes in the general price level. This method, however, possesses all the deficiencies of the current cost method and adds a further flaw. That flaw is the reliance on the general price level. Since a firm generally does not invest in an economy's market basket, there is little likelihood that such figures will predict either the level or the value of cash generation. Furthermore, users are able to create satisfactory price-level adjusted statements from conventional statements with little trouble.[2] The cost of preparing price-level statements therefore, is probably not justified by the benefits.

---

[2] Sidney Davidson and Roman L. Weil, "Inflation Accounting: What Will General Price-Level Adjusted Income Statements Show?" Financial Analysts Journal, January-February 1975.

Something useful is added, however, by exit values, the fourth of the valuation methods dealt with in this paper. They help in predicting future cash inflows from assets that are held for sale and in modifying and updating cash inflow projections. But for assets not held for sale, exit values are irrelevant as such. And, unless supplemented by other information, they are deficient for more general prediction of cash flows. In an exit value income statement, the gross profit number will approximate zero because the cost of goods sold at exit value will be essentially identical to revenues. Therefore, they are not directly helpful for assessing the extent to which cash inflows will result from a given level of cash outflows.

To see these points more clearly, note that, most broadly, current values of assets and liabilities quantify probable cash flows contingent on management's decisions to sell or purchase the assets. Exit values are thus a subset. They constitute probable cash inflows contingent on management's decision to sell the assets. Replacement costs, on the other hand, quantify probable cash outflows contingent on the decision of management to buy replacements for the assets. In fact, the net cash outflows of asset replacement depends on both exit values and replacement costs. The net cash outflow resulting from replacement is the total replacement cost (total cash outflow) less the exit value of the replaced asset (the cash inflow). Both methods are therefore useful for constructing adequate forecasts. Neither is sufficient alone.

Clearly, current values of existing assets and liabilities constitute only some of the probable cash flows. A major portion of cash flows is generated by the operating cycle through the purchase of inputs and sale of outputs, as reported in the fund flow statements. Nevertheless, current values represent sufficient proportion of cash flows to merit collection and dissemination.[3]

Furthermore, financial statements based on any of these methods (including historical cost) do not provide in themselves adequate measures of performance. For instance, under replacement cost or exit value bases, should uncontrollable exogenous changes of these values be considered as reflections on management performance to the extent that they affect income? The deficiency of historical cost accounting as a barometer of performance are of course well known. Thus, as in prediction, while each method provides some valid data which might be used in assessing performance, none can be significant in itself.

Given the strengths and weaknesses of the various valuation methods discussed above, the challenge appears to combine and supplement them in a manner that impounds the strengths of each of the methods, overcomes some of their deficiencies and at the same time minimizes implementation costs.

A Price Deviation Reporting Scheme

We would like to assert two propositions, and use the balance of the paper to explore them. The two propositions are:

(1) the major advantage of applying current value quantification lies in its potential for providing a record of price deviations. Price deviations represent inputs for improving the prediction of cash flows and the assessment of the probabilities of their occurrence.

(2) current values, properly stated, can be useful for predicting probable cash flows and as means for assessing the reliability of forecasts.

---

3. That is, benefits derived from the information are likely to exceed the costs of supplying it. It is noteworthy that the current valuation yields information on probable cash flows but also yields data regarding some of the risk aspects associated with these flows. See, for example, the discussion by Ronen and Sorter in "Relevant Accounting," The Journal of Business, April, 1972, of the role of exit values in providing some measures of risk.

<u>It is the authors' recommendation that the historical record provided by the historical cost valuations be maintained but that both inflows and outflows (i.e., revenues and expenses) be broken down in terms of price and quantity changes.</u>

As alternatives to the proposals currently under consideration, we suggest the following three stages:

1. The first is to improve transactions-based accounting reports by segregating quantity and price dimensions in the statement of changes in financial position (fund statement).

2. The second stage is to segregate quantity and price dimensions of transactions-based data in the income statement and in the balance sheet.

3. The third stage will be to extend the quantity-price segregation beyond transactions data to additionally reflect price changes from the date of transaction to the financial statement date.

Cash flows are obviously determined both by external factors, over which management has no control, and by internal factors, over which it presumably has control. Among external factors are interest rates, overall levels of demand and supply, and exchange rates. These factors may be predicted by relying on market expectations as a whole as reflected in market prices. Management's subjective estimate of this entire set of external factors is an element in the decision-making process and influences the choice of actions taken. These actions, together with the external events that interact with them, determine the probable future cash flows and the uncertainties associated with them.[4]

Management therefore could and probably should explicitly state its assumptions and expectations about the external factors. In other words, it should provide forecasts of cash flows that are conditional on different assumptions. Users could then evaluate the assumptions and make adjustments if necessary in the forecasts for their own decision-making purposes. The breakdown of the forecasts to differentiate the different kinds of factors--those relating to the economy as a whole as distinct from those peculiar to the firm--would help the users of the financial statements to improve their predictive ability. It also would improve their ability to evaluate managerial predictive ability as distinct from performance ability.

Among the significant noncontrollable events likely to influence decisions and to interact with them in producing probable cash consequences, are changes in prices of assets and liabilities. For example, expected prospective changes in prices are likely to affect asset purchase and sale decisions and also their timing, thus affecting the probable future cash flows contingent on these actions. Past changes in prices are also likely to be used as an input in the forecast of prospective changes. These, too, constitute a relevant noncontrollable event that might influence future managerial decisions and also future cash flows.

---

4. The so-called expected-value decision-making model provides one framework within which that noncontrollable events can be seen to influence the decisions that jointly with the events produce cash consequences. Of course, other more sophisticated models could also be used, such as SEU (subjective expected utility model) or NASEU (non-additive subjective expected utility model). Suffice it to say at this point that regardless of which model is chosen as a framework, noncontrollable events interact with the actions taken (and which are influenced by the estimate of noncontrollable events and their probabilities) to produce probable cash consequences.

The nature and consequences of the interaction between changes in current value and decision-making can be illustrated by supposing that management were to provide a detailed probability distribution of future cash flows.[5] Clearly, one of the probable actions by management is to sell existing assets and purchase new ones. The current values of the assets that will thus be sold or purchased will reflect some of the probable streams of expected cash flows. In other words, the current values would quantify some of the points of such a probability distribution.

The same general effect occurs also in the case of the current values of short-term assets and liabilities. The market values of these assets and liabilities reflect some of the cash flows associated with the firm's operations. These include the short-run cash flows generated, on the one hand, by the sale of inventory and the collection of accounts receivable and, on the other hand, by the cash purchase of raw materials and supplies and the discharge of current liabilities to suppliers of inputs.[6]

Current values are thus a reflection of probable cash flows. Moreover, there is a relatively high probability of occurrence of these cash

---

5. In a world of uncertainty, direct forecasts of cash flows are provided in the form of probability distributions. Management would probably feel most comfortable in providing a discrete proability distribution. However, it is not unreasonable to ask management to specify a probability density function of cash flows through responses to a set of questions with respect to the main parameters of the probability function, i.e., mean and variance. In this fashion, the resulting probability distribution of cash flows in the form of present values could be presented.

6. One of the major disadvantages of current values as surrogates is that their usefulness is limited to the near-horizon sufficient for the conversion of current assets and current liabilities into cash. Current values as surrogates will not reflect the contribution of prospective operating cycles on cash flows.

flows, if and when the appropriate decisions are made by management either to sell assets or incur liabilities (for cash inflows) or to purchase assets or discharge the liabilities (for cash outflows). Since these values reflect a consensus of market transactors resulting from supply and demand forces on these cash flows, they are apt to be more reliable than estimates made by a single individual or individuals such as firm's management.[7] The sources for generating information on current values are generally external to the firm. This facilitates independent verification, which, as auditors are well aware, permits a greater degree of reliability to be attached to quantifications.

Research on efficient markets indicates that available information in a market is generally impounded in market prices of securities or other capital assets. For example, fluctuations in the price of the firm's output reflect anticipated changes in demand that is a relevant exogenous factor affecting the firm. Similarly, fluctuations in the market price of inputs would reflect expectations about changing conditions in the supplying industry and in the industries of competing inputs. The market price therefore best reflects the effects of relevant external factors on the firm, although publicly available internal information would also be reflected.

Improved assessment of managerial performance as well as improved prediction of cash flows will result if the data are broken down into distinct and homogeneous components that enable the user to identify the effects of different kinds of events and factors. This will yield better results than working with aggregate figures, as a simple illustration will show.

Suppose we wish to predict the future gross margin of a firm. This can be done in two ways. First, we can analyze the past time series of

---

[7]For a discussion of this particular aspect in more detail and its relationship to the role of exit values as measures of risk, see Ronen and Sorter, op. cit.

gross margin itself, which is the aggregate approach. Or, noting that the gross margin consists of sales inflow (or revenue) minus sales outflow (or cost of goods sold), we can analyze each of these past time series separately.

Clearly, the second method of prediction is superior because the two factors are subject to different economic forces. Sales inflow responds to the underlying demand for the firm's output, whereas sales outflow is influenced by supply factors affecting the firm's inputs. The separate analysis and forecasting of the two disaggregated series should produce a more accurate result than that resulting from the use of the gross margin series, which does not offer the opportunity to distinguish among the different forces at work but lumps them together.

The same approach can be used in developing data for the forecast of probable cash flows resulting from changes in assets and liabilities in general. Again, two components can be identified in the generation of cash inflow contingent on the sale of assets. The first is quantity, a function presumably controllable by management. The second is price, which is determined by external factors such as market supply and demand equilibrium and is not within management's control.

Providing separate series of price and quantity data will aid in meaningful assessments of management performance and in making more sophisticated predictions. The prediction of quantity changes will be based on the assessment of probable managerial decisions regarding purchase and sale of assets analyzed in terms of the relationships of past changes in quantity and price.

An arbitrary base year is chosen and when an asset is purchased, two separate series of data are established. One will reflect the base year prices and the other will reflect the difference between that and actual transaction price. In stage II the result would be an actual record of (1) base-year prices quantification of all assets and liabilities, providing the quantity dimension, and (2) all price deviations between the base prices and transaction prices, providing the price dimension. In the third stage, the price series would be updated to include price changes between transaction dates and current dates.

The two distinct and separated series will provide the means to attain a superior ability to analyze the series and to predict future cash flows contingent on changes in assets and liabilities. Moreover, <u>the separation allows an improved assessment of managerial ability to predict and to perform</u>. Comparing changes in quantity and price allows the assessment of the degree to which external uncontrollable price changes influence managerial decisions to change the quantity of the assets and liabilities.

Price and quantity distinctions should be used to modify the fund statement. In many respects, the fund statement is the most rational vehicle for reflecting the impact of price changes because it shows homogeneous current dollars to start with (if inventory is not defined as a fund item). Adjusting the fund statement would start with adjusted funds provided by operations. To assess the significance of this figure in comparison with past statements, the nominal uses of funds for inventory, plant and equipment, and dividends would be converted into real dollar equivalents. Inventory would be deflated by a specific price index derived from actual transaction data of the particular firm; plant and equipment, by an index appropriate for this category derived from actual firm data as discussed above; and dividends, by a general price level deflator. In addition, the fund statement should disclose material and plant equipment usage in base year and in current terms.

The advantages of our proposal are in reflecting price-quantity deviations in financial statements, including especially the fund statement. Compared to alternative proposals, this method has the advantage of being based, at least in its first two stages, on actual transactions data without suggesting that the difficult problem of changing prices can be solved in terms of a new and improved magic income number based on current cost or price-level adjusted indices. Such single numbers, in any event, are necessarily illusory. No single magic number will be adequate for assessing managerial performance and for prediction. Thus, the thrust of our proposal, rather than replacing one inadequate aggregate measure with another, more costly one, is to disaggregate the available data into relevant dimensions (such as quantity and price, controllable and noncontrollable, factual and interpretive), that allow users to more effectively evaluate management performance and predict future performance.

REFLECTING THE IMPACT OF PRICE CHANGES AND INFLATION IN FINANCIAL STATEMENTS

George H. Sorter and Joshua Ronen

Reflecting the Impact of Price Changes and Inflation in Financial Statements: An Application

G. H. Sorter and J. Ronen

INTRODUCTION

In a recent working paper prepared for this committee, we suggest a scheme to make financial statements meaningful in a period of severe inflation and widely fluctuating prices. The suggested scheme is rather different from traditional proposals advanced by the Financial Accounting Standards Board and the SEC addressed to the same problem. Basically, our proposal consists of disaggregating all items of the fund statement into a quantity and price dimension. For example, sales would be decomposed into two parts: 1) a quantity dimension measured by deflating sales in current dollars into prices of an arbitrarily selected base year and 2) a price dimension measured by the difference between current sales revenue and sales revenue deflated into base year prices.

This allows presentation of all funds statement items in terms of current and base year dollars. It also allows analysts and other concerned decision makers to trace the actual price changes encountered by a firm for both inputs (costs) and outputs (revenues). We also suggest following the same procedure of disaggregation into quantity and price dimensions for all income statement items. In this paper we apply our proposed scheme to two divisions of a multinational manufacturing concern which we here entitle the Alpha Manufacturing Company. We present and interpret the resulting fund and income statements and indicate briefly certain policy implications for analysts and tax authorities.

THE ALPHA MANUFACTURING COMPANY DIVISIONS A AND B

To implement our proposal, we selected two independent operating units of a large manufacturing company. The criteria for selection were the relative size of units, the relative homogeneity of each unit's operation, and distinct differences between the types of operations of the two units. We wanted two operating units within the same company in order to attain a reasonable degree of comparability. We wanted distinctly different independent units, however, so that the results would not depend to a significant degree on the nature of particular operations. The first unit (Division A) engages in continuous processing of products designed primarily for industrial use for specific customer's orders as well as for inventory. The second unit (Division B) manufactures specialized equipment for industrial use. Its operations are diverse and, unlike the first unit, it does not generally produce equipment for inventory, but only for specific orders, typically of large amounts.

Below we briefly describe the procedures for applying the price deviation reporting scheme to the fund and income statements for the years 1973, 1974, and 1975. Both units follow generally accepted accounting principles and finance their operating fund requirements through retained earnings and advances from the parent company.

PROCEDURES UTILIZED

Most of the data for making the desired adjustment to the fund and income statements were readily available. The accounting systems for each unit included schedules of fixed assets and their retirements, showing date of purchase, purchase price, and accumulated depreciation. Also available was a breakdown of materials and parts purchases by major categories.

In choosing a base year, we would theoretically have taken the earliest date on which any equipment retired in the last three years—1973, 1974, and 1975—was purchased. We selected the year 1967 as the base year for two reasons. First, this year was determined to be the appropriate year for Division A, and our wish was to make the adjusted statement for the two units comparable. We therefore decided to select the same year for unit B. Second, purchases of equipment prior to 1967 were relatively minor. The prices prevailing in 1967 with respect to plant equipment and inventory, whose changes are reflected in the fund statements, were used as a base of 100 percent. Indexes for the years 1973, 1974, and 1975 were then developed to reflect the price increases due to inflation in each of the three years relative to 1967.

The price deviations for sales and purchases were generally available from internal accounting records utilized for management reporting and/or from statistics developed to satisfy the requirements of the Wage and Price Control Council. In those few instances where these were not available, appropriate indexes based on the Bureau of Labor Statistics wholesale price index were developed. Price deviations for major equipment purchases were developed from internal records and engineering department analysis of quality and technology changes. For other equipment purchased, as well as for building and building improvements, furniture and fixtures, and so on, the relevant code indexes of the Bureau of Labor Statistics were utilized. In each instance, the actual figures have been adjusted by a constant in order to disguise the involved companies.

INTERPRETATION OF THE RESULTING FINANCIAL STATEMENT

1. The Funds Statements

The funds statements for the years 1973, 1974, and 1975 for Division A are presented in Exhibit I-A, and for Division B in Exhibit I-B. The first four columns of these Exhibits relate to the year 1973. The next seven columns describe the year 1974, while the last seven columns relate to 1975. For each of the years, the first column presents the data in that year's prices. The second column of the first year, and the third column of the succeeding two years present the data in base year (1967) dollars. The third and fourth columns of the 1973 report, and the fifth and sixth columns of the 1974 and 1975 reports show the difference between the current and base year amounts—i.e., the price changes since 1967 in dollars and as a percentage of the base year amount. Columns two and four of the 1974 and 1975 show the percent change of the statistics in the preceding column from their counterparts in the previous year computed using the latter as a base, while the seventh column of years 1974 and 1975 show the percentage change in price per unit relative to the previous year.

The internally generated funds in current dollars are converted to 1967 purchasing power equivalent. The exact steps are described in more detail below, but in a nutshell the internal funds are deflated by an index based on the price changes encountered by the firm itself in its fund requirements. This 1967 purchasing power equivalent is then compared to fund requirements in 1967 dollars.

Finally, the statistical data show consumption of inventory (cost of goods sold) and consumption of plant and equipment in terms of (a) retirement and (b) depreciation, both in current and base year dollars. As will be seen below, these statistics can then be compared to the actual purchases made in base year dollars to measure the maintenance of capital in physical terms, or can be used to assess the ability to maintain capital by comparing them with the funds provided in terms of 1967 purchasing power.

2. The Income Statements

Exhibit II-A shows the income statement prepared in a similar fashion for Department A, and Exhibit II-B the income statement for Department B. The columns are identical with the fund statement columns and the rows are self-explanatory, with the exception of the final figure, which represents current income in 1967 purchasing power by using the same deflator utilized in the fund statement.

To better discuss and interpret the data, the highlights of the fund and income statements of Division A are presented below for the years 1973 and 1974.

3. Highlights of the Two Statements

For 1973 internally generated funds were $93,966. Of this total, $19,206, or 26 percent, represented price changes since 1967. In other words, if there had been no price changes in either sales inflows or operating expenses since 1967, and the physical level of operation was at the 1973 level, internally generated funds would have been $74,760. This is the amount shown in the 1967 column for 1973.

The actual funds used for purchases of inventory, manufacturing services, plant and equipment, and dividends were $89,690. Had there been no price changes in these items since 1967, the identical physical volume of purchases made in 1973 would have cost $70,484. Thus the price change in these items since 1967

ALPHA MANUFACTURING COMPANY
DIVISION A
HIGHLIGHTS
1973

	(1)	(2)	(3)	(4)
FUND STATEMENT HIGHLIGHTS			PRICE CHANGE SINCE 1967	
	1973 $	1967 $	$	%
INTERNALLY GENERATED FUNDS	93966	74760	19206	26
FUND USES	89690	70484	19206	27
EXCESS (DEFICIENCY) OF INTERNALLY GENERATED FUNDS	4276	4276	0	0
GENERATED FUNDS IN 1967 PURCHASING POWER UNITS	93966			
	x.7810			
	73839			
LESS FUND USES IN 1967 DOLLARS	70484			
	3355			
STATISTICAL DATA:				
CONSUMPTION OF INVENTORY	88902	70098		
CONSUMPTION OF PLANT & EQUIPMENT				
(a) RETIREMENTS	354	348		
(b) DEPRECIATION	2486	2340		
INCOME STATEMENT HIGHLIGHTS				
NET SALES	103556	81286	22270	27
TOTAL EXPENSES	101262	79198	22064	28
INCOME	2294	2088	206	10
	x 78%			
INCOME IN 1967 PURCHASING POWER UNITS	1789			

ALPHA MANUFACTURING COMPANY
DIVISION A—HIGHLIGHTS 1974

	(1)	(2)	(3)	(4)	(5)	(6)	(7)
		INCREASE (DECREASE) FROM 1973		INCREASE (DECREASE) FROM 1973	PRICE CHANGE SINCE 1967		PRICE PER UNIT CHANGE SINCE 1973
FUND STATEMENT	1974 $	%	1967 $	%	$	%	
INTERNALLY GENERATED FUNDS	132968	42	81164	9	51804	64	30
FUND USES	133110	48	88396	25	44714	51	18
EXCESS (DEFICIENCY)OF INTERNALLY GENERATED FUNDS	(142)	(103)	(7232)	(269)			
GENERATED FUNDS IN 1967 PURCHASING POWER UNITS	132968						
	x.6690						
	88301						
LESS: FUND USES IN 1967 DOLLARS	88340						
	(95)						
STATISTICAL DATA:							
CONSUMPTION OF INVENTORY	115544	76404					
CONSUMPTION OF PLANT & EQUIP.							
(a) RETIREMENTS	198	98					
(b) DEPRECIATION	3342	3182					
INCOME STATEMENT							
NET SALES	144140	39	88738	9	55402	62	28
TOTAL EXPENSES	135800	34	86344	9	49456	57	23
INCOME	8340	264	2394	15	5946	248	217
	x.6690						
INCOME IN 1967 PURCHASING POWER UNITS	5504						

amounted to $19,206, or a 27 percent price rise. The net result, had there been no price changes since 1967 in any of the factors, is therefore that an excess of $4,276 1967 dollars would have been generated. An amount by coincidence exactly equal to the $4,276 dollars of 1973 dollars was actually generated.

Thus, superficially, one might conclude that, since the price effect on generation of funds was equal or approximately equal to the price effect on the use of funds, the company was neither harmed nor benefited through inflation. However, that would not be correct since the dollars generated in 1973 do not have the purchasing power that 1967 dollars had.

To measure this effect, we deflate the 1973 generated funds by 78 percent. This percentage is computed by dividing $70,484, the 1973 fund uses in 1967 dollars by $89,690, the 1973 fund uses in current dollars. This procedure was followed in order to reflect the deterioration in the power to purchase an "average basket" of fund uses as reflected in the average composition of fund uses over the three years;and the composition of the 1973 fund uses approximates closely this average. This calculation has the effect of showing that inflation had a minimal but adverse effect on the firm, since in 1967 purchasing power units, the excess of funds provided over requirements is only $3,355 rather than the $4,276 that would have been generated in the absence of these changes.

The statistical data provide additional insights concerning the adequacy of fund generation for maintaining capital intact. They show the consumption of inventory (cost of goods sold) in current and 1967 dollars and two measures of equipment consumption. One is depreciation, which quantifies the services of plant and equipment on the basis of their usage time. The second shows retirements, which reflect the lessened capacity of property. Whenever funds used in 1967 dollars are less than consumption measured in 1967 dollars, capital is not being maintained, and whenever funds provided in 1967 purchasing power are less than consumption in 1967 dollars, operations are not generating sufficient funds to maintain capital intact.

Overall, this analysis reflects that fund generation is barely sufficient to maintain capital intact in real terms. That is, using depreciation as a measure of minimal capital replacement, total necessary "real" outlays ($70,098 plus $348 plus $2,340) come perilously close to the "real" value of internally generated funds $73,839.

A similar picture emerges from the income statement highlights for 1973, shown below. Price increases since 1967 were 28 percent. The resulting income figure in 1973 dollars, $2,294, is larger than it would have been had there been no price or cost increases (when income would have been $2,088). However, the net price effect of ten percent on income is clearly not sufficient to compensate for the increases of 27 percent in the prices of inventory and plant and equipment. Thus the expansion potential of the firm is less than if there had been no price changes. This potential is obtained by deflating the nominal 1973 income by the effect of the 27 percent price rise in the uses of funds. It shows that in "real" (that is, 1967) dollars the reported income has the power to add capacity or pay dividends of only $1,789. This figure, when compared to the $2,088 of income in 1967 dollars, reflects the adverse effect of net price changes since 1967.

A totally different picture emerges for 1974. If we look at the table below, we see that in 1974 the price effects become favorable for Division A. Internally generated funds increase by 42 percent (column 2) due to a volume increase of 8 percent (column 4) and a price increase of 30 percent (column 7). (The two variances will not sum to the total percent change because of the joint volume/price effect.) For the funds uses, however, the price variance is only 18 percent, while the volume increase is 25 percent, to combine for a 48 percent increase in funds used. Had there been no price changes in <u>either</u> inflows or outflows since 1967, there would have been a deficiency of $7,232 funds provided by operations (column 3). Because of price changes, however, the actual deficiency in 1974 dollars is $142. In 1974 dollars adjusted for 1967 purchasing power units, it is $95 (column 2). These results are explained by the fact that, since 1967, inflow price increases were 64 percent, while the outflow price rise was only 51 percent.

A similar picture of net gain from price changes is conveyed by the highlights from the 1974 income statement of Division A. Revenue increased by 39 percent from the year before, but the physical output of sales increased by only 9 percent, and the majority of the revenue increase was due to a price change of 28 percent. Total expenses in physical terms also increased by 9 percent, exactly the change in physical volume of output. However, the cost increases were only 23 percent. The net effect on income was a 264 percent increase over 1973, of which only 15 percent was caused by increased volume, and the rest by a 217 percent favorable bottom line price effect. The income statement also reflects the favorable cumulative effect of price changes during 1974 and since 1967. Had prices not changed for either revenues or expenses since 1967, income would have been $2,394. In fact, it actually was $8,340, which, when adjusted for post-1967 purchasing power losses, amounted to $5,504.

A detailed analysis along similar lines of 1975 for Division A and for all years of Division B is left to the reader. (Exhibit I-B displays the fund statement for Division B, and Exhibit II-B contains the income statement for Division B.)

CONCLUSIONS AND IMPLICATIONS

The results support our original contention on the utility of statements constructed on these lines. With basic disaggregation of the data into quantity and price dimension, the analyst can trace the ability of a firm to adjust prices of outputs in response to changing prices of inputs. The analyst can also compare outputs and inputs, revenues and expenses, and funds provided and funds used, not only in overall dollar terms, but also in terms of physical quantities. Since price and quantity changes are not equally controllable by management nor equally predictable, this allows a more informed judgment of management skill and actions, and also provides a more effective predictive tool. The advantages of the proposed reporting scheme, however, do not stop there. The data thus produced can effectively be used for taxation policy. It can probably be convincingly argued that better-offness or income is the ability to expand and/or to pay dividends in real terms. This datum is in fact provided by the purchasing power adjusted income. Additionally, a further loss and tax deduction may be computed to the extent that purchasing power adjusted funds provided by operations are less than total consumption of inventory and plant in real dollars. It would also be possible with this scheme to identify gains or losses from price changes which might equitably be taxed at a different rate from that applied to other gains or losses.

Further, by utilizing the same base year for constructing financial statements indexes as is utilized for national economic indexes, a close integration of company and national income reports and analysis of each is made possible.

Compared with other suggested schemes reflecting the impact of inflation on financial statements, our proposed method seems to have three obvious advantages. First, our scheme provides additional useful information—namely, the price-quantity disaggregation and the adjusted fund statement.

Second, the information here provided is more relevant and understandable in terms of a specific firm being reported on. The reports show actual flows and what they would have been without price changes, and then as a separate calculation presents the net flows adjusted for actual purchasing power changes that this firm experienced. General-price-level-adjusted statements have no assignable meaning for a particular firm, while current cost statements ignore the quantity changes induced by price changes, which, as our Exhibits show, clearly do occur.

Nor do current-cost-adjusted statements provide for a meaningful comparison between outflows and inflows. The current cost of plant and equipment, for example, will produce inflows for the next 20 years. Further, not all of the plant will be replaced in this time period at currently prevailing prices; much will be replaced in the future at prices then prevailing, which fact introduces present value, i.e., discounting problems, as well as expected price change considerations.

Third, and perhaps most important, however, is the fact that our scheme does not deal with "as if" accounting—that is, with what the plant or the inventory would cost at current prices. This "as if" accounting is currently producing horrendous implementation problems. Our reports are more easily understandable and interpretable and much less costly. Since most if not all of our adjustment deals with data and events, the information is or should be available in a sophisticated cost accounting system. Therefore the cost of implementing our scheme should be minimal when compared to alternatives. In conclusion, it seems to us that our proposal provides more information in a less ambiguous manner at less cost than other suggestions. Therefore it should merit further consideration.

EXHIBIT I-A
ALPHA MANUFACTURING COMPANY
DIVISION A—FUND STATEMENTS
1973
(000's omitted)

	(1)	(2)	(3) PRICE CHANGE SINCE 1967	(4)
	1973 $	1967 $	$ (1-2)	% (3÷2)
INTERNALLY GENERATED FUNDS: SALES	103554	81554	22268	27
LESS EXPENSES REQUIRING FUNDS (EXCLUDING COST OF GOODS SOLD)	9588	6526	3062	47
	93966	74760	19206	26
FUND USES				
PURCHASE OF INVENTORY	88078	69236	18842	27
PURCHASE OF PLANT & EQUIPMENT	1612	1248	364	29
DIVIDENDS	0	0		
TOTAL FUND USES	89690	70484	19206	27
NET EXCESS (DEFICIENCY) OF INTERNALLY GENERATED FUNDS	4276	4276	0	
GENERATED FUNDS IN CURRENT DOLLARS (SEE ABOVE)	93966 x 78%			
GENERATED FUNDS IN 1967 PURCHASING POWER UNITS	73839			
LESS FUND USES IN 1967 DOLLARS	(70484)			
EXCESS (DEFICIENCY) OF INTERNALLY GENERATED FUNDS IN 1967 PURCHASING POWER UNITS	3355			
STATISTICAL DATA FOR COMPARISON:				
CONSUMPTION OF INVENTORY	88962	70098		
CONSUMPTION OF PLANT & EQUIP.				
(a) RETIREMENTS	354	348		
(b) DEPRECIATION	2486	2340		

EXHIBIT I-A
ALPHA MANUFACTURING COMPANY
DIVISION A—FUND STATEMENTS
1974
(000's omitted)

	(1)	(2)	(3)	(4)	(5)	(6)	(7)
		% INCREASE (DECREASE) FROM 1973		% INCREASE (DECREASE) FROM 1973	PRICE CHANGE SINCE 1967		PRICE PER UNIT CHANGE SINCE 1973
	1974 $		1967 $		$	%	%
INTERNALLY GENERATED FUNDS: SALES	144140	39	88738	9	55402	62	28
LESS EXPENSES REQUIRING FUNDS (EXCLUDING COST OF GOODS SOLD)	11172	17	7574	16	3598	48	1
	132968	42	81164	9	51804	64	30
FUND USES							
PURCHASE OF INVENTORY	130548	48	86524	25	44024	51	19
PURCHASE OF PLANT & EQUIPMENT	2562	59	1872	50	690	37	6
DIVIDENDS	0		0				
TOTAL FUND USES	133110	48	88396	25	44714	51	18
NET EXCESS (DEFICIENCY) OF INTERNALLY GENERATED FUNDS	(142)	(103)	(7232)	(269)	7090		
GENERATED FUNDS IN CURRENT DOLLARS (SEE ABOVE)	132968 x 66%						
GENERATED FUNDS IN 1967 PURCHASING POWER UNITS	88301						
LESS FUND USES IN 1967 DOLLARS	(88396)						
EXCESS (DEFICIENCY) OF INTERNALLY GENERATED FUNDS IN 1967 PURCHASING POWER UNITS	(95)						
STATISTICAL DATA FOR COMPARISON:							
CONSUMPTION OF INVENTORY	115544		76404				
CONSUMPTION OF PLANT & EQUIP.							
(a) RETIREMENTS	198		98				
(b) DEPRECIATION	3342		3182				

EXHIBIT I-A
ALPHA MANUFACTURING COMPANY
DIVISION A—FUND STATEMENTS
1975
(000's omitted)

	(1)	(2)	(3)	(4)	(5)	(6)	(7)
	1975 $	% INCREASE (DECREASE) FROM 1974	1967 $	% INCREASE (DECREASE) FROM 1974	PRICE CHANGE SINCE 1967 $	%	PRICE PER UNIT CHANGE SINCE 1973 %
INTERNALLY GENERATED FUNDS: SALES	132908	(8)	74256	(16)	58652	79	10
LESS EXPENSES REQUIRING FUNDS (EXCLUDING COST OF GOODS SOLD)	12670	14	6068	(20)	6602	108	40
	120238	(10)	68188	(16)	52050	76	7
FUND USES							
PURCHASE OF INVENTORY	107914	(17)	59908	(31)	48006	80	19
PURCHASE OF PLANT & EQUIPMENT	3834	49	2328	24	1506	65	20
DIVIDENDS	0		0		0	0	
TOTAL FUND USES	111748	13	62236	(30)	49512	80	19
NET EXCESS (DEFICIENCY) OF INTERNALLY GENERATED FUNDS	8490		5952		36738		
GENERATED FUNDS IN CURRENT DOLLARS (SEE ABOVE)	120238 x 56%						
GENERATED FUNDS IN 1967 PURCHASING POWER UNITS	67333						
LESS FUND USES IN 1967 DOLLARS	(62236)						
EXCESS (DEFICIENCY) OF INTERNALLY GENERATED FUNDS IN 1967 PURCHASING POWER UNITS	(5047)						
STATISTICAL DATA FOR COMPARISON:							
CONSUMPTION OF INVENTORY	115754		65032				
CONSUMPTION OF PLANT & EQUIP.							
(a) RETIREMENTS	568		564				
(b) DEPRECIATION	2642		2388				

EXHIBIT I-B

ALPHA MANUFACTURING COMPANY

DIVISION A—FUND STATEMENTS

1973

(000's omitted)

	(1)	(2)	(3) PRICE CHANGE SINCE 1967	(4)
			$	%
	1973 $	1967 $	1-2	3÷2
INTERNALLY GENERATED FUNDS				
SALES	185130	134040	51090	38
LESS EXPENSES REQUIRING FUNDS (EXCLUDING COST OF GOODS SOLD)	39900	24480	15420	63
	145230	109560	36670	33
FUND USES				
PURCHASE OF INVENTORY	144090	101400	42690	42
PURCHASE OF PLANT AND EQUIPMENT	8280	6420	1860	29
DIVIDENDS	0	0	0	0
TOTAL FUND USES	152370	107820	44550	41
NET EXCESS (DEFICIENCY) OF INTERNALLY GENERATED FUNDS	(7140)	1740	(8880)	N.A.
GENERATED FUNDS IN CURRENT DOLLARS (SEE ABOVE)	145230			
	x.7190			
GENERATED FUNDS IN 1967 PURCHASING POWER UNITS	102767			
LESS FUND USES IN 1967 DOLLARS	(107820)			
EXCESS (DEFICIENCY) OF INTERNALLY GENERATED FUNDS IN 1967 PURCHASING POWER UNITS	(5053)			
STATISTICAL DATA FOR COMPARISON:				
CONSUMPTION OF INVENTORY	143040	101770		
CONSUMPTION OF PLANT AND EQUIPMENT				
(a) RETIREMENTS	30	30		
(b) DEPRECIATION	4590	3690		

EXHIBIT I-B
ALPHA MANUFACTURING COMPANY
DIVISION A—FUND STATEMENTS
1974
(000's omitted)

	(1) 1974 $	(2) INCREASE (DECREASE) FROM 1973 %	(3) 1967 $	(4) INCREASE (DECREASE) FROM 1973 %	(5) PRICE CHANGE SINCE 1973 $	(6) PRICE CHANGE SINCE 1973 %	(7) PRICE PER UNIT CHANGE SINCE 1973 %
INTERNALLY GENERATED FUNDS							
SALES	155280	(16)	86100	(36)	69180	80	30
LESS EXPENSES REQUIRING FUNDS (EXCLUDING COST OF GOODS SOLD)	32340	(19)	14520	(41)	17820	123	37
	122940	(15)	71580	(35)	51360	72	29
FUND USES							
PURCHASE OF INVENTORY	99480	(31)	55710	(45)	43770	79	26
PURCHASE OF PLANT & EQUIPMENT	6090	(26)	3750	(42)	2340	62	26
DIVIDENDS	0	0	0	0	0	0	0
TOTAL FUND USES	105570	(31)	59460	(45)	46110	78	26
NET EXCESS (DEFICIENCY) OF INTERNALLY GENERATED FUNDS	17370	N.A.	12120	N.A.	5250	43	N.A.
GENERATED FUNDS IN CURRENT DOLLARS (SEE ABOVE)	122940 x.5690						
GENERATED FUNDS IN 1967 PURCHASING POWER UNITS	68847						
LESS FUND USES IN 1967 DOLLARS	59460						
EXCESS (DEFICIENCY) OF INTERNALLY GENERATED FUNDS IN 1967 PURCHASING POWER UNITS	9387						
STATISTICAL DATA FOR COMPARISON:							
CONSUMPTION OF INVENTORY	98790		55650				
CONSUMPTION OF PLANT & EQUIP							
(a) RETIREMENTS	150		150				
(b) DEPRECIATION	3930		3360				

EXHIBIT I-B
ALPHA MANUFACTURING COMPANY
DIVISION A—FUND STATEMENTS
1975
(000's omitted)

	(1) 1975 $	(2) % INCREASE (DECREASE) FROM 1974	(3) 1967 $	(4) % INCREASE (DECREASE) FROM 1974	(5) PRICE CHANGE SINCE 1967 $	(6) %	(7) PRICE PER UNIT CHANGE SINCE 1973 %
INTERNALLY GENERATED FUNDS							
SALES	172980	11	85290	(1)	87690	103	13
LESS EXPENSES REQUIRING FUNDS (EXCLUDING COST OF GOODS SOLD)	49860	54	25080	72%	24780	98	(12)
	123120	0	60210	(16)	62910	104	19
FUND USES							
PURCHASE OF INVENTORY	99870	0	50490	(9)	49380	98	9
PURCHASE OF PLANT & EQUIPMENT	11730	92	5760	54	5970	104	26
DIVIDENDS	0	0	0	0	0	0	0
TOTAL FUND USES	111600	6	56250	(5)	55350	98	11
NET EXCESS (DEFICIENCY) OF INTERNALLY GENERATED FUNDS	11520	(34)	3960	(67)	(7560)	190	102
GENERATED FUNDS IN CURRENT DOLLARS (SEE ABOVE)	123120 x 51%						
GENERATED FUNDS IN 1967 PURCHASING POWER UNITS	62056						
LESS FUND USES IN 1967 DOLLARS	56250						
EXCESS (DEFICIENCY) OF INTERNALLY GENERATED FUNDS IN 1967 PURCHASING POWER UNITS	5806						
STATISTICAL DATA FOR COMPARISON:							
CONSUMPTION OF INVENTORY	97470		49710				
CONSUMPTION OF PLANT & EQUIP.							
(a) RETIREMENTS	60		60				
(b) DEPRECIATION	3420		3150				

EXHIBIT II-A
ALPHA MANUFACTURING COMPANY
DIVISION A
INCOME STATEMENT FOR 1973
IN CURRENT AND 1967 $

	(1) 1973 $	(2) 1967 $	(3) PRICE CHANGE SINCE 1967 (1-2)	(4) (3÷2)
GROSS SALES	113192	88852	24340	27
SALES DEDUCTIONS	(9636)	(7566)	2070	27
NET SALES	103556	81286	22270	27
COST OF GOODS SOLD				
RAW MATERIALS AND SUPPLIES	56442	48766	7676	16
LABOR AND EMPLOYEE BENEFITS	27564	17338	10226	59
OPERATING EXPENSE	3126	2420	706	29
REPAIRS AND MAINTENANCE	1482	1280	202	16
TAXES	1076	832	244	29
RENTS	76	58	18	31
DEPRECIATION	2486	2390	96	.4
	92252	73084	19168	26
ADD BEG. WIP AND FINISHED GOODS	2542	2254	288	13
DEDUCT END WIP AND FINISHED GOODS	(3344)	(2850)	494	17
COST OF GOODS SOLD	91448	72488	18960	26
GROSS PROFIT			3310	38
SG & A	7910	4976	2934	59
TOTAL EXPENSES	99358	77464	21894	28
INCOME FROM OPERATIONS	4198	3822	376	10
SPECIAL ITEMS	0	0	0	0
INCOME BEFORE TAXES	4198	3822	376	10
INCOME TAXES	1904	1734	170	10
INCOME AFTER TAXES	2294	2088	206	10
INCOME IN 1967 PURCHASING POWER UNITS	1789			

EXHIBIT II-A
ALPHA MANUFACTURING COMPANY
DIVISION A
INCOME STATEMENT FOR 1974
IN CURRENT AND 1967 $

	(1)	(2) %	(3)	(4) %	(5)	(6)	(7)
	1974 $	INCREASE (DECREASE) FROM 1973	1967 $	INCREASE (DECREASE) FROM 1973	PRICE CHANGE SINCE 1967 $	%	PRICE PER UNIT CHANGE SINCE 1973 %
GROSS SALES	155598	37	95792	8	59806	62	28
SALES DEDUCTIONS	11458	19	(7054)	7	4404	62	28
NET SALES	144140	39	88738	9	55402	62	28
COST OF GOODS SOLD							
RAW MATERIALS & SUPPLIES	77088	37	54348	11	22740	42	23
LABOR & EMPLOYEE BENEFITS	32776	19	17862	3	14914	46	15
OPERATING EXPENSE	3630	16	2360	(2)	1270	54	19
REPAIRS & MAINTENANCE	1628	10	1148	(10)	480	42	22
TAXES	1052	(2)	682	(18)	730	54	19
RENTS	182	139	118	103	64	54	18
DEPRECIATION	3342	34	3182	33	160	5	1
	119696	30	79700	9	39996	50	19
ADD BEG. WIP & FINISHED GOODS	3344	32	2850	26	494	17	4
DEDUCT END WIP & FINISHED GOODS	(4156)	24	(2964)	4	1192	40	120
COST OF GOODS SOLD	118884	30	79586	10	39300	49	19
GROSS PROFIT		109		4			
SG & A	9458	20	5154	4	4304	84	16
TOTAL EXPENSES	128342	29	84740	9	443602	51	18
INCOME FROM OPERATIONS	15798	276	3998	5	11800	295	260
SPECIAL ITEMS	0	0	0	0	0	0	0
INCOME BEFORE TAXES	15798	276	3998	5	11800	295	260
INCOME TAXES	7458	292	1604	7	5854	365	323
INCOME AFTER TAXES	8340	264	2394	15	5946	248	217
INCOME IN 1967 PURCHASING POWER UNITS	5504						

EXHIBIT II-A
ALPHA MANUFACTURING COMPANY
DIVISION A
INCOME STATEMENT FOR 1975
IN CURRENT AND 1967 $

	(1) 1975 $	(2) % INCREASE (DECREASE) FROM 1974	(3) 1967 $	(4) % INCREASE (DECREASE) FROM 1974	(5) PRICE CHANGE SINCE 1967 $	(6) PRICE CHANGE SINCE 1967 %	(7) PRICE PER UNIT CHANGE SINCE 1973 %
GROSS SALES	142400	(8)	79560	(17)	62840	79	10
SALES DEDUCTIONS	(9494)	(17)	5204	(24)	4190	79	10
NET SALES	132906	(8)	74256	(16)	58650	79	10
COST OF GOODS SOLD							
RAW MATERIALS & SUPPLIES	72994	(5)	43066	(21)	29928	69	19
LABOR & EMPLOYEE BENEFITS	33718	3	16184	(9)	17534	108	14
OPERATING EXPENSE	3648	1	2134	(10)	1514	71	11
REPAIRS & MAINTENANCE	2514	54	1458	27	1056	72	22
TAXES	1636	56	958	40	678	71	11
RENTS	192	5	112	(5)	80	71	11
DEPRECIATION	2642	(21)	2388	(24)	254	11	6
	117344	(2)	66300	(17)	51044	77	18
ADD BEG. WIP & FINISHED GOODS	4156	24	2964	4	1192	40	20
DEDUCT END WIP & FINISHED GOODS	(3044)	(27)	(1844)	(38)	1260	68	20
COST OF GOODS SOLD	118396	(1)	67420	(15)	50976	75	17
GROSS PROFIT	--						
SG & A	8898	(6)	4272	(17)	4626	108	13
TOTAL EXPENSES	127294	(1)	71692	(15)	55602	78	17
INCOME FROM OPERATIONS	5612	(65)	2564	(36)	3048	119	(44)
SPECIAL ITEMS	796	N.A.	466	N.A.	330	71	N.A.
INCOME BEFORE TAXES	6408	(59)	3030	(24)	3378	111	(46)
INCOME TAXES	2856	(62)	1350	(16)	1506	111	(55)
INCOME AFTER TAXES	3552	(57)	1680	(30)	1872	111	(33)
INCOME IN 1967 PURCHASING POWER UNITS	1984						

EXHIBIT II-B
ALPHA MANUFACTURING COMPANY
DIVISION B
INCOME STATEMENT FOR 1973
IN CURRENT AND 1967 $

	(1)	(2)	(3) PRICE CHANGE SINCE 1967	(4)
	1973 $	1967 $	$ (1-2)	% (3÷2)
GROSS SALES	179580	130020	49560	38
SALES DEDUCTIONS AND OTHER INCOME	5550	4020	1530	38
NET SALES	185130	134040	51090	38
COST OF GOODS SOLD				
RAW MATERIALS AND SUPPLIES	89070	66510	72520	34
LABOR AND EMPLOYEE BENEFITS	42840	26160	16680	64
OPERATING EXPENSE	7890	5880	2010	34
REPAIRS AND MAINTENANCE	1320	990	330	33
TAXES	2280	1380	900	65
RENTS	690	420	270	64
DEPRECIATION	3120	2880	240	8
	147210	104220	42990	41
ADD BDG. WIP AND FINISHED GOODS	2700	290	690	34
DEDUCT END WIP AND FINISHED GOODS	(3750)	(2280)	(1470)	64
COST OF GOODS SOLD	146160	103950	42210	41
GROSS PROFIT				
SG & A	38910	23760	15150	64
TOTAL EXPENSES	185070	127710	57360	45
INCOME FROM OPERATIONS	60	6330	(6270)	(99)
INCOME TAXES	(4890)	(3720)	(1770)	31
INCOME AFTER TAXES	4950	10050	5100	51
INCOME IN 1967 PURCHASING POWER UNITS	3514			

EXHIBIT II-B
ALPHA MANUFACTURING COMPANY
DIVISION B
INCOME STATEMENT FOR 1974
IN CURRENT AND 1967 $

	(1)	(2)	(3)	(4)	(5)	(6)	(7)
	1974 $	% INCREASE (DECREASE) FROM 1973	1967 $	% INCREASE (DECREASE) FROM 1973	PRICE CHANGE SINCE 1967 $	%	PRICE CHANGE SINCE 1973 %
GROSS SALES	148620	(17)	82410	(37)	66210	80	30
SALES DEDUCTIONS & OTHER INCOME	6660	20	3690	(8)	2970	80	30
NET SALES	155280	(16)	86100	(36)	69180	80	30
COST OF GOODS SOLD							
RAW MATERIALS & SUPPLIES	49680	(44)	29700	(55)	19980	67	25
LABOR & EMPLOYEE BENEFITS	42960	1	22260	(15)	20700	93	17
OPERATING EXPENSE	900	(88)	540	(91)	360	67	24
REPAIRS & MAINTENANCE	1380	5	840	(15)	540	64	23
TAXES	3810	67	1980	43	1830	92	16
RENTS	750	9	390	(7)	360	92	17
DEPRECIATION	3000	(4)	2850	(11)	450	18	9
	102480	(30)	58260	(44)	44220	76	24
ADD BEG. WIP & FINISHED GOODS	3750	38	2280	13	1470	64	22
DEDUCT END WIP & FINISHED GOODS	(4440)	18	(2310)	1	(2130)	92	17
COST OF GOODS SOLD	101790	(30)	58200	(44)	43590	75	24
GROSS PROFIT		37		(7)		91	47
SG & A	44340	14	22980	(3)	21360	93	17
TOTAL EXPENSES	146130	(21)	81180	(36)	64950	80	24
INCOME FROM OPERATIONS	9150	N.A.	4920	(22)	4320	86	
INCOME TAXES	1320	126	900	124	420	47	N.A.
INCOME AFTER TAXES	7830	58	4020	(60)	3810	95	195
INCOME IN 1967 PURCHASING POWER UNITS	4384	27					

EXHIBIT II-B
ALPHA MANUFACTURING COMPANY
DIVISION B
INCOME STATEMENT FOR 1975
IN CURRENT AND 1967 $

	(1) 1974 $	(2) % INCREASE (DECREASE) FROM 1974	(3) 1967 $	(4) % INCREASE (DECREASE) FROM 1974	(5) PRICE CHANGE SINCE 1967 $	(6) PRICE CHANGE SINCE 1967 %	(7) PRICE CHANGE SINCE 1974 %
GROSS SALES	164100	10	80910	(2)	83190	103	13
SALES DEDUCTIONS & OTHER INCOME	8880	33	4380	19	4500	103	13
NET SALES	172980	11	85290	(1)	87690	103	13
COST OF GOODS SOLD							
RAW MATERIALS & SUPPLIES	51810	4	28110	(5)	23700	84	10
LABOR & EMPLOYEE BENEFITS	43320	1	20070	(10)	23250	116	12
OPERATING EXPENSE	--		--		--		
REPAIRS & MAINTENANCE	1620	17	870	4	750	86	13
TAXES	2520	(34)	1170	(41)	1350	115	12
RENTS	600	(20)	270	(31)	330	122	16
DEPRECIATION	3600	20	2910	14	690	24	5
	103470	1	53480	(8)	50070	94	10
ADD BEG. WIP & FINISHED GOODS	4440	18	2310	1	2130	92	17
DEDUCT END WIP & FINISHED GOODS	(6840)	54	(3180)	38	3660	115	12
COST OF GOODS SOLD	101070	(1)	52620	(10)	48450	92	9
GROSS PROFIT		34			39240	120	15
SG & A	41700	(6)	19320	(16)	22380	116	12
TOTAL EXPENSES	142770	(2)	71940	(11)	70830	98	10
INCOME FROM OPERATIONS	30210	230	13350	171	16860	126	22
INCOME TAXES	11490	770	7320	713	4170	57	7
INCOME AFTER TAXES	18720	139	6030	50	12690	210	59
INCOME IN 1967 PURCHASING POWER UNITS	9547	114					

CONCLUSION

Conclusion

This volume emphasized the need for and the possibility of providing relevant and useful financial information. This purpose is now of greater than academic interest as evidenced by the increasing attention placed on accounting and accounting reports not only by analysts and accountants, but also by governmental agencies, both legislative houses of the Congress and a Royal Commission of England. Although, "Relevant Accounting" was published in 1972, before the development of the objectives of financial statements, the establishment of the FASB, the increased disclosure requirements of the SEC and the somewhat radical conclusions of the Sandilands Commission, in the main we feel that the central theme of "Relevant Accounting" has been validated, confirmed and in fact, reinforced by these and other events. The central disclosures recommended in "Relevant Accounting" such as current values, forecasts by management, the comparison of these forecasts with actual events, presenting information helpful for the assessment of risk, are all, in one way or another, relevant for the problems and concerns to which recent disclosure requirements and quests for additional disclosures are addressed.

Now, five years later, although the central theme emphasized by "Relevant Accounting" is reinforced by current events, we feel that certain extensions and elaborations on that theme are appropriate. Some of these extensions and elaborations are obvious from the content of this volume. Additional ones are implied by events of today. As evidenced by the last two papers presented, we believe today that the financial statements suggested by relevant accounting should in addition (a) include a fund statement and (b) provide disaggregation of historical quantifications into price and quantity dimensions. This is a natural extension of the emphasis in "Relevant Accounting" on differentiations between exogenous and endogenous factors and the implied necessity to disaggregate information to provide measures for appropriately assessing both. In line with this, we recommend that the historical cost columns, both expected and actual be disaggregated into price-quantity dimensions. Furthermore, we think that management forecasts on which the economic value columns are based, should also be disaggregated in terms of quantity and price dimensions. The price and quantity dimensions embedded in management expectations would then be compared with actual events to produce a disaggregated series of deviations broken down in terms of price and quantity.

The papers included in this volume clearly recognize that we are living in an uncertain world characterized by heterogeneous expectations and beliefs. Throughout, by advocating disaggregations, we reject the notion of simplistic, deterministic, uni-dimensional descriptions of relevant economic events as being inconsistent with our world. We reject simplicity under the general assumption that describing a complex world simplistically does not make it simpler. While our quest for disaggregations and multi-dimensionality should be tempered by the appropriate consideration of the costs involved, our concern for multi-dimensionality and disaggregated information was not arrived at without consideration of such costs. By and large, the disaggregations we call for seem to be less costly than the alternatives that either presently exist or are advocated. By and large, the disaggregations we call for are based on information that is routinely produced within the firm or is easily obtainable. In fact, precisely because we live in an uncertain world, disaggregations are helpful because they allow different users to use disaggregated information in making their assessments of the firm's uncertain prospects.

These considerations lead us to yet further elaborations consistent with but not explicitly dealt with in this volume. Chief among these elaborations would be the explicit consideration and reflection of uncertainty in financial statements. Probabilistic financial statements, more than ever before, now become meaningful and relevant. Tools need to be developed to explicitly incorporate probabilistic information in financial statements and furthermore to define and implement a system that derives deviations of actual events from forecasts. A meaningful system of developing and evaluating deviations needs to be developed. Such deviations should be helpful in assessing managerial ability to forecast, to perform and to lead to corrective action and control. Whether or not such information is provided, we need to reassess the audit function in the context of probabilistic financial statements. What is the auditor's role in attesting to financial statements that incorporate or imply uncertainty? Presently, uncertainty, while not explicitly acknowledged, is present in financial statements and auditors are very uncertain about how to deal with such uncertainty.

We are not deceived into a simplistic belief that this volume contains the solution to a difficult problem. We are mindful of the grave and complex issues related to concepts and implementations of meaningful accounting disclosure which these papers only help to bring into focus. We are fully mindful that these papers represent only a first step, an imperfect step, toward solving some very critical problems. If the first step were required to be the final step, it would be unlikely that any step would ever be taken. This is a time for taking risks in conducting research and suggesting alternatives; to cope with uncertainty, one must be willing to accept uncertainty, not only in the world, but in relation to one's own efforts. But to us the prize of helping to create financial statements that are relevant to and consistent with the world we live in, is worth the discomfort of dealing with uncertainty.

THE DEVELOPMENT OF CONTEMPORARY ACCOUNTING THOUGHT

An Arno Press Collection

Baldwin, H[arry] G[len]. **Accounting for Value As Well as Original Cost** *and* Castenholz, William B. **A Solution to the Appreciation Problem.** 2 Vols. in 1. 1927/1931

Baxter, William. **Collected Papers on Accounting.** 1978

Brief, Richard P., Ed. **Selections from Encyclopaedia of Accounting, 1903.** 1978

Broaker, Frank and Richard M. Chapman. **The American Accountants' Manual.** 1897

Canning, John B. **The Economics of Accountancy.** 1929

Chatfield, Michael, Ed. **The English View of Accountant's Duties and Responsibilities.** 1978

Cole, William Morse. **The Fundamentals of Accounting.** 1921

Congress of Accountants. **Official Record of the Proceedings of the Congress of Accountants.** 1904

Cronhelm, F[rederick] W[illiam]. **Double Entry by Single.** 1818

Davidson, Sidney. **The Plant Accounting Regulations of the Federal Power Commission.** 1952

De Paula, F[rederic] R[udolf] M[ackley]. **Developments in Accounting.** 1948

Epstein, Marc Jay. **The Effect of Scientific Management on the Development of the Standard Cost System** (Doctoral Dissertation, University of Oregon, 1973). 1978

Esquerré, Paul-Joseph. **The Applied Theory of Accounts.** 1914

Fitzgerald, A[dolf] A[lexander]. **Current Accounting Trends.** 1952

Garner, S. Paul and Marilynn Hughes, Eds. **Readings on Accounting Development.** 1978

Haskins, Charles Waldo. **Business Education and Accountancy.** 1904

Hein, Leonard William. **The British Companies Acts and the Practice of Accountancy 1844-1962** (Doctoral Dissertation, University of California, Los Angeles, 1962). 1978

Hendriksen, Eldon S. **Capital Expenditures in the Steel Industry, 1900 to 1953** (Doctoral Dissertation, University of California, Berkeley, 1956). 1978

Holmes, William, Linda H. Kistler and Louis S. Corsini. **Three Centuries of Accounting in Massachusetts.** 1978

Horngren, Charles T. **Implications for Accountants of the Uses of Financial Statements by Security Analysts** (Doctoral Dissertation, University of Chicago, 1955). 1978

Horrigan, James O., Ed. **Financial Ratio Analysis—An Historical Perspective.** 1978

Jones, [Edward Thomas]. **Jones's English System of Book-keeping.** 1796

Lamden, Charles William. **The Securities and Exchange Commission** (Doctoral Dissertation, University of California, Berkeley, 1949). 1978

Langer, Russell Davis. **Accounting As A Variable in Mergers** (Doctoral Dissertation, University of California, Berkeley, 1976). 1978

Lewis, J. Slater. **The Commercial Organisation of Factories.** 1896

Littleton, A[nanias] C[harles] and B[asil] S. Yamey, Eds. **Studies in the Historv of Accounting.** 1956

Mair, John. **Book-keeping Moderniz'd.** 1793

Mann, Helen Scott. **Charles Ezra Sprague.** 1931

Marsh, C[hristopher] C[olumbus]. **The Theory and Practice of Bank Book-keeping.** 1856

Mitchell, William. **A New and Complete System of Book-keeping by an Improved Method of Double Entry.** 1796

Montgomery, Robert H. **Fifty Years of Accountancy.** 1939

Moonitz, Maurice. **The Entity Theory of Consolidated Statements.** 1951

Moonitz, Maurice, Ed. **Three Contributions to the Development of Accounting Thought.** 1978

Murray, David. **Chapters in the History of Bookkeeping, Accountancy & Commercial Arithmetic.** 1930

Nicholson, J[erome] Lee. **Cost Accounting.** 1913

Paton, William Andrew and Russell Alger Stevenson. **Principles of Accounting.** 1918

Pixley, Francis W[illiam]. **The Profession of a Chartered Accountant and Other Lectures.** 1897

Preinreich, Gabriel A. D. **The Nature of Dividends.** 1935

Previts, Gary John, Ed. **Early 20th Century Developments in American Accounting Thought.** 1978

Ronen, Joshua and George H. Sorter. **Relevant Financial Statements.** 1978

Shenkir, William G., Ed. **Carman G. Blough: His Professional Career and Accounting Thought.** 1978

Simpson, Kemper. **Economics for the Accountant.** 1921

Sneed, Florence R. **Parallelism in Two Disciplines.** (M.A. Thesis, University of Texas, Arlington, 1974). 1978

Sorter, George H. **The Boundaries of the Accounting Universe** (Doctoral Dissertation, University of Chicago, 1963). 1978

Storey, Reed K[arl]. **Matching Revenues with Costs** (Doctoral Dissertation, University of California, Berkeley, 1958). 1978

Sweeney, Henry W[hitcomb]. **Stabilized Accounting.** 1936

Van de Linde, Gérard. **Reminiscences.** 1917

Vatter, William J[oseph]. **The Fund Theory of Accounting and Its Implications for Financial Reports.** 1947

Walker, R. G. **Consolidated Statements.** 1978

Webster, Norman E., Comp. **The American Association of Public Accountants.** 1954

Wells, M. C., Ed. **American Engineers' Contributions to Cost Accounting.** 1978

Worthington, Beresford. **Professional Accountants.** 1895

Yamey, Basil S. **Essays on the History of Accounting.** 1978

Yamey, Basil S., Ed. **The Historical Development of Accounting.** 1978

Yang, J[u] M[ei]. **Goodwill and Other Intangibles.** 1927

Zeff, Stephen Addam. **A Critical Examination of the Orientation Postulate in Accounting, with Particular Attention to its Historical Development** (Doctoral Dissertation, University of Michigan, 1961). 1978

Zeff, Stephen A., Ed. **Selected Dickinson Lectures in Accounting.** 1978